From Working Girl
to Working Mother

From Working Girl

to Working Mother

The Female Labor Force in the United States, 1820–1980

LYNN Y. WEINER

The University of North Carolina

Chapel Hill and London

Library of Congress Cataloging in Publication Data

Weiner, Lynn Y., 1951–
   From working girl to working mother.

   Bibliography: p.
   Includes index.
   1. Women—Employment—United States—History.
I. Title.
HD6095.W39   1984   331.4'0973   84-7276
ISBN 0-8078-1612-4

Portions of Chapter 3 first appeared in somewhat different form in the
author's articles: "Sisters of the Road: Women Transients and Tramps,"
published in *Walking to Work: Tramps in America, 1790–1935*, edited by
Eric Monkkonen, by permission of the University of Nebraska Press.
Copyright 1984 by the University of Nebraska Press; and " 'Our Sisters'
Keepers': The Minneapolis Woman's Christian Association and Housing
for Working Women," originally published in *Minnesota History* 46:
189–200 (Spring 1979), copyright by the Minnesota Historical Society
and used with permission.

For Tom, Andrew, and Jeffrey

Contents

Tables

Tables

Figure

Acknowledgments

I take great pleasure in acknowledging the help I have received during the writing of this book.

Sam Bass Warner and Roslyn Feldberg encouraged this study in its earliest forms. Richard Bushman, David Hall, Aileen Kraditor, and Cecelia Tichi were among those at Boston University who taught me how to think about American history and culture. Kathryn Kish Sklar sparked my initial interest in history when I was an undergraduate at the University of Michigan; she has remained a mentor and a friend ever since.

I am also grateful to Northwestern University, where the History Department's Associate Program provided me with an affiliation and with access to an excellent library. The American Historical Association generously awarded me a Beveridge Grant during the final stages of research and writing.

The manuscript was greatly improved because of suggestions and criticisms offered by Thomas Dublin, Alice Kessler-Harris, Eric Schneider, Kathryn Kish Sklar, Winifred Wandersee, and Sharon Weiner. For their useful comments on portions of the book presented at conferences, I thank Estelle Freedman, Brian Gratton, Barbara Hobson, and Ruth Rosen. An early version of the manuscript benefited from discussions with Mary Ann Garnett, Heather Huyck, Linda Lounsbury, Susan Smith, and Meryl Weinreb.

Many librarians and archivists have been most helpful, especially David Klaassen of the Social Welfare History Archives, Mary Ann Bamberger of the Special Collections library at the University of Illinois at Chicago, Archie Motley of the Chicago Historical Society, Dallas R. Lindgren of the Minnesota Historical Society, and the staff of the Schlesinger Library at Radcliffe College.

For granting permission to use their unpublished records, I am indebted to the Child Welfare League of America, the Minneapolis Woman's Christian Association, the Travelers' Aid Association of America, and the Women's Educational and Industrial Union.

I also wish to express my appreciation to the editors at the University of North Carolina Press: to Iris Tillman Hill, for seeing the manuscript through several revisions, and to Sandra Eisdorfer, for her critical eye and excellent suggestions during the editing process.

Finally, my family has always encouraged my efforts, and I would like to thank them, too. My mother, Audrey Allen Weiner, always believed in the potential of her children. My extended family—my father Charles, and Inge Weiner, Sharon Weiner, Tom Hospelhorn, Stuart Weiner, Maria Treccapelli, Alan Weiner, and Robert and Virginia Moher—have remained supportive during the long years of education and writing. My greatest debt is to my husband, Tom Moher. He has been involved in this project from the beginning; his confidence in me, his astute criticism of the manuscript at every stage, and his skill at juggling the demands of work and fatherhood have contributed immeasurably to the completion of this book.

From Working Girl to Working Mother

Introduction

The volatile debate in the 1980s over the social consequences of working mothers is firmly rooted in a historical controversy over the employment of women. Where the absence of men from the labor force has long been considered an anomaly, the presence of women in the labor force has continually inspired controversy, investigation, and reform.[1] The dramatic expansion of the female labor force in modern times has revolutionized the nature of work and family life in the United States.

This book looks at the general history of the working woman in the United States through 1980. The study emphasizes two levels of analysis—the material basis of changing social and economic behavior and the concomitant ideological debate over appropriate female roles, which has in turn affected social reform and public policy.

The female sector of the labor force has more than tripled in the last century, growing from 14 percent in 1870 to 42 percent in 1980. These gains reflect the increasing propensity of women to work. Where just one in seven women worked for wages in 1870, by 1980 one in two women were gainfully employed (see table 1). Moreover, in the course of the last century, the identity of the woman worker has changed. The married woman and the mother have replaced the young single woman as the largest subgroups within the female labor force. This revolution in the female labor force has attracted the attention of historians in recent years. For the most part, however, scholars have studied the history of working women for relatively limited time spans or localities, or for specific occupational, marital, ethnic, or racial groups.[2] There have yet been few attempts to take a long-term historical perspective on the employment of American women.

The long view shows that the expansion of the female labor force occurred in two distinct phases. The first phase was the era of the "working girl."[3] During this period, from the mid-nineteenth century until the early decades of the twentieth century, the single, and often self-supporting, young woman worker became a visible member of the urban labor force. The second phase was the era of the working mother. In this period, from the early twentieth century until the present day, married women and mothers came to the forefront of the female labor force and also dominated the accompanying debate over women and work.

Table 1

Number[a] and Proportion of Working Women
in the U.S. Labor Force, 1870–1980

Year	Total Labor Force	Working Women	Percent of All Women Who Work	Women as Percent of Labor Force
1870	12,160	1,717	15	14
1880	16,274	2,354	16	14
1890	21,814	3,597	19	16
1900	27,323	4,834	21	18
1910	35,749	7,011	24	20
1920	41,017	8,278	24	20
1930	48,163	10,546	25	22
1940	52,711	12,951	27	25
1950	59,223	16,443	30	28
1960	69,234	22,222	36	32
1970	82,048	30,547	41	37
1980	106,066	44,741	51	42

Sources: U.S. Bureau of the Census, *Comparative Statistics for the U.S., 1870–1940*, p. 92, table xv; U.S. Bureau of the Census, *Nineteenth Census of the U.S.*, vol. 1, pt. 1, p. 372, table 78; U.S. Bureau of the Census, *1980 Census of Population*, p. 25, table p. 3.

[a]In thousands.

These two phases of labor force expansion were characterized by factors of class and race. Although poor, black, and immigrant women had long labored in the marketplace for subsistence wages, they had excited little public controversy because they had not been considered subject to middle-class expectations of domesticity. It was when "respectable" groups of women—that is, women who were white, native-born, and nondestitute—entered the labor force that public attention was first drawn to the changing work patterns of women.[4]

The controversy caused by the movement of these women into the labor force led to cycles of reaction and reform based on the desire to reestablish women within the framework of middle-class domestic values. This public response to working women has shaped social policy on issues including wages, housing, job opportunities, and child care. The examination of these policies helps us to understand the origins of such varied reform movements as the Young Women's Christian Associations and the relief programs for dependent mothers and their children.

The first phase of the expansion of the female labor force—the era of the working girl—was marked by the accelerating work rate of young single women. Unfortunately the growth of this trend before 1890 can only be inferred, as the Census Bureau did not categorize women workers by marital status until that decade. By then, however, the population of women who worked included an increased proportion of native-born women, many of them migrants from farms. In 1890, over two-thirds of women workers were single, while married women constituted the smallest marital group within the female labor force (see table 2). The typical woman worker at the turn of the century was unmarried, young, and a domestic servant. Moreover, one out of three urban workers were self-supporting and living away from home.

Society first discovered in the late nineteenth century that these women were working alongside the poor, black, and immigrant women who had always worked for wages without inspiring public comment. The labor of "respectable" women brought them one step away from their prescribed place at home, where middle-class expectations would decree a life of domesticity. Even more removed were the rural women who migrated to the cities to find work. Public opinion maintained that these working girls, adrift from any domestic influence, endangered their physical and moral health and the health of future generations. Popular literature and the records of reform institutions reflect a heated discussion at this time replete with rhetoric about the purity and morality of the working girl. The young single woman worker, in short, was seen as "unfitting" herself for her future role as wife and mother.

The result of this debate over the working girl was an amorphous reform movement that attempted both to extend domestic influences to young working women through such institutions as supervised boarding homes and clubs for working girls and also to protect female health and morality through the regulation of wages and hours of work. By ameliorating the worst conditions facing women entering the work force, these reforms to some degree sanctioned social change. At the same time, however, reform measures characterized by class and gender concerns attempted to bring young women under a form of social control by channeling them into models of housing and work that reinforced domestic values.[5]

In the twentieth century, married women began to enter the labor force. The proportion of wives who work has grown ninefold since 1890, and the proportion of mothers who work has at least doubled. Since statistics for working mothers do not exist on a national level before 1940, however, the latter figure is probably understated (see table 2).

Table 2

Percentage of Women in the U.S. Labor Force, by Family Status, 1890–1980

	1890	1900	1910	1920	1930	1940	1950	1960	1970	1980[c]
				All U.S. Women						
Single	32	34	32	41[b]	28	28	17	16	18	21
Wid.-Div.	11	11	11	—[b]	12	13	15	15	16	19
Married	57	55	57	59	60	59	68	69	65	60
				Total Female Labor Force						
Single	68	67	61	77[b]	54	49	32	23	22	25
Wid.-Div.	18	18	15	—[b]	17	15	16	6	14	15
Married	14	15	24	23	29	36	52	61	63	60
Mothers[a]	—	—	—	—	—	11	26	27	38	40
				Female Labor Force Participation Rate						
Single	41	41	48	44[b]	46	48	51	44	53	62
Wid.-Div.	30	33	35	—[b]	34	32	36	13	46	41
Married	5	6	11	9	12	17	25	32	41	51
Mothers[a]	—	—	—	—	—	28	33	37	43	56

Sources: U.S. Bureau of the Census, *Women at Work*, p. 14, table VII, p. 15, table VIII; U.S. Department of Labor, Women's Bureau, *Employed Mothers and Child Care*, p. 9, table 3; U.S. Department of Labor, Bureau of Labor Statistics, *Working Women: A Databook*, p. 19, table 18; U.S. Department of Labor, Bureau of Labor Statistics, *Marital and Family Statistics of Workers*, p. 5, table 3; U.S. Department of Labor, Bureau of Labor Statistics, *Marital and Family Patterns*, p. 1, table 1, p. 2, table 2, p. 25, table C-1.

[a]Mothers of children under age 18.
[b]Single women counted with widows and divorced women.
[c]Figures for March 1980.

By 1980, the typical woman worker was married, a mother, and a clerical worker.[6] By 1980, too, married women comprised nearly two-thirds of all women workers, fully reversing the trend of a century earlier. This reversal is illustrated in figure 1, in which the declining proportions of single women in the female labor force are contrasted with the rising proportions of married women workers. The steady growth in the numbers of married women workers has been to a large degree a growth in the numbers of middle-income wives in the labor force, particularly after 1940. More recent developments include a startling rise in the proportions of working mothers with very young children.

Figure 1

Composition of Female Labor Force by Marital Status, 1890–1980

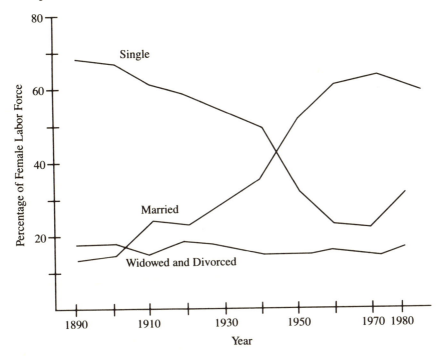

Source: See table 2.

In the course of a century, the working mother has moved from the periphery of the American labor force into the mainstream.

These material changes in the labor force contributed to the changing ideas about women and work that were widely shared by middle-class Americans. As white middle-income married women moved into the labor force in the twentieth century, motherhood, rather than future motherhood, became the subject of concern. As a result, single women workers were no longer considered "controversial" members of the labor force. In the era of the working mother, reformers used psychological rather than moral arguments in the debate over woman's enlarging sphere, reflecting changes in the cultural milieu. "Delinquency" and "neurosis" replaced "purity" and "sin" in the rhetoric about women who worked. The social response to the working mother also reinforced domestic values, but it served to confirm rather than mitigate the controversial status of employed women, particularly if they had children. Because reforms like day care and mothers' pensions were originally meant only for destitute or widowed women, the "respectable" working mother confronted a society that remained unresponsive to her needs for quality child care and for more flexible working conditions. Unlike reforms targeted for the working girl, reforms for the working mother were not shaped in response to rising numbers in the labor force. Rather, social responses to mothers at work emerged in an earlier time as a charitable measure meant to alleviate the consequences of poverty for children.

The shift in the subject of the debate from single to married women reflected both new labor force conditions and changes in the ideology of domesticity. Whereas all "respectable" women had been considered bound by the domestic ideology in the nineteenth century, single working women and working wives in the twentieth century gradually lost their controversial status. For these twentieth-century women, employment practices that were at one time considered suspect were absorbed into the mainstream of acceptable behavior. Their participation in the work force was no longer collectively defined as a transgression of the domestic ideology, as that ideology was narrowed to include only mothers of young children.

The extent to which the domestic ideology will be further modified by the growing population of working mothers remains to be seen. For working mothers, possible solutions to the problem of child care—such as equal parenting responsibilities of both father and mother—strike deep at the heart of the concept of separate male and female spheres. Hence the traditional association of biological difference (reproduction) with social behavior (child care) makes the working mother the gravest threat yet to the standard definitions of family life. Moreover, as more and more mothers of very young children join the labor force, the debate over women's work has become sharply focused on the issue of day care for those children.

This book considers the interaction of work, family, and cultural patterns in the long history of the working woman in America. The historical evidence examined includes both demographic and documentary materials. While government census and survey data are limited by the questions originally asked and by errors in the survey process, they provide the best perspective on national trends and patterns of labor force participation.[7] The writings of government investigators, clergymen, journalists, and working women provide insight into how different segments of the public have responded to the changing female labor force. I have often used specific cases from various cities to illustrate general trends.

The first part of the study examines the development of the era of the working girl. Chapters 1 through 3 look at the growth of the population of self-supporting women in nineteenth-century cities, the "social problem" of purity and future motherhood that emerged after the Civil War, and subsequent social and legislative reforms that were meant to close the gap between behavior and ideology. The second half of the book—chapters 4 through 6—provides a parallel discussion of the era of the working mother. In both cases, changing behavior in the work force fueled a controversy over the employment of women, which itself resulted from the cultural lag between new patterns of labor force behavior and traditional ideas of domesticity.[8] The ideology of domesticity itself has been transformed over time, in a dialectic with changing social and material conditions.

Part One

The Era of the Working Girl, 1820–1920

Chapter 1
"Women Adrift":
The Growth of
an Urban Class

The era of the working girl unfolded in the nineteenth century. By the years after the Civil War, the typical woman worker was young and single. In addition, hundreds of thousands of working women had migrated to cities from American small towns and farms or had immigrated from Europe. By the 1870s, women who worked and lived apart from traditional networks of home and family formed a growing urban class; reformers singled them out with labels such as "homeless women," "women adrift," and "working girls."

By the turn of the century, these self-supporting women were a third of the urban female labor force, and they were also at the heart of a widespread public controversy over the morality of women's work. Yet in modern times young single working women have as a group become socially and historically invisible. The widening of "woman's sphere" in the twentieth century has been accompanied by the acceptance of employment and housing practices that were at one time considered to be a threat to social order.

This chapter examines the history of that generation of single women which first challenged conventional social roles by their entrance into the urban labor force. Immigrant and black women have always worked. But when native-born white women increased their propensity to work, producing in effect a new labor supply, the question of woman's proper place gathered strength in the public debate.

The chapter will first look at the antecedents of the era of the working girl. In particular, this era was shaped by the collapse of paternalistic employment structures in the nineteenth century, particularly the decline in domestic service and factory housing customs which imposed a supervised domestic environment upon working women before the Civil War. This care was thought necessary to insure the respectability of women who worked temporarily before marriage. Ironically, as these customs faded, the supply of young single women who were living on their own increased. The discussion will conclude with a description of the female labor force that had developed by 1900.

Antebellum Women Workers: Maids and Mill Girls

Since colonial times, the urban female labor force included self-supporting women—those who had to work to survive, prostitutes, vagabonds, and widows. By the antebellum era, urban growth and population pressures pushed and pulled thousands of single women to the cities, as young women abandoned the New England countryside to seek work in the burgeoning mill towns and in Boston.[1] But the geographical movement of rural single women did not become a national phenomenon until after the Civil War, when the development of steam railroads and the acceleration of urban and industrial growth launched the journeys of tens of thousands of migrants. At that time, too, the rapid increase in immigration added thousands of foreign-born women to the numbers of female workers living on their own in large cities.

Prior to this time, self-supporting women had not been visible as a social group. Women workers in large cities such as Boston, Philadelphia, or New York were generally considered to be beyond the pale of middle-class respectability; they were usually destitute, black, or immigrant.[2] In smaller communities, however, paternalistic structures allowed thousands of white rural women to migrate, work temporarily, and retain the status conferred by the domestic ideology. In small towns and villages, young women lived as servants with their employers, or they resided in the pseudo-families of supervised boardinghouses. In both cases, they were surrounded by domestic influences and family constraints.

These living arrangements stemmed in part from the colonial axiom that all individuals be attached to those microcosms of social order—well-governed families. In the mid-seventeenth century, for example, the single young person could not legally "be for himself" in Plymouth or Massachusetts Bay, but instead had to reside within an established family unit.[3] This stricture loosened for young men in the nineteenth century. Single men boarded not only with families, but increasingly in commercial boardinghouses and hotels.[4] The expectation for women, however, remained stringent. Woman's respectability rested on her ties to family life. If she could not live within the province of her parents' governance, she was expected to reside within a substitute family environment that insured a modicum of supervision and protection during the years before she married and established her own home.

To some degree, domestic service provided this supervision. Domestic service was the leading occupation for women in the United States through the 1940s, and until the 1920s servants commonly accepted partial payment for their labor in the form of room and board with their employers. A brief overview of the history of domestic service illustrates how the status of the servant evolved.

MAIDS

During the colonial period, female servants were indentured or "redemptioned" whites, or enslaved blacks. White female servants were usually European immigrants who paid sponsors for their passage across the Atlantic with a term of labor that generally ranged from four to five years. Wages were low; at the time of release a servant could expect some food, clothing, and a pittance of money. These early servants were considered to be inferior to their employers; they were stigmatized as a lower social class.[5]

In the early national and antebellum periods, however, the status of domestic service improved to some degree in the northern United States. Particularly in New England, patriarchy fused with democracy to remove the social stigma of domestic work. Antebellum servants were often women born into the same community as their employers. They commonly "attended the same church, sat at the same fireside, ate at the same table, had the same associates; they were often married from the homes and buried in the family lots of their employers."[6] These young women were treated as surrogate daughters "helping" within their employers' households; they were not merely servants laboring for contracted wages.

Significantly, wage-work for single women was at this time socially approved because of the popular belief that workers avoided the sin of idleness and learned "habits of industry."[7] This sanction of women's work evolved because women were needed to meet labor demand. At the same time, social approval rested on the maintenance of moral order and the continuance of quasi-parental supervision.

With the influx of Irish and German immigrants to the United States in the 1840s and 1850s, however, domestic service lost status. Native-born women feared they would lose social position if they competed with immigrant labor. Foreign-born women entered households not as surrogate daughters but as servants of inferior social rank. For these young immigrants, domestic boarding became the female equivalent of the male practice of "boarding out" with strangers before marriage. These women were continuing a long-standing European tradition in which a servant's household membership and the implied protection of her employer sanctioned her departure from home.[8] In Buffalo, New York, for example, newly arrived Irish and German women had by the mid-nineteenth century established a pattern of working for a few years before marriage as live-in servants with the resident native-born families of the city.[9] As domestic service became a major job channel for immigrants, it no longer served as acceptable employment for native-born women between the stages of childhood and marriage.

MILL GIRLS

Factory work developed similarly to domestic service. A system that at one time provided paternalistic safeguards for female respectability declined as immigrants replaced native-born workers in the 1850s and 1860s. The American factory age began at the end of the eighteenth century, when New England "manufactories" hired rural women and children to doff, weave, and spin on factory premises rather than at home. Because labor was scarce, unmarried women had been used to provide an extensive and cheap labor supply for the nascent textile industry.[10]

Many New England factories promoted the Waltham, or boardinghouse, system. Women applying for factory work were required to sign a "regulation paper" promising regular church attendance, strict moral behavior, and residence in a corporation boardinghouse. Men also signed a regulation paper, but for them corporation boarding was not a requirement. Corporation lodgings provided a substitute family environment for young women that effectively transferred parental authority from the farm to the factory.[11]

This moral authority was meant not only to protect the virtue of young women but also to insure factory productivity by maintaining a class of "industrious, sober, orderly, and moral" operatives. Without such a class of workers, the Lowell clergyman Henry Miles suggested in 1846, "profits would be absorbed by cases of irregularity, carelessness, and neglect; while the existence of any great moral exposure in Lowell would cut off the supply of help from the virtuous homesteads of the country." Miles concluded that "public morals and private interests . . . are here seen to be linked together in an indissoluble connection. Accordingly, the sagacity of self-interest, as well as more disinterested considerations, has led to the adoption of a strict system of moral police."[12]

Factory lodgings established to protect the workers were supervised by matrons who were frequently the widowed mothers of operatives and who were often called "mother" by the young residents. Inmates were expected to obey a plethora of rules and regulations, including a strict curfew. Labor historian Norman Ware described the "moral policing" of the Waltham system. "The operatives were told when, where, how, and for how much they must work," he wrote, "when and where they were to eat and sleep. They were ordered to attend church, for which they had to pay pew rent. They were discharged for immoral conduct, for bad language, for disrespect, for attending dancing classes, or for any other cause that the agents or overseers thought sufficient."[13] Discharge was a powerful threat; in Lowell, a blacklisting code guaranteed that a worker dismissed from one mill would not be hired by another.[14]

At the same time, factory boardinghouses attempted to provide the amenities of the country homes left behind by the young migrants. Harriet Hanson Robinson, one of the early "factory girls," nostalgically recalled in her autobiography the pianos, libraries, and carpeted parlors of her factory lodgings, and maintained that the operatives' surroundings were as pure and refined as their own homes.[15] The cultural activities and domestic duties carried on in the boardinghouses—reading, sewing, letter writing—secured a domestic atmosphere of gentility meant to protect both the reputations of the workers and the morality and social order of the factory villages.

This moral strategy succeeded in maintaining the respectability of the Lowell operatives. In 1844, William Scoresby, a British clergyman, visited Lowell and later reported that, among the operatives, "there was not the slightest appearance of boldness or vulgarity; on the contrary, a very becoming propriety and respectability of manner."[16] In the 1860s, the respectability of the Lowell mill girls was still legend. Asa Mercer, an imaginative Washington bachelor, traveled to Lowell to recruit women to migrate to Seattle, a city where marriageable women were scarce. He recruited more than a hundred mill workers, who became popularly known in Seattle as "Mercer girls."[17]

With increasing European immigration and with growing wage and hour demands on the part of the workers, factory employment gradually lost status, paralleling the process that occurred in domestic service. Immigrants were willing to work longer hours for lower wages, the factories filled with foreign-born instead of native-born women, and women mill workers as a group lost the ideological sanctions they had gained in antebellum years.[18]

The era of the "factory girl" was gone by the end of the 1860s. By the 1880s, operative resentment of boardinghouse regulations and the decrease in native-born women seeking jobs in factories led to the abandonment of the Waltham system. The immigrant women who ran the looms and doffed the bobbins did not transgress the class lines crossed by native-born farm women a generation earlier.

By the time of the Civil War, two traditional patriarchal systems that had provided protection and "respectability" for young women who left their families to work were decaying. Domestic work and factory labor no longer offered a mantle of rectitude through the extension of middle-class domestic values. These occupations became provinces of the immigrant, black, and poor women who were already excluded from the pedestal of "pure woman-hood." Rural native-born women were displaced from their approved foothold in the labor force as maids or mill girls, and they were instead expected to remain home as "ladies." Female idleness became a status symbol rather than a disgrace as the domestic ideology was used to heighten distinctions between classes of women.[19]

Still, hundreds of thousands of women who were included in the domestic "place" nevertheless continued to sidestep their prescribed role. As historian Thomas Dublin has pointed out, textile mill workers had often worked not only because of compelling economic need, but sometimes for economic and social independence from their families. These workers worked to build up their dowries, to buy clothing, or to save for an education. And some, like Sally Rice, of Somerset, Vermont, worked for personal satisfaction alone. Sally Rice left home in 1838 and worked as a farm laborer and mill hand. She wrote her parents the next year, "I have but one life to live and I want to enjoy myself as well as I can while I live."[20]

Even after the time that domestic service and mill work lost "respectability," women continued to work for wages outside the home, and a growing propor-tion of them continued to migrate within and between cities seeking housing and employment. The ideology of domesticity never reflected real experience for this segment of the female population.

The Growth of the Female Labor Force, 1865–1900

Although comparative data are not available, it seems that the tendency of young women to work and live away from their homes increased in the postbellum era. In 1889, the United States Department of Labor surveyed 22 cities and found that an estimated 14 percent of the working women studied were living "adrift" from their families. That same year, labor statistician Carroll Wright observed in his report, "The Working Girls of Boston," that while the number of women who were boarders and lodgers was "much less than is generally supposed," still about a third of all working women, *exclud-ing* domestic servants, were living away from home. If servants were included, of course, that proportion would be even higher. In 1891, the United States Department of Labor issued a bulletin on boarding homes and clubs for working women, commenting on the "large working population of women without local homes in great cities."[21]

LABOR SUPPLY

Why did the numbers of wage-earning women, and of self-supporting women in particular, seem to increase so dramatically in postbellum years? A combination of factors may explain the occurrence. Nativity, age, and marital patterns produced a relatively large supply of young single women who for cultural and economic reasons were more prone to seek work outside their homes than were women in previous times. Concomitantly, opportunities on farms were shrinking for women, as labor demand in large cities expanded. Middle-class urban families increasingly sought servants, and factories, mills, and offices demanded female rather than male labor.[22]

There are, unfortunately, few reliable accounts of the self-supporting woman in this era. Some self-supporting women chose not to identify themselves to investigators, believing, one investigator suggested, "that it is more aristocratic, or fashionable, or something else, to state that they live at home, when as a matter of fact, they do not."[23] The richest source on the subject is the Census Bureau's compilation of Twelfth Census manuscript returns, published in 1907 as *Statistics of Women at Work*. This lengthy volume presents information on the nativity, marital status, occupation, and living arrangements for adult women workers in twenty-seven cities and in Brooklyn.[24] An analysis of this information provides a picture of women workers for one year—1900—a year at the height of the era of the working girl.

The majority of women workers at the end of the nineteenth century were young, single, and living at home with their parents. But the practice of young women living on their own had become common in cities by the turn of the century. Of 1,232,000 women workers reported in cities, some 434,000 of them—over a third—lived apart from their parents. In the cities surveyed, boarders and lodgers comprised from 18 to 49 percent of all women workers and from 11 to 34 percent of workers excluding domestic servants (see table 3).

The cities surveyed by the Census Bureau included all those with populations over 150,000 in 1900 except for San Francisco, which was omitted because of the disorder caused by the great earthquake in 1906. Four smaller cities—Paterson, Fall River, Lowell, and Atlanta—were surveyed as well. In general, the relative proportions of self-supporting women in a city were determined by a mix of local conditions and not by any one factor such as size, location, composition of population, or degree of industrialization.[25]

It is evident from the census data that urban women were more likely to work for wages than were women in the United States as a whole. In 1900, 28

Table 3

Percentage of Boarders and Lodgers among Women Workers
for Selected Cities, 1900

Cities	All Boarders	Boarders Excluding Servants[a]	Cities	All Boarders	Boarders Excluding Servants[a]
St. Paul	49	34	Cleveland	32	16
Minneapolis	48	31	Brooklyn	32	13
Boston	44	28	Providence	32	19
New York[b]	41	20	Rochester	31	20
Pittsburgh	40	18	Baltimore	30	16
Kansas City	39	25	Milwaukee	30	14
Philadelphia	38	22	Louisville	27	14
Lowell	37	32	Newark	27	12
Detroit	37	21	Cincinnati	26	12
Washington	36	23	Jersey City	24	11
Chicago	36	21	New Orleans	23	13
Buffalo	35	17	Paterson	21	13
St. Louis	34	16	Atlanta	20	13
Indianapolis	32	19	Fall River	18	14

Sources: U.S. Bureau of the Census, *Statistics of Women at Work*, pp. 218–305, table 28, p. 29, table XX.

[a]"Servant" includes servants, housekeepers and stewardesses, and waitresses.
[b]Includes Manhattan and Bronx boroughs only.

percent of the urban female population worked, compared with 21 percent in the continental United States. Immigrants and the daughters of immigrants were more likely to live and work in the city than were their native-born counterparts.[26]

It is at first surprising to see, in table 3, that Minneapolis and St. Paul ranked highest in the relative numbers of women who boarded away from home and so were presumably self-supporting. Most studies of working women concentrated on the larger cities of the East Coast. The disproportionately higher migrant female population of urban Minnesota can be explained, however, by immigration and migration patterns in the upper Midwest. In 1900, fully four out of five self-supporting women in Minneapolis and St. Paul were immigrants or daughters of immigrants. Immigrants to the upper Midwest arriving before 1890 tended to settle in rural rather than urban districts. Minneapolis and St. Paul therefore attracted the restless daughters of settlers from a large geographic area including Minnesota, Wisconsin, the Dakotas, and Iowa.[27]

But the situation in these hinterland cities was the exception, not the rule. In the more dense urban centers of the East, immigrants settled in cities from the start, and their working daughters were more likely to live at home than with employers or in boardinghouses. In the seaport cities of Boston, New York, and Philadelphia, the majority of women who lived away from home were immigrants and native-born women of native parentage—the latter being migrants from the countryside.[28] Nationally, immigrant women constituted almost half of the female boarding population. Within each racial and nativity group, however, the propensity to live away from home varied. Almost half of all immigrant working women were boarders and lodgers, over 40 percent of black working women were boarders, and over a third of those women born to native-born parents boarded.

But domestic servants skewed this data toward the immigrant population. When servants are excluded, native-born women of native parentage become the first ranked group of boarders and lodgers. The importance of native-born white migrant women will be discussed in chapter 2 as a factor in the growing concern with women who lived apart from traditional family life.

The relative proportions of women workers and boarders by nativity and race reflect larger trends in social history. Immigration to the United States from Europe increased in spurts through the 1800s, peaking in the first decade of the twentieth century, when over eight million aliens entered the country. These immigrants were largely young and single. Through the 1800s, over two-thirds were under the age of 39, and from 1911 to 1920, over 60 percent were single.[29]

Immigrants were also predominantly male. The ratio of men to women was about 3 to 2 from 1820 to 1860 and nearly 5 to 2 from 1900 to 1910. But these sex ratios varied by nationality. Among some immigrant groups were thousands of single women seeking work. Between 1870 and 1890, for example, almost 20 percent of Danish and 30 percent of Swedish immigrants were unmarried women.[30]

How did these women journey to the United States? Many traveled with their families to large cities, others came alone and were met at the stations by relatives and friends, and the rest arrived on their own at American ports without having made arrangements for work or housing. Studies of immigrant women in Boston and Minneapolis found that most initially lodged with relatives or friends before finding work as servants, or in hotels and restaurants where they would also receive room and board.[31]

Internal migration patterns especially favored the development of a class of women boarders and lodgers. At the turn of the century, most Americans still lived on farms or in small villages and towns. But there was little opportunity for employment for women in these rural districts. The inheritance of farms usually went to sons rather than to daughters, and activities were limited for women remaining at home. The 1865 diary of a 19-year-old Wisconsin farm woman portrays a round of life bounded by household and agricultural tasks, school teaching, and loneliness. After a week of teaching, sewing, cleaning, and boiling sugar sap, Sarah Beaulieu wrote, "I think I am getting very much like the old maid that sat down on Monday morning and cried because Saturday did not come twice a week."[32] In a similar vein, the fictional farm girl Rose Dutcher, in Hamlin Garland's *Rose of Dutcher's Coolly* (1895) argued that in an "age of cities" to live in the country was "to be a cow, a tadpole!" On the farm, she complained that "you could arise at five o'clock to cook breakfast and wash dishes, and get dinner, and sweep and mend, and get supper, and so on, till you rotted, like a post stuck in the mud."[33] This farm girl's solution, too, was to go to the big city. Toward the end of the century, agricultural technology further lessened both the opportunity and the need for female labor on farms, contributing even more to the attractiveness of the city for young rural women.

In small towns, opportunities for young women were also limited. Edith H., a 20-year-old from Mankato, Minnesota, wrote the Minnesota Bureau of Labor for help in her search for work. "I want something to do," she pleaded. "There isn't anything to do here because it is a small place and I was tole [*sic*] to go to the cities but to write to you people first as I am a stranger there." Although the state labor bureau had a policy discouraging the migration of young women to the large cities, it is likely that Edith H. joined the stream of eager travelers to Minneapolis and St. Paul.[34]

In general, young single women migrated at a greater rate and at an earlier age than men to seek work in the cities, resulting in both the increase in the female labor supply and the feminization of some urban populations. The movement of migrants to the cities was, unlike that of immigrants, disproportionately female. The migration of women peaked at about the age of 18, while most young men did not leave their homes until they were in their early twenties.[35]

These migration and immigration processes contributed to the relative youth of the urban female working population. Working women in large cities were likely to be younger than working women in smaller cities and country districts. This was most evident in women who were from 18 to 24 years old. Almost half of the women in this age group who lived in cities of at least

50,000 worked in 1900, compared with about a quarter of the same-aged women in rural areas.[36]

A consequence of the younger age of urban women workers was the increased likelihood that they would be unmarried and thus more likely to live away from home. Three out of four white women workers, and four out of five white women boarders and lodgers, were single in 1900. Native-born daughters of immigrants were most likely to be single in both the working and boarding populations. Married women were slowly increasing their tendency to work, especially if they were black, and female heads of household who worked, we will see, were also a growing group. But single women continued to dominate the female labor force at the turn of the century.[37] Patterns of age, marriage, and fertility had important consequences for the female labor supply. The large numbers of unmarried women in the late nineteenth century diminished in ensuing decades, as the female population both aged and married at a faster rate.

There was a relatively large population of young single women in the late 1800s. Since then, there have been lesser proportions of single women in the young- and middle-age groups as the age of first marriages has fallen. But prior to 1900 the majority of women remained single until the age of 25, reflecting both a rising age of first marriage and decreasing marriage rates. More than half of all women from 20 to 24 years of age were single in birth cohorts up to 1884, and a decline in the proportion of single women in that age group prevailed thereafter until 1934 when less than a third of the women between 20 and 24 years old were single (table 4). Women born before 1885— the core of the female labor supply through the early twentieth century—were therefore more likely to remain single for a longer period of time than were women born in succeeding years.

The age of first marriage moved downward from 1890 to 1955. In 1890, the median age of first marriage for women was 22 years; by 1955, the median age was 20.2 years. The decline in the marriage rate was accompanied by a decline in the fertility rate, which dropped from about 55 per 1,000 in 1820 to 20 per 1,000 in 1955. As a result, the population gradually aged. From 1880 to 1950, the proportions of persons under the age of 24 declined.[38]

Demographic factors alone cannot explain why women began to work in this period. The composition of the female labor force reflects cultural and economic transformations as well as demographic trends. As the sociologist Valerie Kincade Oppenheimer points out, analysis of population distribution alone cannot account for changes in female labor force behavior. Rather, explanations for the shifting propensity of some groups of women to work must be sought as well.[39]

Table 4

Percentage of Single Women, by Age, in Birth Cohorts,
1865–1874 to 1925–1934

	Cohort Groups						
Age	1865–1874	1875–1884	1885–1894	1895–1904	1905–1914	1915–1924	1925–1934
15–19	90.3	88.6	87.9	87.0	86.8	88.1	82.9
20–24	51.8	51.5	48.3	45.6	46.0	47.2	32.3
25–29	27.5	24.9	23.0	21.7	22.8	13.3	—
30–34	16.6	16.1	14.9	13.2	14.7	9.3	—
35–44	11.4	11.4	10.0	10.4	8.3	—	—
45–54	9.6	9.1	8.7	7.8	—	—	—
55–64	8.9	9.0	7.9	—	—	—	—
65+	9.3	8.9	—	—	—	—	—

Source: Adapted from Taeuber and Taeuber, *Changing Population of the United States*, p. 153, table 47.

Cultural and attitudinal changes were important factors in the work habits of single women in postbellum years. Traditionally, unmarried women were expected to live within the homes of relatives. Two exceptions, we have seen, were domestic servants and factory operatives who lived in supervised housing provided by employers. Events in the postbellum period—especially urbanization and industrialization—stimulated new work and family processes that led to a life-cycle stage of autonomy for women who were in between the stages of adolescence and an expected adulthood of marriage and motherhood. Moreover, a trend toward higher education combined with widening work opportunities to create among women "a feeling of independence and self-reliance."[40] By the end of the nineteenth century, a period of female economic autonomy— that is, of female self-support—became more common than it had been in previous times.

Urban young women who lived at home with their parents, even those of middle-income groups, did not necessarily remain idle or take in home work, such as sewing, as they might have done in an earlier era. Rather, they increasingly sought employment in shops, offices, and mills. Rural and immigrant women went a step further, leaving their parents' homes to live in the cities among strangers. For all of these women, of course, paid employment was expected to be a temporary activity engaged in only before marriage.[41]

Young women were now working for a variety of reasons. For many young native-born white women a desire for new experiences, independence, personal satisfaction, and excitement impelled them to leave the sanctuary of home. Bessie Van Vorst, in the 1903 study *The Woman Who Toils*, reported that a statement pronounced repeatedly by young factory operatives who had migrated to a New York mill town was: "I don't have to work; my father gives me all the money I need, but not all the money I *want*. I like to be independent and spend my money as I please."[42] Other women echoed this sentiment. In 1908, working women submitted autobiographical essays to *Harper's Bazaar* on the topic "The Girl Who Comes to the City." Among the motivations for employment cited in these firsthand accounts were boredom at home and the "unendurable" life in the country.[43]

Even more women, like most men, worked for economic reasons. Young women worked not only for considerations of independence but also because of changing family-income needs. As middle-class standards of consumption rose, a daughter's salary could make the difference between family subsistence and family comfort. A more compelling reason for seeking work, however, was the need to provide self-support. A large proportion of women workers had no alternative but to work in order to survive. Many of the testimonies in the *Harper's Bazaar* series recounted tales of women who worked because they were orphaned, had to support brothers and sisters, or experienced "family misfortunes" of some kind.[44]

During this period, however, women's wages were inadequate for more than "pin money"—supplemental household income. Women provided a supply of cheap labor for expanding business and industry. Their wages were abysmally low, especially with respect to men in comparable positions. Throughout the nineteenth century, for example, female factory operatives were paid on the average half of what male operatives earned.[45]

In the late 1880s, the urban woman worker was paid an average of $5.68 weekly; when the "lost time" of illness and layoff was taken into account, this sum fell to $5.24. Yet the average cost of living for a self-supporting woman was estimated at $5.51 a week—for housing, food, clothing, the support of dependents, and other expenses. A close look at the data supplied in the 1889 United States Department of Labor report, "Working Women in Large Cities," brings these figures to life. There was, for instance, a bag maker in Philadelphia who earned $4.49 and spent $4.17 a week, a Boston bustle maker who earned $5.19 and spent $4.71 a week, and a Chicago saleswoman who earned $8.42 and spent $7.92 a week. Many women, such as the New York seamstress who earned $4.42 and spent $5.12 weekly, listed "other sources" beyond their salaries as income; these sources probably included sums from their families back home, savings, or, as reformers most feared, money from male friends.[46]

Employers commonly justified their low payrolls by arguing that women worked only for extra luxuries. As late as 1904, an employer reported to the Minnesota Department of Labor that "girls are frivolous, dishonest, and inefficient" and that they worked only for "the excitement, the 'opportunity for ogling customers,' and display of cheap finery."[47] Many employers preferred hiring young women who lived at home with their parents, although some businesses, like hotels and restaurants, paid workers in part with room and board.

Surveys of working women in postbellum decades repeatedly found that many women who worked did so out of necessity. State labor bureau investigations in Kansas, Missouri, and New Jersey in the 1890s found that from 26 to 68 percent of the women studied supported dependents. In 1888, the United States Bureau of Labor found that over half of those surveyed, including women who lived at home with their parents, contributed to family finances.[48] These studies often stressed that boarders and lodgers were responsible for dependents back home as well as for their own self-support.

Like the other investigators, the Bureau of the Census affirmed that many working women labored because of financial need rather than for pin money. In 1907, the Census Bureau noted that, for most women, "it is the necessity of supporting themselves wholly or in part, and perhaps contributing to the support of those dependent upon them, that is usually the impelling motive" for their employment.[49] Of the women surveyed in 1900, over a third were self-supporting and living away from home. Of the remaining two-thirds, 12 percent were "heads of families" supporting dependents as well as themselves. Another 26 percent lived with their fathers, suggesting that the remaining women workers may have supported widowed mothers, destitute siblings, or, rarely, husbands and young children.[50]

These findings were reinforced by the Women's Bureau of the United States Department of Labor in the 1920s. The Women's Bureau analyzed the contributions of women wage earners to family support in 1922 and 1923. Almost all of the women studied who lived at home aided their families, the Women's Bureau found. Of those who lived away from home, nearly half "apparently had sharply defined responsibilities for personal or family support." The Women's Bureau noted that these tasks were accomplished on salaries barely adequate for self-support.[51] Economic need, it is clear, remained a compelling factor in the labor force behavior of many women in this era. But at the same time, the anxious efforts of some investigators to prove that women worked because they had to, rather than because they chose to, to some degree obscured the more complex motivations of women seeking paid employment outside the home.

LABOR DEMAND

Labor demand was as important as demographic, cultural, and economic factors in shaping the supply of labor for the female work force. Women workers were sought by a growing urban middle class desiring household help and by factories, shops, mills, and offices. Traditional female occupations, such as teaching and nursing, were also widening as population growth, mandatory education, and the professionalization of medicine occurred.[52]

The sex segregation of the labor force functioned to insure that labor demand would continue to be sex-specific. That is, as long as certain occupations were labeled "women's work," there would be a continuous need for women workers.[53] Sex segregation also minimized the cultural disjuncture between the need for labor and the cultural expectations of a woman's domestic role. The most common paid occupations for women—domestic service, sewing, nursing, and teaching—were among the occupations traditionally linked to female tasks of household maintenance and nurturing. Moreover, sex segregation guaranteed a supply of cheap labor. The lower status of women's work combined with the domestic ideology to keep female employment subordinate to the primary task of domesticity. This idea that women's work was secondary to family life in turn kept wages down and women unorganized, since so many women workers viewed their wage-earning activities as temporary.[54]

The Bureau of the Census reported with some surprise that women engaged in 294 of 303 recorded occupations in 1900. The only jobs that were exclusively male were those of soldiers, sailors, marines, firemen, streetcar drivers, telegraph and telephone linemen, apprentices to roofers and slaters, and helpers to steam boilermakers and brass workers.[55] But this list is deceiving. An examination of table 5 indicates that most women workers clustered in traditional sex-segregated jobs.

The occupations most often reported by women workers in the cities surveyed in 1900 were domestic service, sewing trades, clerical work, teaching, laundry work, nursing, sales, and textile manufactures. Factors of class, nativity, and race influenced which women entered which occupations. Native-born white women dominated clerical, teaching, and sales work in 1900. Foreign-born women constituted the majority of domestic servants and cotton factory operatives, while black women were half of all laundry workers.

At least 15 percent of the workers in each category were boarders and

Table 5

Percentage of Women Workers in Selected Occupations, by Native Origin and Race, in Selected U.S. Cities, 1900

Occupations[a]	Native White, Native Parents	Native White, Foreign Parents	Foreign-Born White	Black
Domestic service	12	19	47	21
Sewing work	23	41	32	4
Clerical work	41	48	11	—[b]
Teaching	44	42	11	3
Laundry work	7	15	27	51
Nursing and midwifery	32	22	37	9
Sales	30	54	16	—[b]
Cotton mill work	15	26	60	—[b]

Source: U.S. Bureau of the Census, *Statistics of Women at Work*, pp. 198–207, table 26.

[a]Domestic servants include stewardesses and housekeepers, waitresses, and domestic servants; sewing workers include dressmakers, milliners, seamstresses, and tailoresses; clerical workers include bookkeepers and accountants, clerks and copyists, and stenographers and typewriters (typists); teachers include teachers and college professors as well as musicians and teachers of music.
[b]Less than 1 percent.

lodgers, although some jobs were more likely to attract women living on their own than were others. Domestic service, nursing, teaching, and factory work were occupations where at least one in five workers boarded away from home. Other occupations, especially low-paying jobs such as telephone operating and store cashiering, were more likely to be filled by young women still living with their parents.

In general, women workers were most likely to be domestic servants; servants comprised more than a fourth of the urban female labor force in 1900. Almost 276,000 women worked as maids, cooks, waitresses, and kitchen help in private homes, hotels, boardinghouses, restaurants, and businesses. Nearly 80 percent of them received room and board as partial compensation for their labor. For this reason, domestic service was at that time an occupation requiring a population of transient women who were able to leave their parents' homes to live among strangers.

Domestic work was an especially important occupation for Scandinavians.

More than half of all female Swedish immigrant workers, 47 percent of the Norwegians, and 44 percent of the Danish immigrants labored as servants.[56] As David Katzman has noted, domestic service introduced rural and immigrant women to a more urban and modern environment. Indeed, for the unskilled foreign-born woman, domestic work was a major channel into the American culture, one in which she could learn the language and the mores of the middle class through daily contact with its family life.[57]

Sewing workers were the second most populous group of workers. Dressmakers, milliners, seamstresses, and tailors comprised a fifth of the female labor force. Immigrants or the daughters of immigrants made up more than two-thirds of the women in these trades. Additionally, almost two-thirds of the operatives in cotton-textile mills were foreign-born.

Clerical work was the third most important job category for urban women workers in 1900, representing 9 percent of the female labor force. These women—almost entirely native-born and white—labored in city offices as bookkeepers, accountants, clerks, copyists, stenographers, and "typewriters." Stenographers and typists evidenced the greatest increase of all women workers between 1890 and 1900, when the numbers of women in these occupations jumped 305 percent—from 21,000 to 86,000. The feminization of office work was unusually rapid. In 1870, 97.5 percent of the clerical labor force was male. In 1888, the New York City Young Women's Christian Association opened the first typing class for women, and female clerical education soon proliferated. By 1900, women comprised more than a third of the clerical labor force; by 1920, more than half.[58]

Like clerical work, the expansion of sales work opened job opportunities for native-born white women. Sales work for women developed at the same time as clerical work. In 1870, "sales women" were too few to be counted separately in the census records. By 1900, they numbered over 65,000 in the surveyed cities and over 142,000 nationally.[59]

By the 1890s, discussion of suitable work for women often included clerical and sales occupations along with medicine, law, "architecture and decorating," and journalism. These jobs, some argued, would not cause a woman to "lose caste" if she had to earn a living. One advice-book writer contended in 1893 that shorthand writing and typing were skills "well suited to the finer nature and more delicate organization of womankind. . . . The prejudice against employing young ladies in office-work is rapidly dying out."[60] The fast growth of white-collar work as a female sector of the labor force greatly broadened earning opportunities for native-born white women. Expanding labor force needs interacted with cultural expectations to force the widening of the definition of respectable behavior for young women.

The widening of "woman's sphere" in the years after the Civil War engendered deep tensions in American society. By the end of the nineteenth century, the working girl had become symbolic of the movement of women away from traditional domestic pursuits. Investigations into the subject of women and work often focused on the subgroup of self-supporting women who were native-born and white. A coalescence of interest in moral reform, wages, and living conditions sparked the development of a new social problem characterized by race and class concerns as material changes led to ideological debate. All women workers were to some degree controversial, but those living away from home who, because of their class status, were also visibly separated from their "proper place" seemed to pose an especially grave threat to social order.

Chapter 2
The Discovery of "Future Motherhood"

I n the postbellum era new work and migration patterns fueled a widespread controversy about the working woman's effect on morality and traditional family life. As working conditions began to impinge on the lives of "respectable" women, the middle class could no longer ignore the disjuncture between its domestic ideology and the behavior of women who worked for wages. In the lively debate that followed, discussion focused on the impact of industrialism on the single woman worker's moral and physical potential for future motherhood.

This phase of the debate over women and work reflected the concerns of the social gospel and progressive movements. Public discovery of the young working woman mirrored collective anxieties about changing gender roles, moral purity, the displacement of rural tradition by urban culture, and the fate of future generations. The young women who migrated to the cities to work came to symbolize the threat to middle-class ideals of family life posed by economic and social trends of the nineteenth century.

Antecedents of the Debate

The postbellum debate over the employment of women echoed even earlier concerns about women's place in society. In 1836, British author Harriet Martineau observed that American women practiced eight occupations in the workplace: teaching, needlework, keeping boarders, mill work, shoe binding, typesetting, bookbinding, and domestic service. But as early as 1820, women were working in at least seventy-five different kinds of manufacturing occupations.[1] Like their later counterparts, antebellum writers could not reach a consensus on the question of female employment. In the late eighteenth century, there were efforts to sanction the wage-work of women, but by the mid-nineteenth century the rise of the domestic ideology and the worsening of industrial conditions removed that sanction in most occupations, at least for "respectable" women.

Because most of the women who worked in the antebellum era were immigrant, black, or impoverished, the concern with their exploitation never became a widespread social issue, and women workers as a group remained largely invisible to the public. Only the exceptional New England mill workers received much attention, but their status was secured by the paternalism of the textile manufacturers, which undercut any overt threat of independence on the part of the workers. Of the early positions on the issue of women and work, only one—an argument for a separate female domestic sphere—gained much popularity.

One of the early positions on the question of female employment in the United States maintained that women should work for both economic and moral reasons: they were needed in the labor force, and idleness was sinful. Household manufactures, of course, had long permitted women to be economically productive without leaving the protection of the family. But at the end of the eighteenth century the textile industry spawned factories where spinning and weaving were done on shop premises rather than in the worker's home. In 1791, Secretary of the Treasury Alexander Hamilton, in his *Report on Manufactures*, encouraged women to work in the burgeoning factories. Women could then supplement family income, and those who might otherwise be dependent upon the community for support would be "rendered more useful."[2]

Calvinist moralists and manufacturers alike argued that supervised female factory operatives were a boon to the nation's economic order. The factory system, besmirched by the European experience of "dark satanic mills," would be cleansed when transferred to American villages and staffed with bucolic American girls. Female factory operatives would avoid the fate of those unemployed women who were "doomed to idleness and its inseparable attendants, vice and guilt."[3] The women workers at Lowell, Lawrence, and other New England textile towns could work and still retain social status.

At the same time, a few writers countered the proposal that women *could* work with the more radical idea that women *should* work. The feminist themes of Mary Wollstonecraft's *A Vindication of the Rights of Women*, published in England in 1792, were echoed in the United States by Charles Brockden Brown, in *Alcuin: A Dialogue* (1798), and by "Constantia"—Judith Sargent Stevens Murray—a Massachusetts merchant's daughter who penned similar essays in the 1790s.[4] But these proponents of feminism were far ahead of their time and did not reflect popular sentiment.

By the 1820s and 1830s a more conservative viewpoint on the issue of women and work was gaining strength. The middle-class prescription of domesticity maintained that women should not work for wages but should concentrate instead on creating a domestic paradise for husband and children. Even single young women should be preparing themselves for their future domestic role. Male and female social behavior was seen as distinct and immutably tied to the biology of reproduction. Motherhood and the preparation for motherhood were taken to be the foremost concerns of women.

Historians agree that the domestic realm was becoming a distinctly female sphere in the United States in the antebellum era. An older tradition of male dominance within the family eroded as the self-contained household economy of the colonial era disintegrated under pressures of industrialism and urbanization. The patriarchal father no longer governed child rearing and household management with a stern hand. Women gained a new measure of power, although it was sharply limited, as child rearing and domestic economy became their preserve alone. Female education, religion, and manners turned toward the enhancement of the domestic role, as the one-wage-earner family, headed by the father, took root.[5]

As "woman's sphere" became exclusively domestic, adherence to the socially prescribed role became tightly tied to the health of the social order. Families had long been seen as the cornerstone of society. For the clergy, the mother's duty was to raise pious children; for the patriot, it was to raise loyal citizens. As historian Nancy Cott observes, the confluence of religious and secular influences set up a "cultural halo ringing the significance of home and family" for the well-being of society.[6] Female role behavior became imbued with powerful connotations for the future of the nation.

Within this domestic vision the role of the mother became sanctified. Although motherhood had not been an idealized state through the early eighteenth century, "the rise of the moral mother" accompanied the rise of the domestic ideology.[7] The biological processes of motherhood and the social processes of child rearing became symbolic of the possibilities and the limitations of the female role. In this symbolism the separation of childbearing from child rearing was branded immoral, justifying the sexual division of labor and its underpinnings of patriarchy.[8] By the mid-nineteenth century, writers commonly praised the special ability of women to nurture children. Horace Bushnell, Lydia Maria Child, and the authors of the proliferating advice books agreed with the sentiment expressed by Catharine Beecher about "mother" in 1846: "Oh sacred and beautiful name . . . a *whole nation* will have received its character and destiny from her hands."[9]

This domestic ideology placed women firmly within a role that was expected to transcend class boundaries and that reflected the belief that gender roles stemmed from biological differences between men and women. Whereas men were expected to be acquisitive and aggressive, women were thought to represent virtues of self-sacrifice, piety, purity, and nurture. The home came to represent a counterweight to the harshness of modernization, a salve for the husband and father bruised by the daily work encounter. "Woman's sphere" was to be a domestic spiritual oasis within the desert of industrial materialistic culture.

This ideology prescribed expected behavior for white native-born women—they were ultimately to be full-time mothers. Other women, however, continued to work for wages away from farm and home in dusty workrooms and in grimy factories. Although they were a minority of women, their concentration in large cities brought some limited attention to their plight. To some critics, the danger in female employment sprang from the potential for exploitation rather than from concern over role transgression. By the 1820s, urban expansion had created a market for ready-made clothing in the cities, and thousands of women on the East Coast hand-sewed garments for low wages under miserable working conditions.[10] These conditions gave rise to a recognition of the need for work opportunities for women while condemning the culture of industrialism and the exploitative conditions that prevailed. An 1845 report in the *New York Tribune* said of women workers that "their frames are bent by incessant and stooping toil, their health destroyed by want of rest and proper exercise, and their minds as effectively stunted, brutalized, and destroyed over their monotonous tasks as if they were doomed to count the bricks in a prison wall—for what is life to them but a fearful and endless imprisonment, with all its horrors and privations?"[11]

Some reformers argued for the improvement of working conditions for these women wage earners through the expansion of particularly female spheres of work in a sex-segregated labor force. Catharine Beecher, for example, suggested in 1846 that the problem of the female factory worker's ruining her health and the problem of the educated woman without an outlet for her talents could be solved alike by the development of teaching as a woman's profession. This, she wrote, "will prove the true remedy for all those *wrongs of women* which her mistaken champions are seeking to cure by drawing her into professions and pursuits which belong to the other sex."[12]

Publisher and social critic Mathew Carey also proposed that "female" jobs be provided for those women who must earn a living. He was particularly concerned with the plight of urban seamstresses. In his "Appeal to the Wealthy of the Land, Ladies as Well as Gentlemen," published in 1835, Carey offered nine solutions to the problem of exploitative working conditions for women. His recommendations included the expansion of job opportunities, increased job training, and the opening to women of those "low employments" that were monopolized by men.[13]

One of his solutions was for the separation of employment spheres for men and women. Men, Carey suggested, should perform industrial and heavy agricultural labor, while women should take over all domestic, sewing, and sales work—the last still a male occupation in the antebellum years. Carey argued that women were "admirably calculated" for work in retail stores. The *New York Sun*, in 1845, proposed similarly that dry goods store owners hire women exclusively, "dismiss their men to manly occupations, and save for society a thousand women from want and temptation."[14]

The idea that work roles should reflect qualities of gender was reiterated in 1869 by Virginia Penny in her book *Think and Act*. Penny insisted that "a strong, healthy man behind the counter of a fancy store, in a millinery establishment, on his knees fitting ladies' shoes, at hotels laying the plates and napkins of a dinner table, is as much out of place, as a woman chopping wood, carrying in coal, or sweeping the streets."[15] These arguments for distinct employment spheres for men and women extended job opportunities to women who had to work. At the same time, however, a sex-segregated labor market protected many male occupations from encroachment by women and preserved gender roles. Catharine Beecher's proposal for the feminization of the teaching profession, for example, stemmed from a belief that the education of children was a natural function of women.[16]

Some working-class commentators linked the ideology of domesticity to criticisms of exploitative working conditions. In 1845, "Julianna," a writer for the Lowell Female Labor Reform Association, argued that factory life deprived women of domestic attributes. The workers, "instead of being qualified to rear a family . . . have need to be instructed in the *very first* principles of living well and thinking right," she wrote. If the factory system continued, she added, "what . . . will be the mental and intellectual character of the future generations of New England?" The association advocated the establishment of a ten-hour workday in order to prevent damage "to the constitutions of future generations" through injury to women who would one day be mothers.[17]

Women protested their situation elsewhere as well. Needlewomen organized in New York, Philadelphia, and Boston in the 1840s to appeal to the public for higher wages. In 1846 in New York City, seamstresses complained of producing shirts at four cents apiece "while agents of debauchery circulated among them with offers of ease and plenty."[18]

Some working-class men resented the presence of women in industry. The National Trades Union, at their 1836 convention, termed female labor "the most disgraceful escutcheon on the character of American freemen" and noted that women's work "should be only of a domestic nature." Factory work, the unionists insisted, injured both the health and the morals needed for the "culture and bearing of healthy children." They also foreshadowed later criticisms of the use of women to cut wages, contending that women competed for jobs with men and that the female factory operative who worked for low wages was therefore "tying a stone around the neck of her natural protector, Man."[19]

The Discovery of the Working Girl

By the 1860s, changing demographic patterns combined with the effects of industrialism and urbanization to produce a growing class of women workers—"respectable" single self-supporting women. The widening distance between the domestic ideology and women's behavior was bridged by the labeling of self-supporting women as a problematic group—a process that crystallized public unease over larger social changes in work and family life. Because white native-born women who worked most clearly violated norms of sex-role behavior, they captured public attention, bringing attention also to the larger population of women workers, of which they were but a part. The voices of the middle class—journalists, charity workers, reformers, clergymen, and jurists—combined to shape a rhetoric that stressed the dangers of and to women who lived apart from their proper place.

The postbellum phase of the debate over female employment evolved in three stages: the discovery and labeling of self-supporting women; fact-finding and hence legitimization of the problem; and social policy decisions based on a public consensus about the requisites of future motherhood. A fourth stage, the implementation of reform, will be discussed in chapter 3.[20]

The initial discovery of the new problem of the working girl occurred as morality and the economic situation of working women were linked in large cities to the problem of social order. The woman living on her own, it was feared, was prone to behave in an immoral fashion. Women who worked and lived away from home became known as "homeless women" and "women adrift." These terms applied not only to the female boarder and lodger but also to the destitute women of the slums who were literally without shelter and who slept in police stations, public parks, and alleys.[21] The double meaning of these labels buttressed the idea that the woman living outside of traditional family life was on the cutting edge of disrepute. Without the anchor of domesticity, she was adrift in a sea of ambiguous identity.

There was no parallel terminology for "respectable" young men living apart from their families. The "homeless man" was invariably the tramp, the hobo, and the skid-row denizen; the term "self-supporting man" has always seemed redundant. What was controversial for women—living apart from the family while earning a living—was expected for young men. Male boarders and lodgers acquired status through their occupation, wealth, or education.[22] For women, however, traditional identification as daughter, wife, or mother shaped their rank within society in conjunction with class, occupation, and racial status.

The discovery and labeling of "women adrift" first occurred in largely impressionistic newspaper exposés published in the mid-nineteenth century. These articles emphasized the economic exigencies of the self-supporting woman. New York newspapers through the 1860s maintained that tens of thousands of women workers were "in a constant fight with starvation and pauperism." In 1868, a Boston newspaper found 20,000 women toiling for "starvation rates." Urban newspapers across the nation published similar articles through the 1880s. One commentator noted that these stories "arrested the attention of the thinking class to woman's needs as it has never been arrested before."[23]

The heightened concern with working women stressed the physical misery, potential pauperism, and moral danger believed attendant to female employment. Perhaps the best known of the journalistic exposés on working women was Helen Campbell's *Prisoners of Poverty*, originally published as a series in the Sunday edition of the *New York Tribune* in the late 1880s. *Tribune* readers became acquainted with shop girls, domestic servants, and garment workers of New York City, and with women such as Rose Haggarty, a seamstress supporting dependent siblings, who was forced into prostitution by economic need.[24]

This genre of reporting proliferated throughout the country. In Minneapolis, for instance, readers learned of the plight of laundresses, hotel workers, printers, and other women workers in a series of articles by Eva McDonald Valesh, published from 1888 until 1891 in the *St. Paul Globe*. Stories entitled "Song of the Shirt," "Working in the Wet," and "In Cap and Apron" presented readers with colorful portraits of working women, while raising questions about morality, wages, and working conditions.[25]

This publicity about urban work conditions contributed to a public demand for fact-finding agencies. Massachusetts established the first state labor-statistics bureau in 1869; by 1887, twenty-two states had organized similar institutions. In 1885, the Department of Labor was founded in Washington to provide a similar service on the federal level.[26]

The fact-finding efforts of these bureaus confirmed the newly labeled deviance of single self-supporting women. The Massachusetts bureau published the earliest study of urban working women in 1870, corroborating press accounts of low wages, long hours, and the "miserable state of living that was the lot of wage-earning women in the manufacturing towns of Massachusetts."

New York, Maine, California, Iowa, New Jersey, and Minnesota were among the states that followed in the next decade with separate chapters on working women in their annual reports. "No class of wage-earners is more deserving yet receives less attention from reformers, philanthropists, and lawmakers," a typical report from Wisconsin began in 1884, "than the girls and women of cities who are compelled to support themselves, and frequently dependent relatives also, by their daily labor."[27]

Attention to working women continued apace. In 1889, the United States Department of Labor published *Working Women in Large Cities*—a 613-page survey of over 17,000 women employed in twenty-two cities. In 1895, the New York State Assembly appointed a committee to investigate the "condition of female labor" in New York City. They held thirty-six public meetings, heard 258 witnesses, and concluded that "from this terrible and unprecedented condition of affairs arises untold misery, immorality, and crime." In 1907, the United States Senate began a nineteen-volume study of employed women and children. And in 1911, the Debaters' Handbook series, which popularized opposing viewpoints on such issues as capital punishment and the income tax, added a volume of articles on the employment of women, further reflecting the controversial nature of women's work.[28]

As rural and middle-class young women entered the labor force, another genre of reporting emerged. These were the "firsthand" reports of investigators examining the experience of women's work at the turn of the century. Though limited by a middle-class and often patronizing perspective, these accounts remain a valuable source about the lives of working women. "First-person" investigations such as Bessie and Marie Van Vorst's *The Woman Who Toils* (1903) and Cornelia Parker's *Working with the Working Woman* (1922) were typical of the reports written by middle-class women posing as workers; Bessie Van Vorst cast off her "Parisian clothes" to don "coarse woolen garments" and a "shabby felt sailor hat" to transform herself into a "working girl of the ordinary type."[29] Other firsthand chronicles were written by "respectable" women who had to work, such as Dorothy Richardson, in *The Long Day* (1905); the anonymous author of *Four Years in the Underbrush: Adventures of a Working Woman in New York* (1921); and the young women submitting essays to *Harper's Bazaar* for the 1908 series, "The Girl Who Comes to the City."[30]

This wealth of literature reflected a new urgency about the controversial status of the working woman. Most commentators agreed that acquired characteristics—such as debilitation resulting from overwork—could be transmitted through heredity to children, and hence the work life of young women, though temporary, could permanently damage their future lives as mothers.[31] They differed, however, in proposals for change. Conservatives argued that women could and should return to their proper sphere at home, reflecting assumptions rooted in the domestic ideology of the mid-nineteenth century. Radicals on this issue, like earlier feminists, encouraged women to participate in any kind of work they desired and proposed that women not be barred from traditionally male occupations. Progressives took a middle view. They accepted the fact that women were working, but proposed that domestic influences and protections be extended into the work and living environments of self-supporting women. The social structure rather than the behavior of workers would be transformed. Like earlier activists, progressives sought a way to mesh the realities of women's work with ideological prescriptions about future motherhood.

The conservative viewpoint held that the working woman transgressed her proper place in society. Advocates of domesticity viewed gender roles as inflexible and upheld the idea of patriarchy, particularly the economic dominance of men. The conservatives focused their arguments on the status of white native-born women. These commentators, blind to the realities of economic need for so many women, contended that since working women had voluntarily left home, they could just as easily return.

The subject of interest for many conservatives was the young farm girl whose innocence and purity were contrasted to the depravity of urban life. The "ideal farm girl," a *Farm Journal* writer suggested in 1903, should accept her future as a mother in a quiet country home. For the girl who rebelled against her lot, moral disaster was inevitable:

> The farm girl is all right until she gets herself worked into the notion that she is capable of something higher than helping her folks at home—that there is a "career" for her that will lead on to wealth and distinction, and she must leave the paternal roof and go in pursuit of the good things she feels sure are laid up for her somewhere. When she feels herself pretty well assured that she is of better stuff than her mother, and that she will marry no "hayseed" for a husband and settle down for life to domestic drudgery as she did, there is trouble brewing for her that will sooner or later overwhelm her.[32]

The picture painted here of domestic drudgery could not be attractive to many high-spirited young women, but the alternative was presented in even less desirable terms. If farm life were hard and dreary—and articles and readers' letters in the rural women's magazines attested to lives of isolation, loneliness, and adversity—life in the city was presented as no less than the road to ruin.[33] The problems of nonwage work in a rural home did not inspire public debate; the consequences of the rejection of that life did.

These opponents of women's work claimed that employment was for many women a frivolous choice motivated by a shallow desire for excitement. One writer with this point of view was Bessie Van Vorst, who posed as a factory hand in Pittsburgh and in Perry, a New York mill town, in 1903. Van Vorst stated that the native-born woman "works for luxury until the day when a proper husband presents himself." She added that "the American woman is restless, dissatisfied. . . . For natural obligations are substituted the fictitious duties of clubs, meetings, committees, organizations, professions, a thousand unwomanly occupations." She proposed that those women who worked for any reason but dire necessity should leave the labor force, where they only competed with their impoverished self-supporting sisters. If a woman desired to earn extra money, Van Vorst concluded, she should work in such industrial arts as lace-making, goldsmithing, or bookbinding, tasks "more consistent" with her destiny as a woman.[34]

Instead of absorbing lessons in cooking, budgeting, and child care, critics charged, women who worked learned ultimately useless tasks, developed a taste for extravagance, and, perhaps worst of all, nurtured a dissatisfaction with mundane domestic life. Women, one writer claimed, were becoming "mentally and morally unfit" for the traditional female role within the family.[35]

This growing unfitness for motherhood, some believed, was related to the failure of education for women. Opposition to higher education for women in this era came from critics who contended that schooling in anything but domesticity encouraged an "incoherent rebellion" against wifehood and motherhood and fomented invalidism and physical disability. The psychologist G. Stanley Hall, in his study *Adolescence*, published in 1904, presented a typical argument against "excessive intellectualism" in young women. "Just as a man must fight the battles of competition, and be ready to lay down his life for his country," Hall stated, "so woman needs a heroism of her own to face the pain, danger, and work of bearing and rearing children, and whatever lowers the tone of her body, nerves, or *morale* so that she seeks to escape this function, merits the same kind of opprobrium which society metes out to the exempts who can not or who will not fight to save their country in time of need."[36] Hall, along with others, argued against training women for careers that were "disfunctional" for their roles as future mothers.[37]

The belief that women were innately limited by biological constraints was common. Dorothy Richardson, author of *The Long Day*, suggested in an essay published in 1906 that the reproductive potential of women brought special dangers to their efforts to expand their sphere of activities. Women, she argued, could not develop the "equal industrial abilities" of men because "as potential mothers they are functionally limited mentally and physically."[38]

This perspective was taken also by the social critic Henry Finck, who suggested in a widely circulated 1901 essay, "Employments Unsuitable for Women," that the woman who chose to work "coarsened" herself and lessened her chances for successful marriage and motherhood. He criticized women who left home to work, claiming that "girls should be taught that, except under the stress of poverty, it is selfish as well as suicidal on their part to go out and work." He wrote, "Men still prefer, and always will prefer, the home girl to any other kind. They want a girl who has not marred her beauty and ruined her health by needless work, or rubbed off the peach bloom of innocence by exposure to a rough world."[39] For women who did have to work, Finck recommended only those jobs which insured that women "remain womanly":

> Having once discovered the charm of the eternal womanly, man will never allow it to be taken away again, to please a lot of half-women who are clamoring for what they illogically call their "rights." Men will find a way of making these misguided persons understand that it is as unseemly for them to be—as many of them are now—butchers, hunters, carpenters, barbers, stump speakers, iron and steel workers, miners, etc., as it would for them to try to take the places of our soldiers, sailors, firemen, mail carriers, and policemen. All employments which make women bold, fierce, muscular, brawny in body or mind will be more and more rigidly tabooed as unwomanly.[40]

Finck concluded that employments which did not threaten female purity and "womanliness" should be accessible to them, but he cautioned, "Let this be regarded, not as a special privilege and an indication of social progress, but as a necessary evil, to be cured in as many cases as possible by marriage or some other way of bringing the workers back to their deserted homes."[41]

Like the conservatives, feminists were for the most part concerned with the situation of middle-class women; unlike the proponents of domesticity, however, they sought expanded rather than constricted work opportunities. In lyceum lectures and in publications, feminists promoted the idea that women should be able to choose employment instead of marriage as their primary role. In 1865, Mary Abigail Dodge argued that "respectable" women should be able to work without the danger of losing their class status. "Let a poor girl go to work, and it is nothing at all," she wrote. "She is obligated to do it, and society does not so much as turn a look upon her; but let a girl go out from her brown-stone five-story house, from the care and attendance of servants, to work for three or five hours a day . . . and immediately there is a commotion."[42] Dodge asserted that women should consider the independence of work preferable to the dependence of an unhappy marriage. Women, she maintained, need not accept "the debasement of [themselves] which an indifferent marriage necessitates. It is better to be not wholly well placed than to be wholly ill placed."[43]

Kate Gordon, of Mount Holyoke College, responded directly to Hall's attack on higher education for women. She suggested in 1905 that Hall's characterization of women was of "a very apotheosis of the vegetable" and that the domestic sphere for women that was so strongly advocated by Hall was but "one of a large number of possible occupations for women."[44]

In response to Henry Finck's essay on occupations unsuitable for women, suffragist Ida Husted Harper insisted that women had the right to work when and if they pleased. Not all women, she pointed out, had the opportunity to "stay at home and take care of their peach-bloom."[45] The active encouragement of widening work opportunities for women was on the radical edge of postbellum thought. More common was the idea that some women were going to work, for better or for worse, and that reformers should improve the conditions that surrounded working women bereft of domestic influences.

Conservatives sought to recapture a past in which women did not work for wages outside of the home, and feminists looked to a future of equality. But progressives acknowledged present realities about women who worked, and they interpreted the controversy of women's employment as one of exploitation rather than one of role transgression. At the same time, progressives argued that society should be adjusted to provide economic and moral security for working women who were still fundamentally domestic beings.

Progressive reformers were influenced in their approach to the problem of the working woman by their attempt to rebut conservative accusations that women worked for supplemental income alone. Investigators produced survey after survey that attempted to demonstrate that even the women at home were often wholly or partly dependent upon their own wages for self-support.[46] Moreover, progressive reformers believed, if the economic situation of the working woman who lived at home was precarious, what of the woman who lived on her own, and who had to purchase rent, food, and other necessities of life on her all-too-meager salary? The remedy, they argued, was the melioration of harsh working conditions.

The progressive viewpoint reflected a changing cultural climate of reform. The laissez-faire view of William Graham Sumner and others, which supported the doctrine of the "survival of the fittest," had been increasingly countered by advocates of social change in the latter part of the nineteenth century. The maxims of the social gospel and progressive movements maintained that social conditions were not fixed but were malleable and that the greater good was the active shaping and reshaping of society to advance ideals of social harmony and justice.[47]

The social gospel was a creed of "applied Christianity" preached by Protestant clergymen such as Washington Gladden and Walter Rauschenbusch in the late nineteenth and early twentieth centuries. The gospel held that sin and salvation were social concerns, particularly in the cities beset by the effects of rapid growth and industrialism. "Our cities are the battle ground of Christian civilization," Washington Gladden contended. "They are destined to become, more and more, the arena upon which our greatest conflicts for liberty and order and morality are to be waged."[48] These conflicts included the fight against such "sins" as government corruption, the toleration of prostitution, and the exploitation of urban workers.

The social gospel gained an enlarged forum in 1908, when the Federal Council of the Churches of America was founded in Philadelphia by thirty-three Protestant denominations. Among the declarations for social justice espoused by the council was the need to "safeguard the physical and moral health of the community" with the protective regulation of women's work conditions.[49] The social gospel provided a religious sanction and an evangelical rhetoric for the doctrines of the progressive reform movement. Henry May has demonstrated the links between the two movements in the widespread "social awakening" of late nineteenth- and early twentieth-century cities faced with the adjustment to industrialism, particularly in the challenge to the laissez-faire doctrine and the search for a better society through the gradual reform of American capitalism.[50]

The progressives were particularly preoccupied with children. As the historian Robert Wiebe has noted, to the progressive "the child was the carrier of tomorrow's hope. . . . Protect him, nurture him, and in his manhood he would create that bright new world of the progressives' vision."[51] Hence the interpretation that working women endangered their future motherhood magnified the progressive viewpoint while reinforcing traditional values about women's role in society. The protection of working women from physical and moral danger became even more tightly linked to the harmonizing of social order when the well-being of future generations was at stake.

In his "Prayers of the Social Awakening," the clergyman Walter Rauschenbusch encapsulated the viewpoint about working women:

O God, we pray Thee for our sisters who are leaving the ancient shelter of the home to earn their wage in the store and shop amid the press of modern life. Grant them strength of body to bear the strain of unremitting toil, and may no present pressure unfit them for the holy duties of home and motherhood which the future may lay upon them. Give them grace to cherish under the new surroundings the old sweetness and gentleness of womanhood, and in the rough mingling of life to keep the purity of their hearts and lives untarnished. . . . If it must be so that our women toil like men, help us still to reverence in them the mothers of the future.[52]

Rauschenbusch here effectively summed up the progressive interpretation of the working woman—that she endangered her future motherhood through the vulnerability of her health and morality and that domestic values still prevailed. Rauschenbusch also believed that protections should be extended to the woman outside the home that would extend the vision of "woman's place" into the industrial environment.

A major theme of progressive reformers was that unregulated conditions of employment imperiled the physical health of the young women who would one day be mothers. In *Women and Industry*, Annie MacLean stated that harsh working conditions "make for a weaker generation to replace the present one."[53] The widely circulated Debaters' Handbook on the employment of women opened with the statement that work risked a young woman's "future usefulness" and asked, "Can society afford to maintain any system of industry that involves the physical, mental, and moral neglect of children through the employment of girls and women?"[54] Some reformers suggested that an especially dangerous aspect of industrialism was that young women who worked were not preparing for their future roles as mothers. The lack of domestic education was linked by the United States Senate investigators to infant mortality. In a 1912 study of Fall River, Massachusetts, the researchers found that "the mother's ignorance of proper feeding, of proper care, and of the simplest requirements of hygiene" was the major cause of infant death.[55]

Social-gospel advocates agreed that women workers were a special class requiring protection because of their status as future mothers. Walter Rauschenbusch wrote in 1917 that "women . . . demand special attention because life springs from their bodies. They alone can exercise the sacred function of maternity, which is higher than the production of goods. Their capacity to bear and rear sound children is the most important physical asset of the race."[56] This argument reached its apex when the United States Supreme Court upheld the constitutionality of a workday limited to ten hours for women laundry workers in Oregon. In the landmark 1908 case *Muller* v. *Oregon*, Justice

David Brewer deemed that female dependence and physiology justified protective legislation. A working woman's long hours of standing on her feet, he wrote, "tends to injurious effects upon the body, and as healthy mothers are essential to vigorous offspring, the physical well-being of woman becomes an object of public interest and care in order to preserve the strength and vigor of the race."[57] As we will see in chapter 3, protective legislation became one of the remedies proposed for the problem of the self-supporting woman.

Work itself was seen as a demoralizing influence on young women workers. Some observers, such as Virginia Penny, argued that women gained sharpened wits and quickened perceptions because of their work experiences, and the United States Senate investigation countered accusations that the "new occupations" of women led them into immorality.[58] Carroll Wright, of the Massachusetts Bureau of Statistics of Labor, had similarly defended the virtue of the working girls of Boston in 1889. These young women, he argued, were "making an heroic, an honest, and a virtuous struggle to earn an honorable livelihood."[59]

But most commentators appeared to agree with the Wisconsin Vice Commission, which stated that working conditions contributed to immoral behavior. "In many stores and factories men and women of all degrees of morality and immorality mingle with promiscuous familiarity," the commission noted, adding that "it must also be stated that the requirement that women employees shall stand all day, and the active nature of the day's work cause a severe nervous strain, leading to fatigue and weakening of the will power by the time the day is ended."[60] A state factory inspector in Minnesota concurred, observing in 1912 that the "moral tone" of factories and laundries was low because of the familiarity of working men toward working women, "the prevailing practice of telling suggestive stories," unsanitary conditions, and a "spirit of discontent." She also suggested that the monotony of the work routine caused women to seek the "rest in excitement. . . . Imagine spending ten hours a day washing dishes in a restaurant . . . putting eyelets in shoes, or feeding towels in a mangle. . . . The machine is master, the operator is slave. . . . I remarked recently to a foreman that the girls must be tired. He said, 'No, they are so used to it, they are like the machine, they don't feel it.'"[61] The routinization of work, the inspector declared, deadened the sensibility of workers and increased their vulnerability toward immoral behavior.[62]

Whereas the criticism of industrialism in the antebellum era resulted in an isolated movement to ease women into "female" occupations, now reformers vigorously strove to adjust industrial society itself to meet standards of domesticity. Jane Addams argued that "as working women enter fresh fields of labor

. . . society must endeavor to protect them by an amelioration of the economic conditions which are now so unnecessarily harsh and dangerous to health and morals."[63] This amelioration would occur through a series of remedies by which reformers attempted to safeguard the "future motherhood" of the hundreds of thousands of young women who had abandoned their traditional place within the home.

Chapter 3
The Working Girl and
the Social Order

*T*he ideological controversy over the status of the working girl in the late nineteenth century led to extensive reform efforts to protect her physical and moral health. From about 1865 to 1920, reformers attempted to "soften the harshest experiences" of working women through the provision of such ameliorative measures as Travelers' Aid services, boarding homes, and recreational programs, which would extend domestic values into the lives of those women considered to be most "adrift" from their proper place. From about 1890 to 1923, another reform was increasingly advocated—the protection of future motherhood through the improvement of conditions in the workplace itself.

In both cases there was a recognition of social change. Young women were joining the urban labor force in increasing numbers and would continue to do so. But there was also the assumption that the working life of the young girl was temporary and that marriage would pull her back into the domestic domain. As a result, reform measures were for the most part targeted for the young, inexperienced, but "respectable" woman worker, and other groups of women, such as older career women or black women, were largely ignored. At the same time, the health of the social order would be preserved. If the entrance of single women into the labor force promised great social change, the extension of these reform measures would help to control and regulate the effects of that change.

The effort to protect the working girl was an urban phenomenon. The city was viewed as hostile to the preservation of domestic values both because of the visibility of prostitution and because of behavior practices of urban women workers that were widely believed by the middle class to be immoral, such as the patronage of dance halls and saloons. The virtue of the young country girl was believed to be especially endangered by exposure to urban life. The story of Nelly Haynes, told in *The Household* magazine in 1892, was typical for its contrast of rural virtue with urban depravity; Nelly's beauty and ambition prod her to leave the dull country town of "Mantlewood" for the glitter of the big city. There her path leads, inevitably, to prostitution and squalid death.[1]

Prostitution in this era was more than a mere rhetorical symbol of role transgression. Prostitution was quasi-legal in most American cities from the 1870s through the 1910s. Reglementation—a system of controlling prostitutes through a monthly fine system and regulated red-light districts—kept prostitutes highly visible. St. Louis, Washington, Chicago, New Orleans, and Minneapolis were among the cities tolerating wide-open "vice zones" in the 1870s and 1880s.[2]

Young working women were seen as vulnerable to the lures of prostitution for two reasons—low pay and loneliness. It was commonly thought that prostitutes were recruited from the ranks of poorly paid working women, many of them turning to vice because of the higher standard of living they thought they could achieve. Whereas the average working woman at the turn of the century could earn from $4.00 to $6.00 weekly, the prostitute could earn from $50 to $400 in the same amount of time—if she were young and attractive.[3] Prostitutes themselves testified that low wages motivated their downfall. In 1888, a Minneapolis prostitute told a newspaper reporter, "I tried for three years to support life on the wages I was paid as a cashier in a big store. . . . I gave up the struggle at last. . . . They call me unworthy of any person's notice now, but I don't starve and freeze since I quit being respectable."[4]

Other women told of the need for love, acceptance, and social life as a reason for their turn to prostitution. The vulnerability of young women living outside of domestic influences was the subject of a series of articles in the 1910 *Ladies' Home Journal*. The anonymous author of "My Experiences in New York" described life for a young migrant, lonely and frightened, and warned that the unsupervised working girl could be easily led into temptation and immorality, at worst, or a dreary "unnatural" life as a single career woman, at best.[5]

Reformers feared that young women seeking entertainment and friendship might turn to the commercial manifestations of urban culture—dance halls, saloons, and amusement parks. These aspects of city life could be so dangerous, William Sanger suggested in 1858, that inducements should be provided "for young women to leave the city, thus removing them from its baneful influences to a part of the country where their own labor would give them the means of a comfortable subsistence and a virtuous life."[6]

Others feared that danger was even more overt. Fears of "white slavery" abounded in cities in this era, as reformers saw panderers ready to pounce on unwary country girls at every way station and on every street. Ernest Bell, a minister and leader of the Illinois Vigilance Association, warned mothers in 1910 that "the country girl is in greater danger from the 'white slavers' than the city girl . . . because [she is] less sophisticated, more trusting and more open to the allurements of those who are waiting to prey upon [her]."[7]

But most reformers recognized that warnings alone would not prevent young women from seeking work in the city. They instead mounted a "purity crusade" in the postbellum era. Groups including the National Purity Congress, incorporated in 1895, and the vice commissions of dozens of cities proposed that red-light districts be outlawed and preventive moral measures be supported. They would thus suppress the immediate problem of prostitution while offering working women some alternatives to the dismal living conditions that, they believed, led inexorably to immorality.[8]

Reform of the Urban Environment

Efforts to protect women workers from the lures of the urban environment through ameliorative measures were dominated by middle-class charity workers. These philanthropists believed that they shared a common sisterhood with young women less fortunate than they. The statement of the Minneapolis Woman's Christian Association in 1886 was typical of this sentiment: "Dear Sisters, . . . The shops, factories, and stores are full of girls— many of them away from home and friends. They are our young sisters and we shall be held accountable by God for their safe-keeping. We *are* our sisters' keepers."[9] Although these reformers often declared that the shared status of gender was more important than the notion of class, their activities belied this concept. If class were obviated, it was because reformers assumed that working women shared, or could share, in their middle-class ideals.[10] The protection of working women was promoted through the extension of middle-class domestic values through such institutions as Travelers' Aid, boarding homes, and recreation clubs.

TRAVELERS' AID

One remedy for the problem of the working woman that took shape in the 1860s was the institution of Travelers' Aid—a movement that brought the geographic mobility of young women under the watchful guardianship of moral reformers. Travelers' Aid had begun in the United States in 1851, when the former mayor of St. Louis, Bryan Mullanphy, bequeathed over $300,000 for a "fund to furnish relief to all poor emigrants and travelers coming to St. Louis on their way, bona fide, to settle in the West."[11] By 1866, when the

Boston Young Women's Christian Association (YWCA) was founded to protect migrant women, the idea of Travelers' Aid had narrowed to mean protection for young women and the concomitant prevention of urban prostitution.

The Boston YWCA, in its first annual report in 1867, expressed the attitude
that had been embraced by the Travelers' Aid movement for nearly half a
century:

> It is well known that many young women come to the city from homes in
> the country where they have enjoyed the blessings of parental affection
> and care and guardianship. Their world circumstances necessitate their
> separation from loved ones and compel them to seek employment where
> there is a larger demand for it. They generally come inexperienced,
> unacquainted with the difficulties which are before them, obliged to
> seek their homes where snares are spread on every side, with no kind
> hand to lead, or wise and judicious acquaintance to advise. It was felt
> that some agency should be devised that would *meet young women on
> their arrival in the city*, conduct them to proper homes and counsel
> them.[12]

The first Travelers' Aid work of the YWCA was to advertise referral services
for housing and employment in railway depots and in circulars sent to clergymen throughout the New England countryside. By 1875, YWCAs, state labor
bureaus, and other groups had established similar services in Providence,
Hartford, Cleveland, New York, and Minneapolis.

By the 1880s, reformers determined that young migrants needed more than
an address posted on a depot wall. In 1885, the Brooklyn Society of Friends
funded the nation's first full-time Travelers' Aid worker. She sat in the terminal of Grand Central Station, distributing cards and notices, and was soon
advising hundreds of young migrants. By the 1890s, Travelers' Aid workers
were common sights in the train and boat stations of most large cities.

The matrons, wearing brightly colored sashes and badges, attempted to
protect young women by distributing religious tracts, providing addresses and
train schedules, promoting supervised boardinghouses, and publicizing employment agencies run by benevolent groups. They counseled young runaways
who had not yet "fallen" into disrepute, sent pregnant unmarried women to
rescue missions, and occasionally advised penniless young women to return to
their parents' homes in the country. Matrons monitored the depots from 6:30 in
the morning until 10:00 at night in some cities, and most kept extra cots in
their own lodgings for women in need of emergency housing. Chicago matrons in 1893 reported aiding over 4,500 persons, 17 of whom were young
women rescued "directly from the hands of evil persons."[13]

Some Travelers' Aid organizations also provided more extensive transient lodgings for women. "Women's hotels" and transient homes were often located near train depots for the use of women traveling through the city. Unlike the boarding homes, the transient lodgings were open to a broader group of women, including older women with children and pregnant single women. The Travelers' Aid Home in Minneapolis, for example, was founded in 1909 to "provide a temporary home under healthful influences"; the home accepted lodgers for up to two weeks' residence for free, in some cases, or for from fifteen to fifty cents a night for those who could afford to pay.[14]

New York philanthropist Grace Hoadley Dodge, later the president of the national YWCA, spearheaded the drive to unify the diverse Travelers' Aid organizations into a single group at the turn of the century. She became the national spokesperson for Travelers' Aid work, attending international conferences of station workers and speaking widely on the importance of modern social work organization. The need for Travelers' Aid work was imperative, Dodge wrote in 1906, because "pure womanhood" alone no longer protected virtue. "[T]he changes in economic condition that have brought millions of girls from the shelter of the home into the dangerous independence of the factory, the shop, or the office," Dodge argued, "and the general relaxation of standards accompanying a growing cosmopolitanism, have worked together to make it unhappily true that a girl's innocence, instead of being her safeguard, may prove to be her worst enemy."[15] In 1905, Dodge promoted the founding of the New York Travelers' Aid Society, which united such diverse groups as the YWCA, the Council of Jewish Women, and the Female Auxiliary Bible Society.[16]

In 1912, the concept of Travelers' Aid reached the White House, when Illinois Vice Commission members visited President Woodrow Wilson to discuss the relationship of women's work to immorality. Illinois Senator Niels Juul advanced the idea that Travelers' Aid homes be government-sponsored: "The government takes care of a pound of tobacco. It follows the commodity from Kentucky or Virginia across the state line, and even counts the number of cigars made out of that pound of tobacco. If the national government can devote so much time to a pound of butterine, it can surely devote some time to the care of womanhood traveling from one state to another."[17] But the attempt to elevate Travelers' Aid work from voluntary local reform to state policy failed, and Travelers' Aid remained in the domain of women reformers and state labor board workers. In 1917, Dodge's efforts toward unification came to fruition, and the National Travelers' Aid Society was formed.[18]

From the 1860s through the 1920s, Travelers' Aid services centered on the perceived needs of young migrant women for moral protection in the city.

During the same era, reformers attempted to provide another service for the girl living on her own—the extension of a middle-class domestic environment through the subsidized and supervised boarding home.

BOARDING HOMES

Self-supporting women faced limited choices for housing in late nineteenth-century cities. One government report estimated in 1889 that over half of the women found alone in large cities lived with private families, 29 percent lived in boardinghouses, and 8 percent resided in lodging houses. Toward the end of the century, the practice of lodging with families and in small, family-like boardinghouses gave way to large commercial lodging houses, "housekeeping apartments," and a related café and restaurant culture.[19]

Women seeking housing were often barred from the "better class" of accommodations by low wages and social biases. Landladies often preferred male renters, as they believed women living alone would lessen the "respectability" of their lodgings. The prejudice against women living outside of families was noted by George Ellington in his book, *The Women of New York: Or, the Underworld of the Great City*, when he wrote in 1869 that the "lone woman" looking for a room in New York City was often assumed to be "not a good woman, but quite the contrary."[20] This point of view proved long-lived; as late as 1935 the arbiter of middle-class manners, Emily Post, maintained that "in the world of society no young girl may live alone," lest "Mrs. Grundy" set tongues to wagging.[21]

Reformers feared that the kind of housing available to poorly paid working women imperiled their health and morality. Too many working women, argued the United States Department of Labor in 1889, lived in "narrow crowded streets, where drinking shops, gambling houses, and brothels abound." In these districts, the Labor Department observed, were the "ordinary homes of the poorer paid among the working girls in large cities."[22] Cheap boarding and lodging houses lacked a parlor, investigators noted, and the woman alone could not be expected to entertain her male friends in her bedroom and remain respectable. The lack of a parlor became a keynote for reformers, who warned repeatedly that women might all too easily turn from their dingy, parlorless houses to frequent instead "the warmth and brightness of the dance houses and saloons, where they must of necessity meet undesirable and unsafe acquaintances."[23]

Studies of working and living conditions in cities emphasized the dangers of cheap lodgings. In 1869, Virginia Penny related the tale of two boardinghouses in New York City that were patronized by men who chose their lodgings "for the influence they might obtain over the girls." Nearly forty years later, Albert Wolf's 1906 study of lodging house culture in Boston included two narratives of respectable women residing in lodging houses who were distressed by their close proximity to gambling, prostitution, and alcoholism.[24]

These housing conditions attracted the attention of purity reformers, who proposed to extend "family influences" to self-supporting women in the form of supervised boarding homes. Unlike homes for immigrant women that were training grounds for domestic servants, or the antebellum rescue homes for prostitutes, these boarding homes were intended for the "respectable" women who were temporarily, and regrettably, on their own.[25]

The boarding home, proponents promised, would extend family influences to women who worked by providing affordable lodgings, religious services, and supervised leisure-time activities in a respectable location. The 1889 report of the United States Department of Labor contrasted the meager surroundings of cheap commercial boarding and lodging houses with the life offered by supervised boarding homes:

> A quiet, respectable street; clean halls and stairways; a neat parlor, and usually a library or reading room . . . young men allowed to call almost every evening, and permission accorded the girls to remain out after 10 o'clock under proper escort for special entertainments; religious services regular and earnest, but not obtrusive or compulsory; a matron ready with sympathy or suggestion . . . an air of refinement pervading the house and surrounding the inmates; no rough associations or immoral influences; such conditions make a veritable home where girl or woman may live in accordance with her individual nature, sheltered from intrusion, self-supporting, self-respecting, useful, respected, and even beloved.[26]

The first boarding home that offered permanent residence to nondestitute women was established by the Ladies Christian Union in New York City in 1856. The Young Woman's Home contained sewing, laundry, meeting and dining rooms, two parlors, and sleeping rooms. Its interior was, according to one reporter, a display of "neatness and taste."[27] By 1877, at least twenty similar homes had been organized in cities including Boston, New York, Cincinnati, and Denver. Most of these were founded by women's organizations like the YWCA, WCA, and such church groups as the Sisters of Mercy. Some public-spirited individuals sponsored homes as well. In Chicago, Cyrus McCormick, the founder of International Harvester, funded a large YWCA residence. In New York City, department-store magnate Alexander Turney

Stewart founded the much-publicized, opulent, and short-lived Hotel for Working Women.[28]

By 1898, there were at least ninety boarding homes opened in forty-five cities. These homes could house over 4,500 women at one time; because many boarders and lodgers were temporary, large numbers of women passed through the homes yearly. In 1898, over 30,000 different women registered at the nation's boarding homes, and the United States Department of Labor reported that over 120,000 different women had patronized the homes since the first temporary supervised lodging for women was established in 1848.[29]

The boarding homes ranged from large to small, modest to splendid. At one end of the spectrum was the Chicago YWCA on Michigan Boulevard, a seven-story building containing some three hundred single and double bedrooms, a library, parlor, auditorium, gymnasium, laundry, bathrooms, dining rooms, and classrooms. Less ambitious but more typical were the small institutions like the Minneapolis Woman's Boarding Home, which housed 70 women, or the St. James Guild Boarding Home in Philadelphia, which accommodated 12 women.[30]

Most of the homes accepted both temporary and permanent boarders. In many cities, YWCAs and WCAs established separate homes for permanent boarders and transients; the latter were Travelers' Aid services often labeled as "branch homes" that followed less strict daily routines. In houses that accepted both kinds of residents, long-term boarders often resented the transients. In Boston, for example, the "permanent" boarders at the YWCA home preferred to live on the upper floors, for those on the lower floors were likely to return from work to "find a stranger asleep in the other bed, or an unfamiliar hat and coat over the chair."[31]

Typical conditions of admission to the boarding homes were that women be of "good character" and provide references—a stipulation also common in many commercial hotels in the nineteenth century. Admissions officers usually insisted that women earn wages of less than $5.00 a week, demonstrate a lack of "natural protection" in the city, be white, young (usually under the age of 30) and unmarried. Although most clubs were sponsored by Protestant women's groups, many accepted any "respectable" white applicants. Some homes were open exclusively to Catholics, Jews, various ethnic groups, and blacks. Although prices ranged from $1.00 to $7.00 weekly, most homes charged about $3.00.[32]

Most of the boarding homes were intended to meet the needs of rural migrants, women who were, according to the Chicago YWCA, "orphaned, so far as natural protections are concerned" but still "lofty in sentiment."[33] The Minneapolis Woman's Boarding Home officials welcomed "all honest women but prefer to aid the young and inexperienced. The innocent, unsophisticated country girl comes all unprepared for a city life of trial and temptation. She comes fresh from green fields, and the liberty of home life, to work in [a] stuffy factory, or dusty office."[34] The Young Woman's Home in New York City reported a similar concern with a "respectable" class of women. Of their boarders in 1865, the Woman's Home officers reported, "Many of them are the daughters of clergymen and other distinguished gentlemen. . . . Of 29 inmates, in 1865, 18 were artists, one a copyist, three were teachers, eight dressmakers and seamstresses. . . . Many young ladies tarry here while completing their education."[35]

A study of forty-three homes in 1898 indicated that domestic workers—including servants, waitresses, and nurses lodging on their days off—comprised a quarter of the boarders; office workers and store cashiers were 13 percent; saleswomen were 11 percent; and sewing women were 11 percent. Students, missionaries, teachers, and others also boarded. Factory workers made up only 3 percent of the boarding population.[36] These figures, however, are deceptive. Of the homes reporting domestic servants—and only half of them reported any at all—two-thirds of the servants were found in only four homes—the St. Mary Home in Detroit, the French Evangelical Church Home in New York, the House of Mercy in Cincinnati, and the WCA home in Cleveland.[37]

Many of the homes barred domestic servants, laundry workers, black women, and factory operatives, reflecting their concern with the white native-born women dispossessed of their status by the need or desire to work. For the native-born women, the homes acted as a buffer between the urban environment and the domestic ideology. Although they worked for a living, they still lived "at home," and so their bodies, reputations, and status remained protected.[38]

This protection was insured by the matron, who, as the Providence, Rhode Island, YWCA officers noted, was intended as a substitute mother who "attends to all the details of house keeping and presides over the home as a mother does in her family."[39] The matron admitted applicants and saw that lodgers ate meals at the ringing of one bell and that they turned out the lights at the ringing of another—usually by 10:30 at night. Sunday and daily worship services were often mandatory. In some cases, members of the sponsoring organization regularly visited the homes to transmit "ennobling influences" so that the young boarders, in turn, could "become a power of good in their homes" when they eventually married.[40] In all of the homes, moral behavior and daily routine were strictly regulated, as the rules of the Buffalo, New York, WCA Home in 1898 typified:

1. Applications for board may be presented to the matron. . . . Satisfactory testimonials of character will be required. . . . No boarder will be allowed to remain whose conduct is not satisfactory. . . .
3. Rooms must be well aired every morning, and kept in all respects neat by the occupants. . . . The use of the bathroom will be carefully adjusted, occupants of each room being assigned its use on certain days and hours. . . .
6. Family worship is held daily, which all are required to attend. It is expected that no boarder will absent herself from these exercises without a reasonable excuse to the matron. . . .
7. All visitors must leave the house promptly at 10 p.m. . . . when it is expected that all boarders will retire to their respective rooms and perfect quiet will be secured. . . .
8. All visitors will be received in the parlors, and, under no circumstances taken into the other parts of the building without the knowledge and consent of the matron. Men callers will be received only on Tuesday and Thursday evenings.[41]

Although strict rules were upheld in the homes, amenities were also provided. A parlor—often with a piano—was made available to boarders and their guests. But the problem of the parlor was not as easily solvable as it seemed. Some surveys indicated that young women lived in boardinghouses with parlors but still preferred to entertain in their bedrooms, or in public places, for the communal parlor lacked privacy.[42] Recognizing that young women desired more privacy than was afforded in a common parlor, some homes, such as the Boston YWCA Franklin Square House, set up several small parlors that could be reserved and used privately. Homes also typically provided libraries of books and magazines, savings and loan programs, low-cost vacation or convalescent retreats, and emergency-loan funds for unemployed or sick lodgers.[43]

More than half of the homes surveyed by the Department of Labor in 1898 provided free meals and deferred rent to unemployed boarders. The Minneapolis Woman's Boarding Home, for one, provided free temporary housing for women actively seeking employment; in 1879, two women were allowed to stay and "pay what they could, as they found it impossible to pay their board even at the reduced rate."[44] For many women, had there been no such emergency service, their only alternative resource would have been lodging in the police station, or fending for themselves on the streets.[45]

The "safety-net" feature of the boarding home movement was illustrated by an investigation published in the *Chicago Chronicle* in 1887. "Miss Hayseed's

Adventures" recounted the experience of the reporter Elinor Raymond Maxwell, who garbed herself in old clothes and "a sailor hat of an ancient block" and then set off to discover what would happen if she landed in Chicago "without a cent in her purse and no friends to meet her." Maxwell found her way paved by friendly police officers and Travelers' Aid workers, who sent her to the local YWCA. There she was given a free room, meals, and an offer of work as a servant.[46]

Boarding home proponents also argued that structured leisure time would advance the cause of moral purity. The Minneapolis WCA, for example, cautioned in 1888 that "an ounce of prevention is worth a pound of cure, and were this work of guiding the leisure hours of young girls looked after, there would be less need of reformatories."[47] In many homes, young women read poetry in literary societies, studied typewriting, stenography, languages, dressmaking, and cooking, and formed enthusiastic athletic teams.[48]

Some women expressed gratitude to the homes for providing them with a substitute family. They contributed aphorisms, news articles, short stories, and gossip to publications sponsored by the organizations. Boarders of the Minneapolis WCA homes, for example, published a newsletter, aptly titled the *Annals of No Man's Land*, in the 1910s and 1920s. Much of the material in these publications emphasized the importance of friendships made between women who had arrived in the city as strangers, reflecting the importance to many women of the sociability of the homes. One poem, about the Pillsbury Home, expressed this common theme:

> P is for the port in distress
> I is for the incense of friendship
> L is for two lights in the fog,
> S is for the spirit of kinship
>
> .   .   .   .
>
> Little bachelor girl finally finds "home"
> Maybe it isn't so bad after all
> To go limping along alone.[49]

Some boarders also demonstrated their appreciation for the homes in their decisions to marry in the parlors of their residences.[50]

But other women harshly criticized the boarding homes. Labor Department investigator Mary Fergusson observed in 1898 that many working women disliked the supervised homes because of the "odor of charity," the discipline, and the institutionalism.[51] This view was reflected in Minneapolis, where young women petitioned the officers of the Woman's Boarding Home in 1885 to change the name of the home, "as the present name is obnoxious on many accounts." Their petition was tabled, and two years later, some of the boarders took matters into their own hands and destroyed the nameplate on the building. In 1922, a similar opinion was registered by a New York clerical worker, who suggested, "Don't call whatever you build a 'Home for Women;' girls must feel self-respecting."[52]

Other women resented the rules and regulations. When Louise Bosworth, of the Boston Women's Educational and Industrial Union, surveyed Boston's women workers in 1911, she found that to many "the rules of an institution are shackles; the customs to which inmates must conform are fetters."[53] In 1883, journalist Helen Campbell told the tale of "Katy," a young New York City shop girl, who said, "I've a good mind to live at the 'home' only I should hate to be bossed 'round, and you can't get in very often either, it's so crowded."[54] Maimie Pinzer, a reformed Philadelphia prostitute, wrote that at the YWCA "the atmosphere in such a place would make me want to do something hideously wicked, just to see what it was like."[55] And a young worker, "Minnie," was reported by Clara Laughlin in *The Work-a-Day Girl* in 1913 as saying:

> Maybe you could stand it if they wouldn't always be tryin' to improve you. You come home at night dead tired after sellin' brass tacks or makin' paper boxes, and they set you up in the parlour an' have a missionary woman tell you how the Chinese girls bind their feet. It's awful—when what you're dyin' for is a chance to shake a leg. You have to get a permit to stay out after 10:30. And you gotta pray before you eat and pray before you sleep, an' give an account of everything you do. . . . You kin try one o' them places if you want to—I've had enough o' them.[56]

Still, the homes were crowded and received more requests for admission than they had places. In Manhattan in 1921, for example, fifty-eight organized homes reported long waiting lists for admission.[57] The discrepancy between the criticisms and the demand for places lies in part in the class differences among working women. Working-class women, particularly those who were servants or factory operatives, testified that boarding homes were oppressive and didactic; rural migrants and others of "respectable" origins saw instead a reflection of the homes they had left behind. This self-selection was buttressed by the policies of the homes, which accepted only office workers, students, or sales clerks. In 1890, Clare De Graffenreid of the Department of Labor charged that selection policies meant that "the most deserving are barred out by the class distinctions which mark almost every stage of philanthropy."[58]

The partial subsidization of the homes by charity came under criticism as well. Despite the subsidies, many poorly paid workers still found the homes too expensive and located too far from the factory districts. Others argued that the subsidized homes hurt the fight for higher wages. Critics maintained that employers justified low wages by pointing to the boarding homes, saying that they were not responsible for the dangers of low wages when cheap and safe housing was available. Some corporations that were notorious for the low wages paid to their women workers sponsored boarding homes. Fairfax Hall, for example, was a boarding home established by the Illinois Bell Telephone Company for its switchboard operators by the 1920s.[59]

The boarding-home movement provided housing for a limited number of women. It offered long-term shelter to several thousands of women who saw themselves as "respectable" and in need of the protection of a form of family life. It provided temporary lodgings to larger numbers of women from rural areas who needed help in adjusting to urban culture and who patronized the homes only until they earned enough money to live on their own, or found other women with whom to set up housekeeping apartments.[60] But the boarding-home movement did not meet the needs of many factory operatives, domestic servants, older wage-earning women, mothers, or black women. Nor did it address the housing needs of working women who desired a place to live without the constraints of a tightly regulated home operated by moralistic philanthropists.

Many women preferred another solution to the housing problem—cooperative housekeeping. Although some commentators suggested that cooperative housekeeping would allow women to live well and even "keep a girl to do the housework," working women who shared rooms testified to a less genteel life. Most women living together worked and divided costs and housekeeping tasks. A young woman who had migrated to New York in 1902, for example, wrote how upon arriving in the city she was advised that cooperation with other women was the alternative to becoming a part of the "submerged tenth." She rented a five-room apartment with four other women.[61]

While cooperative housekeeping kept costs down, still boarding for full-time workers sometimes proved difficult. One young woman complained to the Minnesota labor commissioner in 1888: "Four of us hired a large room. We cooked, sewed, washed and ironed for ourselves and managed to live. Our wages were $3.00 per week apiece, but our clothes were always so shabby that we didn't go to parties evenings or to church on Sunday. We were so tired after doing our work that we had no time to read or do anything but sleep."[62] By the end of the century, some women attempted to formalize these housekeeping arrangements by establishing boarding clubs. Unlike the boarding homes, which were hierarchical in structure, the clubs were cooperative and self-governing. The Eleanor Club of Chicago, for example, was founded in 1898 to provide housing, recreation, and dining facilities to women able to pay a set rate. Another example of cooperative housing was a New York City boarding-house for some fifty residents that was established with a loan from the International Ladies' Garment Workers' Union; the tenants paid rates high enough to repay the loan and secure an independent status.[63]

These clubs offered members considerably more autonomy than was available in the supervised boarding homes. Maggie Toomey, the treasurer of Chicago's Jane Club, for example, said in 1892 that cooperative clubs differed from boarding homes "in as much as we have no rules and no matron to order us around. We do as we please—in most things. Here every girl has a say in the affairs of the club. . . . [I]f she cares to go out of an evening she does so, and lets herself in with a latch-key."[64]

Whether cooperative housekeeping was formal or informal, it was the housing of choice for growing numbers of women. A Minneapolis social worker explained this choice in 1917. "From my own point of view, and that of most of my friends," she stated, "a boarding house life, even the best of its kind, is a poor apology for living, and we all agree if we had the problem of home finding to face we would settle it by combining and taking an apartment."[65] In 1922, a survey of working women in Manhattan found that most women, given a choice, preferred the independence of living in housekeeping apartments. Although less than a fifth of the store, office, and factory workers surveyed lived in apartments, more than two-thirds listed the housekeeping apartment as their preferred housing arrangement.[66]

Recognizing that many young women could or would not live under the supervision of the philanthropic boarding home, and that the majority of young women workers lived at home with their families in any case, reformers also advocated another method for extending the influence of domesticity into the urban environment—recreation clubs, which would provide an alternative to commercial entertainments.

RECREATION CLUBS

The concern with the leisure-time activities of working women expressed by the proponents of boarding homes was also evidenced in the establishment of recreation clubs for women. Jane Addams was among those who criticized the culture of commercial recreation for its demoralization of women. "The whole apparatus for supplying pleasure is wretchedly inadequate and full of danger to whomsoever may approach it," she warned in 1909.[67] Five years later, Addams further admonished that "the modern city sees in these girls only two possibilities, both of them commercial: first, a chance to utilize, by day their new and tender labor power . . . and then another chance in the evening to extract from them their petty wages by pandering to their love of pleasure."[68]

Reformers believed that the pleasures of the city appealed to the sensual instincts of workers exhausted by long days of labor. In 1912, the U.S. Senate investigation described the situation for the working woman: "The dance hall with a saloon connection is probably the most harmful, but it is by no means the only dangerous opportunity for recreation within her reach. The cheap theater with its highly miscolored pictures of life; the penny vaudeville, the moving picture show, the summer resort of one kind or another—in all she is liable to find abnormal excitement, dangerous companionship, and every incitement to begin the course which leads so many to harm."[69] Hull House reformer Louise DeKoven Bowen also warned of the dangers of commercial entertainment. The clientele, moral tone, and sexual mores of the dance hall, she argued, were but "feeders to the underworld." Other forms of urban pleasure, including excursion steamers, amusement parks, and theaters were pathways on "a road easily leading to destruction."[70] Some organizations were formed in the postbellum era to counter the attractions of these amusements by offering alternative programs of recreation. The YWCA was the best known and longest-lived of these, pioneering not only in Travelers' Aid and housing work but in recreational reform as well.

When the first YWCA in the United States was founded in Boston in 1866, it was meant to meet "the temporal, moral, and religious welfare of young women who are dependent on their own exertions for support." Early YWCAs were established by young "business women"—white-collar workers and students—or by philanthropists. By 1915, there were YWCAs in over two hundred cities, each attempting to build "Christian character" and extend domestic influences to young working women. Among the services offered by urban YWCAs were not only employment bureaus, boarding homes, and housing registers but also libraries, cafeterias, bicycle and rowing clubs, gymnasium and physical culture classes, vacation lodges, and recreation clubs. By 1889, the YWCA began "extension work" in factories, leading noon prayer meetings accompanied by a melodeon carried from factory to factory. Soon city associations were setting up recreation clubs for factory operatives. The YWCA in Dayton, Ohio, for example, organized the "Busy Girl's Half Hour" at the National Cash Register factory, offering talks on health, dress, and morality.[71]

The YWCAs were only the best known of a host of similar organizations concerned with providing recreational outlets for young women. There was also the Massachusetts League of Girls Clubs, founded in 1889 to provide recreational programs for women workers.[72] Nationally, the Association of Working Girls Societies was founded in 1881 when Grace Hoadley Dodge began her efforts toward club work with an inauspicious meeting with a group of silk factory workers. The operatives disrupted the first meeting by overturning benches and jeering, one worker later saying, "You ladies do not know us; you do not know the temptations, the trials; you do not care for us. The girls in this factory feel so bitterly toward you all." But Dodge eventually succeeded in securing the cooperation of the workers to create the association. By 1890, there were seventy-five clubs representing over 2,000 women. Their goal was to "lighten the burdens of the working girl, to increase her efficiency, and to elevate her character" through classes, club work, and moral instruction.[73]

In addition to these groups, the National League of Women Workers was founded in 1897 and by 1914 consisted of one hundred clubs of 14,000 members. Working women met regularly in groups like the Friendly Associates, of Boston, or the Amethyst Club, of Pittsburgh, where they upheld ideals of "nonsectarianism, self-government, and self-support." Club members, most of them factory operatives, participated in activities designed to develop character, citizenship, loyalty, and efficiency. They could also take advantage of savings and loan programs, insurance plans, and industrial training opportunities.[74] Finally, there were the vacation clubs. Organizations such as the YWCA, churches, and boarding homes sponsored lodges or summer camps where young working women could find relatively inexpensive vacation accommodations.[75] Reformers intended these clubs not only to encourage efficient work habits but also to be morally elevating. And some clubs also stressed lessons on physical development, sex education, decorum, and such topics as "qualities of womanhood" and "social relationships."[76]

Many women reformers believed that activities like recreation clubs brought the "wealthier, more educated, better placed women" into relations with "the poorest and most friendless." The Department of Labor, in 1889, noted that in working girls' clubs "earnest, intelligent and cultivated women acknowledge the close bond of sisterhood with rough, ignorant girls, and by tact, patience and gentle influence develop the best that is in them."[77] Club proponents believed that their work would help to "obliterate class lines" by stressing the shared status of womanhood. Journalist and club leader Jane Croly, for instance, wrote in 1891 that club life protected and stimulated young women. The club member's mind "no longer dwells upon her little attempts at finery, or the small jealousies and complexities of daily life. She is in a measure removed from them, and rises superior to them," Croly maintained.[78] But some working women resented the patronizing attitude of reformers who denied class divisions while exemplifying them. Rose Phelps Stokes reported how the philanthropic clubwoman looked "from the working woman's viewpoint" in 1906: "Not long ago, in one of the principal settlement houses of

New York, a very fashionably dressed woman, a lorgnette dangling from her fingertips, opened the door of a working girls' club, uninvited, and, raising her lorgnette to her eyes, surveyed the group before her, and, as though desiring to compliment the girls, remarked in the hearing of all, 'What a very attractive looking lot of working girls these are!' This sort of thing is by no means rare."[79] Stokes suggested that working women disliked condescension but that they readily recognized "true friendliness" and good will.[80]

Some working women organized their own clubs for self-support. A New York woman who worked in a publisher's office at the turn of the century, for example, formed a club with her friends in order that they might help each other secure better jobs. In two years they had 80 members. "We learned comradeship and the moral support this gives," she wrote in *Harper's Bazaar*.[81] In large cities, working women also organized self-governing lunch clubs, where they cooperated in managing cafeterias, rest rooms, libraries, and parlors. In Chicago, for instance, the Noonday Rest Club enrolled some 700 members by 1896; the Oguntz Club in the same city reported 150 clerical and factory workers among its members.[82]

Club work, along with housing and Travelers' Aid efforts, was a patchwork response to deeper problems facing women workers in large cities. The response of women's benevolent groups to the conditions of work and wages in cities was to try to obviate what they saw as the moral danger resulting from low wages and the separation from home. By the 1910s, another response to the discovery of the working woman gained strength—the attempt to alter the worst abuses in the world of work itself.

Reform of Working Conditions

The conditions of work encountered by young women in this era were criticized on several counts. We have seen that some commentators argued that the familiarity of men and women workers in stores and factories led to immorality; in this era the low wages and long hours attendant to women's work also were linked to physical and moral debilitation. While some reformers argued that the solution to the problem of immorality was to remove women from the workplace and return them to a home environment as domestic servants, a more widespread effort attempted to improve the abysmal conditions of store and factory work by promoting minimum-wage and maximum-hour laws.

THE PROMOTION OF DOMESTIC SERVICE

Some reformers contended that domestic service was the "natural vocation" for women and that the removal of women from industry and into middle-class homes would insure their moral protection. Julia Ward Howe was among those supporting this idea. She wrote in 1891, "When I see, as I often do, our American girls deteriorating in health, and not unseldom in character, through the experience of the shop and the factory, I feel a deep regret at the thought of the refined and well-ordered homes in whose comforts and good influences they might so easily be sharers, their service being to the right-minded an occasion of respect and gratitude, not of supercilious patronage or fault-finding."[83] Howe was joined by state labor commissioners, some manufacturers, and such organizations as the Women's Educational and Industrial Union, organized in 1877, in the promotion of domestic service as a field well fit for female needs and abilities. Minnesota Labor Commissioner John O'Donnell, for one, stated in 1901 that "it is my belief that there is no better place for the female wage-earner to be employed than in our American homes, surrounded by an atmosphere of refinement."[84] A New York writer criticized society for stigmatizing domestic work, arguing that "in all our large cities thousands of girls employed in stores and factories could live far more comfortably and qualify themselves to be excellent housewives by accepting situations in private families."[85]

Some critics suggested upgrading domestic service to meet the status needs of young native-born workers and proposed that the women form unions, associations, clubs, take classes, and demand better treatment from employers. At Chicago's Hull House settlement, for example, the Bureau for Women's Labor hoped to organize women workers to raise the standards of domestic service, with the aim of "diverting young girls from the drudgery of the cash girls' bench and the mill, to the life of the home."[86] And some young women did find domestic service to be acceptable work. A number of them told Lucy Salmon, according to her 1901 study of household servants, that their occupation provided vacations, good wages, and, most important, domestic influences. "I like a quiet home in a good family better than work in a public place, like a shop," one woman stated. Another said, "When I came to _____ and saw the looks of the girls in the large stores and the familiarity of the young men, I preferred to go into a respectable family where I could have a home."[87]

But most native-born white women rejected these arguments. Young women in survey after survey cited as reasons for their distaste for domestic service the days of ten hours or longer, the lack of free evenings and privacy, isolation, low wages, and maltreatment.[88] The advantages of domestic service paled next to the loss of status, lack of freedom, and monotonous work routine. A list of "daily duties" for servants, published in a 1904 handbook, had the servant rising at 6:00 A.M., preparing, serving, and cleaning up after meals, making beds, dusting and cleaning, and cheerfully answering the door.[89] "There is a very bitter feeling against housework among the shop girls," the Minnesota labor commissioner reported in 1888. In Wisconsin, 94 percent of the women surveyed by the state Labor Bureau in 1901 preferred factory to domestic work. In Boston, the Women's Educational and Industrial Union surveyed 564 factory operatives and shop girls to encourage a switch to domestic work, but only 26 women considered the change.[90]

Many women protested the low status of domestic work. "Girls who work in factories are more respected," a servant told the Minnesota labor commissioner. "I worked for one family who used me like a dog around the house. I will never do that kind of work again," stated another.[91] Lucy Salmon wrote of male factory operatives who would invite to their parties young self-supporting milliners, stenographers, and salesclerks but who drew the social line at servants.[92]

The low status of domestic work, established by the mid-nineteenth century, was reinforced in this era by efforts of some groups to channel immigrants into middle-class homes as servants. Mary Gove Smith, of the Boston Women's Educational and Industrial Union, argued that special homes for immigrant women could help train them for appropriate work as servants. "The girl who comes perhaps from the mud hut of some little Austria-Hungarian village sees in the model immigrant's home new possibilities," she wrote. "Cleanliness, order, system are about her, and she realizes vaguely or definitely, as her intelligence permits, that progression means the formation of new habits, of adaptation to new modes of life, of new ambitions."[93] Smith cited as an example the immigrant home in East Boston, which accommodated 35 to 40 women and promoted "the atmosphere of home." Thirty similar homes were established by the 1910s for Protestant, Jewish, and Catholic immigrants in New York City, Baltimore, and Philadelphia.[94]

The motive in promoting domestic work for immigrant women was not to preserve respectability as much as to prevent immorality and maintain a well-regulated class of servants. In 1904, women's groups in Boston, Philadelphia, and New York established the Inter-Municipal Committee on Household Research to study conditions of domestic service, publicize needed remedies, and endorse approved employment agencies.[95]

One member of the committee argued that employers needed to be protected from their servants, reporting that the demoralizing effects of "promiscuous mingling" on ship, in lodging houses, and in intelligence offices (employment bureaus) could permit situations in which "the girl passes from these surroundings with their increment of dishonesty, promiscuousness, and vice directly into the presence of an American family. . . . [S]ince she . . . becomes a member of our households, it is a grave question as to how far the atmosphere of lax morality which she brings with her may extend."[96]

The committee believed intelligence offices were especially dangerous to the welfare of young immigrants. Two-thirds of all servants were hired from these agencies, and critics charged that the offices were corrupt institutions from which women were often sent to brothels or to households "about whom nothing is known." Between 1904 and 1909, fourteen agencies in New York City had their licenses revoked for sending women to "immoral places" and brothels. Reformers recommended licensing and inspection legislation to protect the unsophisticated immigrant woman from immoral practices and unsanitary conditions.[97]

There was concern, too, for young black women who migrated north to find work as domestic servants. Francis Kellor condemned the practice of southern employment agencies that sent agents into rural districts to recruit servants for northern households. "Men grotesquely dressed," she wrote, "carrying drums, . . . parade through the smaller towns, and cry the rare opportunities offered by the agency to any girls who wish to go North, shouting 'Fall into line! Free passage! No fees!' " Once north, Kellor stated, these young women were often sent to brothels or forced to work without wages because they had signed exploitative contracts, or they were "turned loose" upon the cities without work. Kellor and others recommended that the protections proposed for immigrant women, such as lodging houses and licensing of agencies, be enacted for these young black women as well.[98]

There had long been criticisms of domestic service as a breeding ground for prostitution. In the 1870s, the Boston Female Asylum reported that young women placed in homes as servants complained of sexual advances made by the husbands and sons of their employers' households.[99] Several surveys of urban prostitution in this period discovered that about a third or more of the women studied had first been domestic workers. In 1888, the Department of Labor found that of 3,866 prostitutes studied, a third had first been domestic workers—the largest single occupational group from which prostitutes came. In its 1911 report, "Relation between Occupation and Criminality of Women," the Department of Labor learned that the most frequent previous occupation of women prisoners and prostitutes was domestic service, and not factory work or saleswork as had been commonly hypothesized.[100] This link of vice to domestic service helped to entrench its low status, and efforts to upgrade the reputation of domestic service as an occupation for native-born white women failed.

WORKING WOMEN'S ASSOCIATIONS

Others recognized that most women would not be talked into leaving the industrial labor force and attempted instead to improve conditions and safeguard motherhood by promoting the associationism of working women. Unions had long been a traditional method by which men had bettered their conditions of work. After 1860, women's trade unions, which had been only sporadically active since the 1820s, multiplied. Laundresses, cap makers, and shoe workers were among groups that united to improve conditions.[101]

A powerful public demonstration of the women's union movement occurred in 1903, when 35,000 women in twenty-six trades were organized in Chicago. That year, a labor-day parade included the performance by women marchers of the following song:

> Shall song and music be forgot
> When workers shall combine?
> With love united may they not
> Have power almost divine?
> Shall idle drones still live like queens
> On labor not their own?
> Shall women starve while thieves and rings
> Reap where they have not sown?[102]

But the participation of women in unions was limited by traditional attitudes; most women did not define themselves as workers but saw their employment as a temporary measure before marriage. Moreover, many employers blocked the formation of unions, and predominantly male unions were often hostile toward women workers. In 1905, a survey of union membership in fifteen occupations revealed that over 20 percent of the men but only 3 percent of the women in the surveyed trades were union members. Even during World War I, the peak period of union organization for men, less than 10 percent of women in manufacturing occupations belonged to unions. In 1924, a Women's Bureau study found that barely 140,000, or less than 5 percent, of women workers were union members.[103]

Although most women were not organized in trade unions in this period, some did participate in other kinds of groups that attempted to improve working conditions. Protection leagues, for example, were an early form of women's labor activity. The Boston Women's Educational and Industrial Union was founded in 1877 to "aid, strengthen, and elevate women, by drawing them into a bond of unity." The union formed committees to protect women's legal rights and to redress complaints about salary disputes. In New York City, the Working Woman's Protective Union was founded in 1868, and by 1890 had collected, through court action, some $41,000 for 12,000 women "who would otherwise have been defrauded of their hard-earned wages." Similar organizations were founded in Philadelphia, Indianapolis, Chicago, and St. Louis.[104]

The Consumers' League, which was instrumental in research and lobbying for hour and wage legislation, was another important organization for women. The league originated with the New York City Working Women's Society, which was organized in 1886 by young garment workers and cash girls who first met to protest harsh working conditions. Their early activities included the support of strikes, advocacy of legislation to hire female factory inspectors, and the study of local working conditions. In 1890, an investigation of saleswomen resulted in the formation of a committee to publish a "white list" of stores that dealt "justly with their employees." The first list, which included only eight establishments, was publicized in an effort to convince consumers to patronize only approved stores, hence pressuring employers to raise the standards of employment. This committee became the New York Consumers' League in 1891. By 1900, there were sixty-four Consumers' Leagues in the United States and a national league that aimed to "abolish the sweatshop."[105]

By 1903, the Working Women's Society itself was absorbed into a second organization—the Women's Trade Union League. The league was a federation of women's unions and middle-class sympathizers which worked with the American Federation of Labor to assist women in the formation of unions. Like some of the earlier working-girls clubs, the league emphasized the importance of contacts between women of different classes in a ritualized social context. Although some garment, textile, laundry, and shoe workers did succeed in organizing, their success was still limited to relatively few women.[106] It was the achievement of protective legislation, promoted of course by the unions, which altered the environment for thousands of working women.

PROTECTIVE LEGISLATION

By the end of the nineteenth century, many of those concerned with the issues of women and work realized that unions would not be the remedy to improve working conditions for women, nor would strictly ameliorative measures succeed. Protective legislation, advocates argued, would safeguard future motherhood not by the extension of domestic influences, but by the insurance of economic security and the protection of health. Laws mandating maximum hours of work and minimum wages were enacted by state governments in this period in an effort to protect the physical and moral health of working women.

Proponents of protective legislation defended their proposals on the basis of the needs of young self-supporting women who were then at the forefront of the debate over women and work. But at the same time, as laws were enacted to protect this group, the population of the female labor force was beginning to shift as older, married women began to increase their numbers in the labor force. Laws that were designed to protect young temporary workers were in fact often applied to older workers or to single career women who did not desire work restrictions. For these latter women, the legislation of hours and wages forged an especially tightly linked "chain of protection."[107]

Many voices were heard in the debate over labor legislation. Social reformers and politicians argued that women's employment should be regulated in order to preserve the health of future mothers, to counter oppressive conditions of long hours and low wages, and to set standards that could be applied to men as well as to women. Opponents included businessmen who saw legislation as interference with their constitutional right to make contracts with their employees, and those who maintained that restrictions would damage business opportunities. Some feminists, particularly those in the National Woman's Party (the sponsor of the first Equal Rights Amendment proposal in 1923) also opposed protective legislation contending that it implied inequality under the law. Legislation intended for young, inexperienced workers needing protection, the feminists argued, unduly restricted older women who were competing with men for jobs. Hence laws meant only for women would doom women to inferior status in the workplace. Trade unionists were divided between those who thought protective legislation would enhance union goals, others who sought to use legislation to keep women out of certain occupations, and still others who saw legislation as a threat to organizing efforts. Women workers, for the most part unorganized and unwilling to participate in state legislative commissions, were rarely heard.[108]

Arguments favoring protective legislation often rested on commonly held assumptions about differences in the physical capabilities and social responsibilities of men and women. Azel Ames, Jr., a physician and investigator for the Massachusetts Bureau of Labor Statistics, wrote in 1875 that "the normal, the God-appointed work of women . . . is that of the home and the mother, the rearer, the trainer, the blessing of man." Ames was an early advocate of laws regulating hours, wages, sanitary conditions, and the kinds of work women could do. "The highest moral and physical well-being of a race," he claimed, "demands that there will be nothing in its conditions of life and labor that shall injure the richness and purity of the chief source whence its existence and its best influences come."[109] Nearly forty years later, this same argument was still being advanced in favor of protective legislation. In 1913, a Connecticut state commission concluded that the "physical well-being of woman is essential if we are to have a strong and vigorous race, and when through overstrain and exhaustion woman's vitality is lowered, her fitness for motherhood may be destroyed, and her children will pay the penalty with weakened or vitiated physical vigor. Therefore as a potential mother the state has a right to protect her."[110] Similarly, Marie Pfeiffer, a Pennsylvania silk worker, told a YWCA convention in 1920 that working conditions should be improved so "our next generation will be strong." "Weak women will mean a weak race," she argued, "unless we give them some help. The girls in industry today, I feel, are the mothers of the next generation."[111]

Many progressive-era reformers believed that women were weaker than men in energy, strength, and powers of "persistent attention" and that they were vulnerable to disease and to injuries of the "generative organs." Dozens of studies were marshaled in legal briefs and in state investigations to support the contention that unregulated industry rendered women unfit for motherhood. Citing statistics of infant mortality, morbidity, and lowered birthrates, these studies attempted to determine the effects of unsanitary working conditions, low wages, and long hours on the lives of young women in their childbearing years.[112]

Hours

Among the earliest labor legislation in the United States were laws restricting the maximum hours of employment. By the 1890s, hours laws were often justified on the basis of the need to protect the physical health of future mothers. Hours legislation has a tangled history, beginning in the antebellum era as a drive for the improvement of factory conditions for male as well as female workers. As early as 1842, Lowell factory operatives had demanded a ten-hour day, and union agitation had led seven states to enact general hours statutes between 1847 and 1855. These early laws, however, were ineffective because they mandated only that workers not be "compelled" to work more than ten hours a day.[113]

By 1867, the ten-hour movement had narrowed to exclude men. This reflected the efforts of organized labor to improve conditions in textile factories, which employed large numbers of women and children. Labor's strategy was to facilitate acceptance of a general reduction in mill hours by shortening hours for women. As one labor historian noted, unionists hoped "to fight the battle from behind women's petticoats."[114]

Massachusetts enacted the first effective ten-hour law for women who worked in manufacturing employments in 1874. In 1893, the Illinois legislature passed an eight-hour law for women, but the state supreme court struck down the law, ruling that it interfered with the employer's right to freedom of contract and that it also denied women equal protection under the law. This and other rulings rendered most hours laws ineffective, and women continued to work in some industries up to eighteen hours a day.[115]

Hours laws received new life in a 1908 Supreme Court ruling, *Muller* v. *Oregon*. The Court deemed that the effects of long hours on women's health justified legislation to limit the number of hours per day of work. Between 1909 and 1917, forty-one states wrote new or improved hours laws for women, often extending the scope of the law to cover both factories and mercantile establishments. The working day was limited to nine hours and the working week to fifty-four hours.[116]

The working night, as well as the working day, also became a subject of legislation. In the United States, night-work laws for women were passed in four states between 1890 and 1904. In 1906, fourteen European nations endorsed the Bern Convention, which prohibited the employment of women from ten at night until five in the morning. In Massachusetts, the law again was intended to improve textile-industry conditions, where unionists sought to counteract a growing trend to overtime evening work by barring night work for women, hence forcing the mills to close by six at night. Most state night-work laws, however, were blocked by court injunctions, and women continued to work late hours in industries such as laundries, telephone and telegraph offices, and factories.[117]

In 1913, the New York State Court of Appeals ruled in the case of *People* v. *Charles Schweinler Press* in favor of a state law barring night work for women, and by 1928 ten states had outlawed women's night employment in at least two industries. But there was wide variation in the state regulation of working hours. In Kansas, the law for some industries was extensive, mandating limits to the hours of employment, requiring minimum periods for rest and for meals, and barring night work. In other states, including Alabama, Florida, Georgia, and Iowa, there were no hours regulations at all.[118]

Hours laws were viewed by advocates as a panacea for a variety of social ills. In 1890, Clare De Graffenried of the Department of Labor declared: "Each reduction in the hours of work, from sixteen to fourteen, from fourteen to twelve, from twelve to ten, has occasioned immediate and enormous improvement in the condition of the laboring classes. Shorter hours tend not only to provide occupation for millions of unemployed, but they will stimulate production and widen our markets by multiplying wants; they will make education possible, and conduce to a higher social and moral development in the home."[119] Hours laws for men, in contrast, were justified by the need for workers to remain healthy to insure efficiency and public safety. By 1912, thirteen states restricted miners to eight-hour days, and drug clerks, railroad and streetcar workers, and federal employees were among other men who were subject to maximum-hour statutes in some states.[120]

For women, hours laws were often defended as necessary to protect future motherhood. In 1870, the Massachusetts Bureau of Statistics of Labor suggested that long hours of work made women "unfit for the reproduction of their kind." The Maryland Bureau of Industrial Statistics stated in 1896 that more than ten hours of work daily led to weary women "with no pleasant anticipations for the morrow." The bureau queried in its report, "What lives are these for future wives and mothers? Future generations will answer." In 1908, the Michigan Bureau of Labor contended that working long hours "injures the mothers of our citizens. . . . We shall begin to see that . . . for the injury to the women, the mothers, the homes, and the rising generation, there must be special laws for the conditions under which women work."[121]

The United States Supreme Court agreed with the concept that women had special needs for regulated working hours. In 1908, Louis Brandeis submitted to the Court a 113-page brief prepared by Josephine Goldmark in the case of *Muller* v. *Oregon*. The brief cited more than one hundred studies purporting to show that long work hours damaged women's health and imperiled industrial output. "Deterioration of any large portion of the community inevitably lowers the entire community physically, mentally, and morally," Brandeis and Goldmark noted. "When the health of women has been injured by long hours, not only is the working efficiency of the community impaired, but the deterioration is handed down to succeeding generations. . . . The overwork of future mothers thus directly attacks the welfare of the nation."[122]

The evidence submitted in the Brandeis brief did not prove a causal relationship between the employment of women in industry and sex-related dangers to health and morals. In fact, some proponents of labor legislation argued that the "procreative power" of men was also injured by night work.[123] But the Court's decision relied heavily on the arguments about the dangers of long work for future motherhood. Justice David Brewer wrote for the majority:

The two sexes differ in structure of body, in the functions to be performed by each, in the amount of physical strength, in the capacity for long-continued labor, particularly when done standing, the influence of vigorous health upon the future well-being of the race, the self-reliance which enables one to assert full rights, and the capacity to maintain the struggle for subsistence. This difference justifies a difference in legislation and upholds that which is designed to compensate for some of the burdens which rest upon her.[124]

In 1913, Brandeis and Goldmark prepared a similar argument for the New York Court of Appeals in defense of a law barring night work for women. They maintained that women night workers suffered from the same dangers as those who worked long hours by day, but that they endured additional burdens of increased exhaustion, deprivation of sunlight, the moral dangers of traveling on the streets after dark, difficulty in finding respectable boarding places where they could return at odd hours, and exposure to the increased vulgarity of men night workers. The Court found these arguments convincing, deeming that "the health of thousands of women working in factories should be protected and safeguarded from any drain which can reasonably be avoided. This not only for their own sakes, but as is and ought to be constantly and legitimately emphasized, for the sake of the children whom a great majority of them will be called on to bear and who will almost inevitably display in their deficiencies the unfortunate inheritance conferred upon them by physically broken down mothers."[125]

Some discussion of night work for women recognized that the problem of night work included the married woman who chose to work at night in order to meet family responsibilities during the day. But, in general, reformers focused on the subject of hours for single women, as the length and spacing of work hours remained correlated to the state's need for healthy future mothers. In 1928, Mary Hopkins of the Women's Bureau offered a typical defense of night-work laws: "It is the state's imperative concern to see that the vitality [working women] should pass on to their children is not prematurely sapped or endangered by night work."[126]

The Women's Bureau claimed that maximum-hour statutes benefited men as well as women. "Just as the polling place has become cleaner and more presentable since women have started using it," the bureau stated, "so has the factory in many instances shown the influence of the higher standards which are imposed where women work." The bureau also indicated that there were few cases of women encountering undue discrimination because of hours legislation and that more women had been hired to take the place of overtime workers.[127]

But some women workers disagreed. In Chicago, women ticket agents for the elevated railroads protested in 1911 when their schedules were cut from twelve to ten hours a day because of a new law limiting the hours of women's employment. In New York, women printers won an exemption from a night-work statute in 1924, successfully arguing that they would otherwise be deprived of their livelihoods. In other cities and states there were cases of women being fired or shifted to less remunerative shifts because of hours laws.[128]

Wages

The minimum wage was the second link in the "chain of protection." State labor bureaus in the 1880s and 1890s had related the low wages of women workers to the prevalence of prostitution in cities. By the 1910s, the concern with the morality of self-supporting women led to public pressure for the regulation of women's wages. City and state vice commissions, labor bureaus, trade unions, and purity reformers joined in the advocacy of a "living wage" for women workers.

In 1910, the National Consumers' League initiated the promotion of minimum-wage laws, and other groups, including the Progressive party and the Women's Trade Union League, followed with similar demands for legislation. Massachusetts enacted the nation's first minimum-wage law in 1912, and eight states passed similar statutes the following year. By 1917, seventeen states had laws legislating women's wages. These laws set minimum weekly salaries for women workers by city, industry, age, and experience, establishing a separate wage scale for apprentice workers.[129]

Like hours legislation, minimum-wage laws were for the most part defended on the grounds of protection for future mothers. But where hours laws focused on the physical well-being of women, laws that regulated wages were seen as critical for the preservation of public morality at a time when low salaries forced many women to seek supplemental sources of income.

Fears of prostitution continued to keep the controversy over working women in the public eye. Robert Bremner has credited a popular novel, *The House of Bondage* (1910), with bringing increased attention to the link between low wages and immorality. In this novel, an innocent country girl is deceived into leaving rural Pennsylvania for New York City, where she is tricked into a life of prostitution in a brothel. Although she manages to escape, she returns to the prostitute's trade after failing to find employment at a wage sufficient for self-support.[130]

Fears about the morality of women were reflected in the state minimum-wage campaigns. In California, clubwomen adopted the following slogan: "Employed womanhood must be protected in order to foster the motherhood of the race." Voters in that state agreed in a 1913 general election that the absence of subsistence wages "is the cause of ill health, lack of strength for a good motherhood, and frequently degeneracy and prostitution for the weakest."[131] In Chicago, the city Vice Commission reported in 1911 that "there is no doubt that many girls do live on even $6 and do it honestly, but we can affirm that they do not have nourishing food or comfortable shelter, or warm clothes, or any amusement, except perhaps free public dances, without outside help. . . . Is it any wonder that a tempted girl who receives only $6 a week working with her hands sells her body for $25 when she learns that there is a demand for it and men are willing to pay the price?"[132]

Manufacturers and employers countered that morals were not related to wages and that most of their young women workers were in any event not self-supporting. Julius Rosenwald, the president of Sears, Roebuck and Company, testified before the Illinois Vice Commission that "we make it a point not to hire any girl for less than $8.00 a week who does not live at home." Manufacturers claimed that a minimum wage would force them to replace inefficient women workers with more efficient men and that the law of supply and demand would be abrogated.[133] Some women trade unionists joined in the opposition to the minimum wage. In California, women labor activists charged that a minimum wage could too easily become a maximum wage, undermine union-scale rates, inhibit organization efforts, and bar women from certain occupations.[134]

States considering minimum-wage laws debated the economic needs of young self-supporting women as a guideline for the establishment of salaries deemed necessary for the "reasonable comforts and conditions of life." These wage levels were determined by legislatures, administrative commissions, and advisory boards that gathered survey data, examined payrolls, and suggested theoretical budgets to support suggested wage levels.

Estimated budgets varied widely. Of seven states that investigated cost-of-living data by 1915, suggested weekly budgets for women living on their own ranged from $7.30 in Kansas to $10.48 in Oregon.[135] Wage boards also varied on the proportion of income to be spent by women on various items but shared a concern with the minutia of the working woman's life. As one historian observed, boards "would come to sword points over a relatively minor matter; for example, whether a working girl was entitled to a new hat every year or car fare for Sundays as well as weekdays."[136]

The clothing budget arrived at by the Minnesota Minimum Wage Board demonstrates this extraordinary effort to mandate the working woman's economic life down to the last detail:

Item	Price
1 heavy waist	$ 1.50
4 heavy waists at $1.00	4.00
1 stocking cap	.50
1 pair cloth gloves	.25
1 pair mittens	.50
1 pair leather gloves	1.00
2 suits heavy underwear	2.00
4 suits summer underwear	2.00
2 summer dresses	7.00
1 skirt	4.00
4 pair shoes	13.00
1 pair rubbers	.50
2 working aprons	.50
1 winter coat . . .	9.00
1 suit . . .	9.50
1 heavy dress	8.00
1 slicker	3.00
1 Sunday dress	7.50
3 nightgowns at .75	2.25
2 hats at 3.00	6.00
2 corsets	4.00
4 corset covers	1.40
3 underskirts	2.40
1 and a half dozen handkerchiefs	.90
2 pair dress shields	.50
2 ties, ball string, . . . misc.	1.50
12 pair stockings	3.00
Margin for unforeseen necessities	4.30
Total annual expenditure	$100.00[137]

Wage boards also estimated weekly costs for food, rent, laundry, carfare, medical bills, church gifts, insurance, club dues, amusements, vacations, books, magazines, and newspapers.[138] Savings were not considered; the budgets assumed that women were entitled to a minimal standard of living, and nothing more.

But wages legislated in the states did not even meet the minimum cost of living, nor did they allow for support of dependents. The methods used to determine the "living wage" were criticized by some observers for unnecessary stringency and inaccuracy. Elizabeth Brandeis, the author of several articles on labor law, noted that "these women, all of whom were self-supporting, necessarily had to live in some fashion on what they earned."[139] Some women continued to deny themselves food or clothing in order to make ends meet, a practice documented in several investigations from the 1880s through the 1910s.[140]

In 1920, a Minneapolis factory worker, Naomi M., wrote to the Minnesota Wage Commission that working women attending the public minimum-wage meetings had presented a most incorrect picture of their lives:

> I'll begin by saying that it is impossible for a girl to live in "comfort and in health" on eleven dollars per wk. as all the others who spoke at the meeting said. Of course there are many who are doing so, and no one took the trouble to tell you how they do it. . . . The majority of the girls who receive only $11 per week have a "friend" who will help them out, but there are girls who have high ideals of life and are trying to live up to them who will not accept such help. I am in this class, and I have lived on eleven dollars a week, but I had to go hungry most of the time. You see, if I ate all I wanted there would be nothing left for clothing, so when I would contemplate buying a new dress or hat or shoes, that meant that I would have to go on a diet for several weeks, and my daily menu was usually an apple for breakfast, a sandwich and cup of coffee for lunch and maybe another sandwich or a bowl of milk toast for supper. I was amused at all the girls who spoke Friday eve. They said they spent about a dollar a day for food. They were too proud to tell the honest truth, just how little they eat. Of course if they ate nourishing food such as they should eat it would cost them about $1.25 per day. But the girl who gets only $11.00 per week goes hungry to work every day.[141]

The writer concluded that a minimum wage should be $18.00 per week "in order to meet the needs of comfort and health." But the wage set in Minnesota that year ranged from $10.25 to $12.00 per week, Naomi M.'s recommendations notwithstanding.[142]

The Women's Bureau compared the state minimum wages to the cost of living indexes and found that in many cases legislated wages did not meet the "necessary cost of living." Adjustments in minimum-wage rates year by year rarely kept pace with inflation. In 1920, nine states had established minimum-wage rates that were from $2.00 to $7.00 lower than cost-of-living estimates.[143]

Some observers argued that the minimum-wage statutes, though flawed, were still a step in the right direction. Rose Schneiderman stated that while minimum-wage rates did not "permit the full expression of life," still they helped to elevate wages to some degree.[144] Minimum-wage rates were most effective in raising salary levels for young, inexperienced women workers, particularly in states and in occupations where wages were traditionally low. In Oregon, for example, in the year following the enactment of a wage law, there was an upward trend in the salaries of inexperienced women workers under the age of 18, who were paid the newly established apprentice salaries.[145] But there was less visible benefit for older, more experienced workers, who reported static or even declining salaries.

Some working women complained that they were under new pressures to work harder because of the legislation of wages. One department store supervisor protested to investigators from the United States Bureau of Labor Statistics: "It's mighty fine for the young girls beginning now, but for us, who have worked our way up from the bottom to near the top, to have to see that the wherewithal is made to pay the younger girls a living wage is making us pay a heavy price for the benefit of the next generation."[146] There were other reports of women fired when they completed their stint as apprentices, when employers were ordered to increase their salaries, or when men were willing to work for less than the set rate for women. But it is difficult to discern the actual influence of the minimum wage on salaries, as other factors affected the economy during the 1910s. These factors included a rise in price levels, acceleration of industrial production, and a curtailment of immigration with a resulting labor shortage in some occupations, particularly during wartime.[147]

Minimum-wage laws for women were ultimately doomed by court rulings. The freedom-of-contract argument was invoked by the Supreme Court in *Adkins* v. *Children's Hospital* in 1923 to overturn the minimum wage in the District of Columbia. Justice George Sutherland argued for the majority that physical differences between the sexes, used to justify hours laws, did not apply to wages. As a result, minimum-wage laws were either overruled or fell into disuse in most states. It was not until the New Deal, when National Recovery Act codes and the Fair Labor Standards Act mandated government control of working conditions in occupations relating to interstate or foreign commerce, that labor legislation was revived.[148]

The Disappearance of the "Working Girl"

The eclipse of protective legislation was accompanied by a diminishing public interest in the status of self-supporting women. The ameliorative reforms discussed earlier lost ground during the 1920s. Travelers' Aid, for example, began to turn in new directions. By the 1930s, Travelers' Aid had redefined its role to include men as well as women travelers, and it became widely involved in social welfare during the depression, as its governing principle shifted from "moral protection" to "social casework."[149] Boarding homes also changed, some closing because of lack of patronage, and others turning into residences without excessive rules, and certainly without the attempt to re-create a hierarchical family environment.[150]

Demographic changes had led to a lessened visibility of self-supporting women by the mid-1920s. Stricter immigration laws and urbanization, which led to a smaller rural population from which migrant women might come, stemmed to some degree the tide of in-migration, at least as reflected in statistics on the proportions of women boarders and lodgers in cities. Joseph Hill, of the U.S. Census Bureau, suggested in 1929 that the relatively lower numbers of self-supporting women in cities was connected to patterns of urban growth. Rapidly growing cities, like Atlanta, reported higher proportions of female boarders and lodgers than did cities experiencing a decline in the rate of population increase. Of eleven cities surveyed by the Census Bureau in 1920, ten reported decreases in the relative numbers of women boarders and lodgers since 1900. St. Paul, for example, found 44 percent fewer women living on their own in 1920 than in 1900. Hill suggested that this occurred as "city conditions were becoming more settled, and home or family life for working women was becoming more common or general, as a natural result of retardation in the growth of that city."[151]

But the apparent decrease in the relative proportions of self-supporting women living on their own must also be viewed in the context of other factors. First, the occupational patterns of women were changing. By 1920, fewer women were servants, and more were clerical and sales workers. The domestic servant was no longer as likely to be a single young woman as much as she was likely to be an older married or widowed woman doing "daywork" to support her family. Since so many young single servants of the earlier era had roomed with their employers, the decrease in their numbers necessarily affected the enumeration of women who lived away from their own homes.[152]

Second, attitudes toward single women workers had changed. The self-supporting woman, once considered controversial, was by the 1920s viewed as a normal figure in the labor force. Her work and life outside the home became more acceptable. The domestic ideology was no longer thought to include the unmarried daughter; her status was no longer imperiled by employment and lodging away from home. This change was acknowledged by a Toledo, Ohio, real estate agent, who remarked in 1926 that, while "he remembered the time when he would have considered it very questionable if detached women had wanted to rent an apartment," he now thought that self-supporting women "are [as] desired as tenants as well as anyone else."[153] The first generation of women living on their own had provided a bridge between the older hegemony of domesticity and the modern, though still limited, diversity of roles for single women.

Finally the composition of the female labor force itself was changing. Young single women still continued to work. But at the same time, by the 1920s older married women had begun to enter the labor force in increasing numbers. As we shall see in chapter 4, the movement of married women into the labor force occurred as child labor declined. At least to some degree, mothers took the place of their children as contributors to family income.

The increase in the numbers of working wives and mothers led to a shift in the debate over women, work, and social order. At the 1923 Women's Industrial Conference, Commissioner of Labor James Davis argued, "We can do no greater service to humanity and the future of the Nation than to stir American public opinion that this evil shall vanish once and for all from American industrial life."[154] The evil was no longer the malevolent effect of industry on the young woman who would one day be a mother. What was now at issue was the growing labor force participation of the older woman who already had children at home.

Part Two

The Era of the Working Mother, 1920–1980

Chapter 4
The Transformation of
the Female Labor Force

During the twentieth century, the working wife moved from the periphery of the female labor force into the mainstream. In 1900, fewer than one in ten married women worked for wages. By 1980, married women comprised almost two-thirds of the female labor force, as one in two of all married women worked (see table 2). Scholars have suggested that demographic changes, including the decline in the relative proportion of single women in the population, a long-term drop in the fertility rate, and urbanization, have contributed to the dramatic rise in the number of married women who work.[1] But at least as important an influence on the rising work rate of wives have been changing social values about women, work, and family life that have interacted with changing factors of labor supply and demand.

As we have seen, the movement of single women into the urban labor force in the late nineteenth century was characterized by a growing visibility of the "working girl"—the white native-born woman worker. Similarly, the movement of married women into the job market was characterized by the entrance of white middle-income wives into the labor force. At the same time, the work behavior of mothers shifted. At the turn of the century, mothers who worked often did so while their children were very young. They left the labor force when their sons and daughters were old enough to join the ranks of child labor and thus contribute to family income. By the mid-twentieth century, mothers typically did not work while their children were young but entered the labor force at the time that their youngest child entered school. This pattern was eroding by the 1970s, when even mothers of preschool-aged children were joining the labor force at an accelerating pace.

This chapter charts the history of the working wife and mother through three periods in the twentieth century. From 1900 to 1940, middle-income white wives typically did not work outside the home. The female labor force was comprised mainly of single, widowed, and divorced women, and the wives who did work were for the most part poor and black. From 1940 to 1970, the married woman overtook the single woman as the largest group in the female labor force, and the participation rate for white married women rapidly accelerated. In the era from 1970 to the present, mothers—particularly mothers of young children—have become the fastest-growing group of workers. In each period, changes in labor supply, labor demand, and social values have interacted to shape the composition of the female labor force.

The Working Wife from 1900 to 1940

Relatively few wives worked at the turn of the century. Sixty-seven percent of women workers in 1900 were single, and only 15 percent were married. Just 6 percent of the population of married women worked, in contrast to 41 percent of single women (table 2).

Working wives came from a different population than did single women. They were much more likely to be black or poor. At the turn of the century, black wives were eight times as likely to work as were their white counterparts. Only 3 percent of white native-born married women worked, compared with more than a fourth of black wives. This affected the overall composition of the female labor force. In 1900, when two-thirds of single women workers were native-born whites, nearly half of the married women workers were black.[2]

As a rule, wives who worked in this era were poor women who needed to help support their families. Whereas it had become commonplace for single young women to work even if their families could have supported them, most wives worked only because of severe economic need. The work of wives was considered "a final defense against destitution" rather than an expected activity.[3] Married women worked only when other family income was insufficient for survival.

In this period there was an inverse correlation between family income and the employment of wives. Married women worked when their husbands earned low wages, were ill, or were unemployed. Katherine Anthony's investigation of working mothers on the west side of New York City in 1914 found that the employment of married women dropped as family income rose. "The mother works when she must," Anthony reported, "and when necessity is less stringent she relaxes her efforts outside and gives more attention to her home."[4]

A 1918 Philadelphia study also found that most wives who worked did so only because of desperate family circumstances. Three-fifths of the families with working mothers interviewed by the Philadelphia Bureau of Municipal Research lived on incomes less than the minimum standards set by the bureau for a family consisting of a husband, wife, and three children under legal working age. Of women with husbands who were employed, three out of four wives worked because their husbands' earnings were too low for family support.[5]

Some twenty years later, this inverse correlation between family income and the employment of wives still prevailed. A 1940 examination of families in seven cities showed that four to five times as many wives of low-income men worked as did wives of wealthier men. In general, the higher the husband's income, the lower the tendency of the wife to work.[6]

The relatively common practice of child labor, particularly at the turn of the century, also affected the work of married women. In 1900, nearly one out of five children aged from ten to fifteen years were employed.[7] The younger the age of children in working-class families at the turn of the century, the more likely the mother was to work outside the home. But as children reached the age of nine or ten, their mothers left the labor force, as both sons and daughters had better opportunities for earning higher wages.[8] Fourteen-year-old Fannie Harris, who worked for a necktie manufacturer, gave testimony before a committee of the New York legislature in 1895 that illustrates the process by which children replaced their mothers in the labor force:

Q. Have you got any older brothers and sisters?
A. I have an older sister.
Q. Does she work?
A. Yes, sir.
Q. Does your mamma work?
A. Now she ain't working because I'm working, but before, when I didn't work, she worked.

· · · · · · · · · · · ·

Q. And if you don't go to work then your mamma will have to work?
A. Sure.[9]

As we shall see, the pattern of wives working when their children were too young to work, and then staying home when the children were old enough to find employment, was reversed by the mid-twentieth century. By then, mothers of young children withdrew from the labor force, reentering when their youngsters were old enough to attend school.

The social stigma attached to the working wife was a strong deterrent to women entering the work force. Until the 1940s, paid employment outside the home was considered to be respectable only for single women or for widows who took over the management of their family businesses. For the married woman, paid employment could bring social anathema; the working wife was often considered to be beyond the pale of middle-class respectability.

But there was in this era a foreshadowing of a new employment pattern for married women. A minority of wives worked not because of absolute economic need but because of relative economic need—the desire to better the standard of living for their families. In 1915, the United States Bureau of Labor reported that some women textile workers hoped to "raise the family scale of living" with their earnings.[10] The 1918 Philadelphia study of mothers in industry found that 18 percent of the working mothers surveyed listed as their reasons for employment "personal preference." Many of these mothers were planning to build up family savings or earn enough for a family vacation.[11] Also in 1918, of 590 mothers working in the meat-packing plants of the Chicago stockyards, over a fourth worked in order to help their families buy property, discharge debts, or educate their children.[12] In 1920, a Census Bureau study discovered that on occasion a woman would work "not strictly from necessity but rather from choice, for the sake of securing a better living for herself and her husband than his income alone could provide."[13]

Some of the immigrant women interviewed in a 1925 Women's Bureau study also cited a desire to improve their families' standard of living. Theresa M., for example, a Hungarian immigrant with an employed husband and three children, worked as a roller in a cigar factory. She worked not to fend off family starvation, but to make things "nice"; her earnings helped her family to build a cellar, install plumbing and electricity, and buy a washing machine.[14] From 1920 to 1940, historian Winifred Wandersee suggests, family values were becoming redefined under the pressures of a rising standard of living and new consumption patterns. Although most married women still resisted work for wages in this era, those who worked did so not only because of absolute need, but also because employment opportunity was favorable or because the material comfort of their families superseded traditional concepts of women's role. Those who worked for the last two reasons "represented a change in family values, aimed at satisfying new needs rather than avoiding a poverty-level existence," Wandersee states. "But these women were able to rationalize their activities outside the home within the existing framework of traditional family values by defining their work in terms of the economic needs of the family."[15] This redefinition of family roles, however, was still nascent in 1940. For most married women, the inverse relationship between their employment and the income of their husbands remained powerful. It was not until the 1950s and 1960s that attitudinal change caught up with the factors of labor supply and demand, as increasing numbers of wives worked for reasons other than family subsistence.

In general, in the period before 1940, married women were reluctant to seek employment outside the home, and with good reason. Their lack of training and lack of commitment to full-time work, along with employer preference and the social values that led to a loss of status for working wives, relegated married women to the most menial and low-paying of jobs. As a result, married women and single women did different kinds of work. Although the majority of single women, we have seen, worked in domestic service at the turn of the century, still nearly 20 percent of them were employed in the white-collar occupations of clerical, sales, and telephone and telegraph work. In contrast, most married women workers were farm laborers, laundresses, domestics, or home pieceworkers; less than 2 percent of them was employed in occupations that could be defined as white-collar work. The kind of work performed predominantly by married women was the lowest status work; for example, married women were the majority of oyster canners and preservers—workers in a trade characterized by the government as one "in which . . . conditions were more unpleasant and the wage level lower than in any other industry studied."[16]

The occupations undertaken by wives in part reflected their need to work in occupations that would mesh with their need for time at home. Mothers in New York City in 1914 preferred jobs in neighborhood factories where conditions were worse than in other places but where they were closer to their homes. Wives often worked in jobs with short hours or night hours so that they might leave the care of their children to their husbands. Jobs that were not sought after by single women because of oppressive conditions or odd hours were taken up by married women who had little choice. A Philadelphia office cleaner reported of her choice of night work in 1918 that "single women want their evenings, but the married women can get along without a good time."[17]

Much of the work of married women was performed within their homes and was undercounted by the Census Bureau. As late as 1920, at least one-fourth to one-third of married women workers were home workers.[18] In rural areas, wives toiled on family farms or as sharecroppers; in cities, they produced piecework in the clothing, artificial flower, or cigar trades, took in laundry or dressmaking, or kept boarders. Thus they could tend their children while earning a wage and often put their children to work as well.[19]

Clothing pieceworkers, for example, often taught their children to help out at an early age. *New York Tribune* reporter Helen Campbell described how young children assisted their mothers with clothing production in the late 1880s. She wrote of a New York overall maker who said of her children, ages seven and five, "I couldn't do as well if it wasn't for Jinny and Mame there. Mame has learned to sew on buttons first-rate, and Jinny is doing almost as well. . . . We'll do better yet when Mame gets a bit older."[20] Elizabeth Butler stated in her 1907 study of Pittsburgh working women that in families living in the "outwork" districts of the city, "as fast as children could hold a needle they were pressed into service" as button makers, thread pullers, and machine operators.[21]

Some women, impelled by economic need, worked a variety of low-paying jobs. The Bureau of Labor Statistics reported the story of a widowed mother who worked nine hours a day in a bookbindery. As janitor of the building where she lived she cleaned halls before she left for work in the morning; in the evening, after cooking and cleaning, she colored picture postcards at the rate of fifteen cents a hundred. "She said that she often went to bed too tired to sleep and felt more tired when she got up in the morning than when she went to bed," the bureau stated.[22]

But perhaps the most common means of income for married women in this period was cooking and cleaning for boarders and lodgers. In 1901, nearly one in four urban families investigated by the Bureau of Labor reported that boarders brought them an average of $250 yearly—a sum representing over a third of the average annual family income, which was estimated to be $749.50.[23] Half of the New York City families studied in a 1907 report took in one or more boarders. Most of the wives who took in boarders and lodgers did not consider this activity as an occupation but rather as part of routine house-keeping duties. The Census Bureau agreed; it considered boarding and lodging housekeeping to be a formal occupation only for those whose primary means of support was the care of five or more boarders.[24]

One factor retarding the entrance of wives into the labor force in this era was the value placed on work within the home. Working-class wives might keep boarders and make clothing for their children; middle-income wives placed a higher value on child care, leisure, and housework. For both groups, home work was preferable to work outside the home.[25]

Before 1940, most wives and mothers who worked for wages outside the home remained on the fringe of the female labor force. Their children and husbands had greater opportunities for employment, and when married women sought work it was in the occupations with the lowest status. Married women worked outside the home only when they had to. Women's Bureau investigator Caroline Manning reported that "trouble, if not tragedy, had cast its shadow" over most of the working wives in the 1920s.[26] But developments in the supply and demand for female labor had begun in this era which would accelerate after 1940, bringing into the labor force white middle-income wives who worked not because of trouble or tragedy but because of choice.

Forces for Change, 1940–1970

Although the number of married women who worked increased steadily through the twentieth century, the greatest gains were made after 1940. From 1940 to 1970, married women increased their work rate each decade by at least 28 percent. As a group, married women became the most important source of new workers in the United States. From 1951 to 1961, wives accounted for nearly half of the total growth of the American labor force.[27]

The change in the racial composition of the female married labor force was also dramatic. In 1890, only one in fifty white wives was employed; black wives were more than ten times as likely to work. But after 1940, the labor force rate of white married women accelerated. The decade from 1950 to 1960 saw the greatest growth for white wives, as their work rate jumped from 17 to 30 percent. By 1970, the differential in work rates between black and white wives had narrowed further (table 6).

The transformation of the female labor force has been attributed to a number of factors. Analysts have cited demographic changes as responsible for the rising work rate of married women. They have noted that women in 1970 were older, less likely to have children, more likely to be living in cities than in rural areas, and more likely to have college degrees than they were in 1900.[28]

These changes alone, however, could not account for the fast rise in the female labor force participation rates after 1940. For native-born white women, especially, the key factor in work behavior has not been changing family structures or urbanization but rather a rising propensity to work, which reflects a change in social values.[29] Work for wages outside the home came to

Table 6

Percentage of Married Women in the Labor Force, by Race, Selected Years, 1890–1980

	1890	1900	1920	1930	1940	1950	1960	1970
All women	5	6	9	12	17	25	32	40
White	2	3	7	10	14	17	30	39
Black	23	26	33	33	32	36	47	51

Sources: Brownlee, "Household Values," p. 200, table 1; Durand, *Labor Force in the U.S.*, pp. 216–17, table A-7; U.S. Bureau of the Census, *U.S. Census of Population, 1960*, pp. 501–6, table 196; U.S. Bureau of the Census, *Nineteenth Census of the U.S., 1970*, pp. 688–89, table 216.

be valued as highly as was nonwage work within the home and the status of domesticity. In short, changes in the nature of work and in the role of women explain why the labor force participation rate of married women was so much higher than what can be explained by demographic factors alone.

Population changes did in part affect the supply of women available as workers. The relatively high proportion of single women in the nineteenth century gradually diminished. In 1958, economist Gertrude Bancroft commented on the "almost complete disappearance of the spinster and the increasing proportion of married women in the population."[30] The proportion of single women fell from about a third of all women in 1890 to about a fifth in 1970. Yet, although the proportion of single women fell by 14 percent, their representation in the female labor force fell from 68 to 22 percent—a decline of over three times what could be expected on the basis of increasing marriage rates alone.[31]

Whereas women were more likely to be married in the mid-twentieth century, they were also likely to bear fewer children. The decrease in the birthrate, a result of birth control as well as of changing family ideologies, has been cited as a factor lessening the burden of housewifery and thus increasing the tendency of married women to work outside the home.[32] There has been a gradual decline in the fertility rate of American women since at least 1810.[33] And from 1920 to 1970, fertility rates fell from 117.9 births per thousand women to 87.9.

The relationship between declining fertility and the rising employment of wives, however, must be viewed with caution. Despite the "baby boom" of the 1950s and 1960s, the labor force participation rate of wives did not decline but instead continued to rise. From 1940 to 1960, when the fertility rate jumped from 72.9 to 118.0, the work participation rate of married women still rose by 88 percent.[34]

The overall drop in the fertility rate, combined with rising life expectancies, did lead to a gradual aging of the population. In 1890, the largest age group in the adult female population was the group from 16 to 24 years, and over half of all adult women was younger than 30 years old. Eighty years later, in 1970, the largest age group of women was in the population aged 35 to 44, and over half of all adult women was older than 35.[35]

This aging of the population was reflected in the female labor force. In 1900, the largest age group of women workers was from 16 to 20 years old, but in 1970, the largest group was aged from 35 to 44. Still, the aging of the population alone could not account for the changing female labor force composition. The work rate increased in every age group for married women from 1900 to 1970, most markedly for women between the ages of 20 and 24 and for women over the age of 35. In every age group, married women increased their labor force participation at a much greater rate than did single, widowed, or divorced women.[36]

Another factor suggested as influential for the rising work rate of wives was the continued urbanization of the population that occurred in the twentieth century.[37] Historically, women in cities have been more likely to work for wages outside the home than have women in rural areas. In 1900, when 28 percent of women in large cities worked, only 18 percent of women in smaller cities and country districts were employed.[38] In 1950, apparently residence was still a factor in women's employment. Then, 22 percent of nonfarm white wives and 35 percent of nonfarm black wives worked for wages, compared with 13 percent of white wives and 18 percent of black wives who lived on farms.[39] But this determinant is complicated by the fact that farm wives, who often contributed to the work on their family farms, were viewed as unpaid family laborers and therefore were not counted by the Census Bureau as wage earners.[40]

The final demographic factor that seems to have altered the female labor force has been the growth in education for women, which has occurred since 1940. Before World War II, women earned about 20 percent of bachelor's and first professional degrees. By 1940, women received over 40 percent of those degrees, and by 1968, nearly one in five women had secured a college diploma.[41]

More and more educated and skilled women from higher-income families entered the work force. A study of the census returns of 1940 and 1950 showed that the inverse correlation between the rate of female employment and median male income in 1940 and earlier was reversed for white women by 1950. The more a woman was capable of earning, because of increased education, the more likely she was to work.[42] Still, many college-educated married women did not work in this period, so the factor of education by itself does not explain the growth rate of married women in the labor force.

Demographic changes may have contributed to the enormous influx of wives into the labor force in this era. But we must also consider other factors that led married women into the job market, particularly changes in the nature of work and in the role of women within the family.

Work outside the home had become less demanding in terms of time and relatively more profitable. The reduction in the weekly hours of work made employment more attractive to women who performed the dual jobs of wage earner and housewife.[43] The average hours of work in manufacturing occupations fell from an estimated fifty-nine a week in 1899 to forty in 1939, and a corresponding acceptance of the eight-hour day in white-collar work made employment still more feasible for women with children.[44] Moreover, a rise in real wages over time may have encouraged more women to work outside the home. Economists have pointed out that as wages rise leisure time becomes more expensive. From 1890 to 1960, real income tripled, while the participation rates of married women in the work force increased sixfold.[45]

A related factor was the value of work performed at home and rendered by wives in services such as child care, food preparation, and household maintenance.[46] Some scholars have argued that the proliferation of laborsaving devices in the twentieth century eased the burden of housework and hence provided wives with more time for outside employment. The electricity-powered washing machine and refrigerator have been linked to a reduction in the time needed for household tasks.[47] But inventions related to the mechanization of housework, such as the vacuum cleaner and electric iron, were widely used before 1940, prior to the time when the work rate of married women accelerated.[48]

Moreover, the spread of laborsaving devices appeared as domestic servants disappeared from middle-class homes, and higher expectations for housekeeping may have added to rather than subtracted from the hours put into those tasks by middle-income women. The average household spent more time on laundry work in 1964 than in 1925, for example. Washing machines and electric driers eased the physical burden of clothes cleaning, but most families now had more clothes that were washed more often.[49]

The age and presence of children in the home also affected the propensity of women to work. As we have seen, in the first third of the twentieth century, mothers worked, if ever, when their children were young. As children became old enough to find jobs, their mothers dropped out of the labor force. By mid-century, this pattern had been reversed. In 1950, only 12 percent of women with young children worked outside the home (see table 7). By 1960, more than a third of the women with school-aged children were employed, a higher rate than married women with no children living at home. By 1970, nearly half of the women with children aged from six to seventeen worked. Clearly, the life-cycle pattern described for turn-of-the-century working women had changed. By mid-century, mothers of young children were not commonly employed but instead worked after their children had entered school.

The entrance of these mothers into the labor force occurred as their children were moving out of the labor force and into the schools. The proportions of children who worked for wages decreased in the years that mothers began to work. In 1870, 13.2 percent of all children from ten to fifteen years old were employed. By 1900, 18.2 percent of children in this age group worked; one out

Table 7

Percentage of Married Women in the Labor Force, by Presence and Age of Children, 1948–1970

	1948	1950	1960	1970
With no children under 18	28.4	30.3	34.7	42.2
With children aged 6–17 only	26.0	28.3	39.0	49.2
With children under 6	10.8	11.9	18.6	30.3

Source: U.S. Department of Labor, Bureau of Labor Statistics, *Handbook of Labor Statistics, 1978*, p. 64, table 14.

of four boys and one in ten girls reported wage-earning activities.[50] After the turn of the century, however, child labor diminished. By 1920, 11.3 percent, and by 1930, 4.7 percent of children in this age group worked.[51]

The decrease in child labor occurred in part because of a movement to abolish the employment of children. Reformers feared that children who worked were not being properly educated, and they pushed for laws to prohibit the work of children and to mandate compulsory schooling.[52] Thus the changing pattern of family economics saw the increasing employment rate of mothers at the same time as children were being moved out of the labor force.

Even as the presence of children in the home was becoming less of an influence on a mother's decision to work, so the dollar amount of her husband's paycheck was becoming less important. Economists predicted that the work rate of married women should decrease as their husbands' incomes rose.[53] As it turned out, a rapid rise in the labor force participation of middle-income wives in the 1950s and 1960s confounded this expectation.

Investigators examined the labor force participation of married women as a function of their husbands' incomes for 1950, 1959, and 1968. For 1950, there was a fairly linear negative correlation between the two variables, as the work rate of wives fell as their husbands' income rose. By 1959, and even more in 1968, this trend began to erode. By 1968, the work rate of married women was highest for those whose husbands' annual incomes were close to the then national average of about $6,500.[54]

These income studies reflect the increasing propensity of married women to work for reasons other than absolute economic need. Middle-income wives had begun to seek employment to achieve both personal satisfaction and to raise their family standards of living. Union women surveyed by the Women's Bureau as early as 1950 reported that they worked for objectives beyond family survival. The level of economic need had been enlarged to include items that at one time were considered to be luxuries. These women worked to buy a house or car, pay bills, or educate their children. Two out of three women members of the Brotherhood of Railway and Steamship Clerks, for example, worked to make house payments. One out of four of the International Association of Machinists listed the education of their children as a work objective.[55] These women might argue that they worked to support their families, but the definition of what constituted family support had changed to reflect higher expectations of consumption needs.

Attitudinal factors about women's work outside the home had more influence on certain groups of women than on others. For women for whom work was not a role transgression, such as poor women, such factors as the age of their youngest child may have been more critical in their decision whether or not to work. But for middle-income women, the shift of values that increasingly permitted women to work without losing class status probably was one of the more important factors influencing their work decision.[56]

As the supply of women workers grew to include married women, the demand for female labor was rising. Historians differ on the nature of the pull of the labor market for wives. William Chafe has argued that World War II was a watershed for American women, prompting a "revolution" in the labor force by bringing the first large numbers of married women into the marketplace.[57] Other scholars suggest that the war did not initiate this process but instead temporarily speeded up the trend of increasing demand for female labor. Leila Rupp, for one, dismisses the importance of the war for the history of women's work, arguing that "the influx of women into the labor force during the war had nothing to do with . . . long-term changes, and had no permanent impact on the female labor force."[58] It seems clear that the long-term effects of occupational segregation that were established by the turn of the century influenced the growing demand for women workers. There were well-defined spheres of women's and men's work, as certain jobs, such as elementary school teaching and typing, were deemed women's occupations, and others, such as construction work and accounting, were designated for men.[59]

The years from 1900 to 1960 were characterized by the general decrease in the need for farm labor and a concomitant increase in the demand for white-collar workers. The demand for manual labor and service work has remained relatively constant over that period. The trend for men is quite clear. When men's efforts were no longer required on the farm, they turned to manual and service jobs and, to a lesser extent, to nonclerical white-collar work. At the same time, women, and particularly married women, were filling the growing demand for white-collar workers. It was office work, which had become women's work, for which demand was now the greatest. For married women, farm, manual, and service work gave way to white-collar work by mid-century.

As labor demand opened up new opportunities for women, the gap that existed at 1900 between married and single women workers narrowed. Although single women were about twice as likely to hold white-collar jobs as were married women in 1900, by 1960 there was little difference in the occupational distribution of married women and women workers in general.[60]

The shift of wives to white-collar work especially favored the employment of white women. Black women found barriers to work opportunities in offices because of higher educational requirements and because of institutional racism. In 1960, when two in five white wives worked in clerical or sales occupations, only one in ten black married women was in the same category.[61]

Whereas the expansion of work opportunities for women was the more important factor in the overall demand for female labor, the short-term experiences of millions of married women during World War II were also significant. During the war, there were great gains in the female labor force. Over 6 million women, three-fourths of them married, took jobs for the first time between 1940 and 1945. These women increased the size of the female labor force by more than 50 percent.[62] This pattern differed from the experience of women during World War I, when only 5 percent of women war workers had joined the labor force for the first time.[63]

During World War II, women produced engines, guns, shells, and tanks in war plants and took 2 million new clerical jobs. The aircraft industry reflected the influx of new women workers. In April 1941, 143 women were employed in seven aircraft factories. By October 1943, these same factories had hired 65,000 women—an increase of over 450-fold.[64] By 1944, both married and single women were working in greater proportions than previously; single women had increased their labor force participation rate by 15 percent, and married women by 6 percent.

But layoffs and demotions reduced the female labor force after the war. By the end of 1945, one out of four women in industry had quit or been laid off. Between 1945 and 1946, more than 3 million women who had worked during the war had dropped out of the labor force.[65] Still, millions of women continued to work after the war, taking advantage of work opportunities that had been expanding for decades. For married white women, the most important gains came not from 1940 to 1950 but from 1950 to 1960, when they increased their work rate by 13 percent—the fastest rise per decade up to that time.

The forces of labor supply and demand were interactive. Shortages of single women combined with increased job opportunities to create a demand for married workers, and increased job opportunities in the female sector of the labor force in turn attracted more of them into the job market as social values about the economic role of women began to change. The patterns of labor supply and labor demand that were established at mid-century had shaped a female labor force that by 1970 differed markedly from the female labor force of 1900.

The Working Wife and Mother in the 1970s

By 1976, 62 percent of the female labor force was married—the exact proportion of women workers who had been single in 1900. In the 1970s, trends favoring the work of married women continued.

The working wife was no longer likely to be black or poor. Racial differences in the work rates of married women continued to narrow; in 1978, 58 percent of black wives worked, but the rate for white wives had risen to 47 percent. Black women were also beginning to obtain relatively higher-status jobs; the proportion of black women who held clerical jobs nearly tripled between 1960 and 1976. By 1980, nearly half of all employed black women were white-collar workers.[66]

At the same time, the service sector of the economy—which included white-collar work—continued to grow. The ratio of service-to-goods producing jobs widened from 1.5 to 1 in 1950 to nearly 2.5 to 1 by 1976. By 1979, too, clerical workers had become the largest occupational group for women in the United States, overtaking manual and service jobs.[67]

The tie between a woman's employment and her husband's income, loosened in the postwar era, became undone in the 1970s. Between 1967 and 1974, the labor force participation rate of women whose husbands earned $2,000 to $6,000 rose by 11 percent, but the work rate of wives whose husbands earned over $30,000 a year jumped by 38 percent. A 1974 survey found that among women with children under the age of eighteen, employment rates for middle-income wives were the highest. Whereas participation rates continued to rise for women in all income categories, the overall rate for married women rose as their husbands' incomes rose to the annual salary level of $7,000 to $10,000, and dropped off thereafter for women whose husbands earned over $10,000 a year. In 1978, this trend continued, as the highest proportion of wives who worked—more than half of all married women—had husbands who earned from $10,000 to $20,000 a year.[68] Finally, the fertility rate continued to drop, falling from 87.9 in 1970 to 66.4 in 1979, at the same time as the female labor force participation rate increased by 10 percent.[69]

But the 1970s, while continuing the labor force trends of the postwar era, also saw some new developments. First, there was a sharp increase in the numbers of female-headed households. The proportion of single-parent families, most of them headed by women, more than doubled since 1950, comprising 18.9 percent of all families by 1978. From 1970 to 1978 alone there was an increase of over 2.5 million single-parent families. This trend, a result of the rising divorce rate and the rise in the numbers of babies born to unmarried mothers—was important because female-headed families were so much poorer than two-parent families. Forty percent of single-parent families in 1978 lived on incomes below the poverty level—a status held by only 6 percent of families with two parents living at home.[70]

The other major change in the labor force involved the rapidly growing work rate of mothers of very young children. In 1950, only 12 percent of mothers of preschool-aged children worked. In 1969, fewer than one in four mothers of children under the age of three worked, and by 1979, this percentage had risen to over two in five.[71] In 1978, a new subgroup of working women was recognized by the Census Bureau for the first time. These were the mothers of infants under the age of one year. The Census Bureau found that in 1978, a startling 30 percent of mothers with infants under a year old worked, at least part-time, and 41 percent of mothers with children under the age of two were also employed.[72] The practice of mothers of young children staying at home and out of the labor force, evident in the 1950s, was apparently eroding. And although economic pressures were partly responsible, as they were in 1900, changing social values also played an important role.

Developments in the supply-and-demand factors in the female labor force in the twentieth century resulted in a changing identity for the woman worker. The single self-supporting woman had been replaced in the job market by the wife and mother. In turn, the working wife who had been black or poor at the turn of the century was by the 1970s more likely to be middle income and white. Because of her class status, the working wife and mother could no longer be treated strictly as a charity case or be ignored. The concern with the protection of the future motherhood of the single woman, which had been the cornerstone of the public debate over working women in the early twentieth century, now shifted to a concern with the protection of motherhood itself.

Chapter 5
The Discovery of the Working Mother

The married woman who worked for wages had long been considered to be an aberration, a "social accident" of scant public significance.[1] Because she was usually poor or black, her status elicited little controversy. Reform efforts aimed at the child care or health needs of the working mother were in general secondary to the larger measures meant to protect the working girl. By the 1920s, however, the female labor force was beginning to be affected by the increasing work rates of white middle-income wives. The disjuncture between the domestic ideology and the employment patterns of women resulted in the discovery and labeling of a new social problem. The working mother replaced the working girl as a symbol of female role transgression and social change.

The development of the debate over the work of married women mirrored a narrowing of the domestic ideology. By the 1930s, daughters who worked for wages before marriage were no longer considered to be "adrift" from their proper place. But the domestic role prescription still held strong for married women and mothers. As Robert and Helen Lynd noted of public opinion in "Middletown"—Muncie, Indiana—during the 1930s, "there is more indulgent tolerance of a business-class girl's working between school and marriage, but when she marries, 'all that foolishness stops.' "[2]

Once married, a woman was expected to devote full time to home activities. These activities were increasingly less economic in scope, as home production of goods for family consumption and for industry was rapidly diminishing.[3] Rather, a new emphasis on a mother's role in meeting the emotional needs of her family was taking hold in American culture. "The chief concern over the family nowadays," a sociologist suggested in 1933, "is not how strong it may be as an economic organization but how well it performs services for the personalities of its members."[4] A mother's responsibility for the nurture of her husband and children gained new importance as her economic responsibilities, whether making overalls at home as piecework, sewing clothes, or baking bread for her family, lessened.

The work of married women in the period from 1920 to 1940 provoked questions about the moral, economic, and psychological aspects of a woman's role as wife as well as mother. After 1940, these concerns narrowed still further; the work of wives without children and of mothers of children in school gradually came to be accepted. But the employment of mothers of young children captured public attention. This was the bottom line for the controversy over women and work. The consequences of a woman's employment outside the home on the physical and psychological health of her young children became the center of public debate.

Working Mothers before 1920

Before 1920, the concern with married women in the work force was subordinate to the concern with single women. When the labor of married women came to light, two themes were expressed that would shape the controversy throughout the twentieth century. Even after the composition of the female labor force shifted toward the working wife and mother after the mid-twentieth century, public opinion about these women was still mired in the outdated conceptions of the nineteenth century.

The first theme advanced in the nineteenth century was about the effect of the employment of mothers on the health and upbringing of their children. For the most part, this aspect of the debate focused on poor women; some critics feared that their work caused them to neglect their children and thus contributed to such social ills as delinquency and dependency. Moreover, the effect of long hours of toil on a mother's well-being and, in turn, on her progeny was seen as consequential for the future of the working class.

Carroll Wright said in his 1875 report of the Massachusetts Bureau of Labor Statistics that the work of married women in factories was an evil "sapping the life of our operative population, and must sooner or later be regulated, or, more probably, stopped."[5] The United States Industrial Commission, in 1902, maintained that married women debilitated by hard work would give birth to sickly children, thus weakening the "physical and moral strength of the new generation of working people."[6] The problem of the "mother who must earn" was, like the problem of the working girl, one of the effects of a woman's work on her children.

The second theme in the discussion of working wives in this era stemmed from the rare but highly visible employment of middle-class married women, who consciously sought work as an alternative to their domestic role. For these women, work was seen as a matter of choice rather than of necessity. By taking jobs, they were seen as deliberately transgressing their proper place.

The challenge posed by this role transgression was exemplified in the writings of Charlotte Perkins Gilman. In *Women and Economics*, published in 1898, and in *The Home*, published in 1903, Gilman argued that the financial independence brought by earning a paycheck was critical for the freedom of women, and she proposed that the employment of wives be encouraged by the establishment of communal kitchens and nurseries.[7] But Gilman's ideas were on the edge of contemporary thought. More common was the contention that the issue for middle-class women was not how to combine work and marriage but how to choose between them.

In an 1893 article in the *North American Review*, Mary Hawes Terhune argued that women faced a choice between "counting room and cradle." It was, she advised, not a matter of equal alternatives. For the woman who chose life in the counting room, Terhune warned, "native branches have been pruned to make room for the alien. If the result satisfy her, it is because she has unsexed herself. If longings for the shelter, the sacred joys and loves of wifehood and motherhood have survived through the unnatural process, she is an object of pity."[8] This point of view was also expressed in the popular women's magazines of the era. An article in the 1900 *Ladies' Home Journal*, for example, stressed the primacy of homemaking as the sphere of women. "An American Mother" instructed *Journal* readers that "if fate has denied to any woman a home, a husband, and a baby, let her take up art, or medicine, or blacksmithing. . . . But to claim that these are higher occupations than her own craft—the high calling of wife-hood and motherhood—is the most shallow and dangerous cant."[9]

While the employment of married women was not seen as a social problem on a large scale before 1920, still the themes evoked throughout the twentieth century were taking shape in the earlier period. The problem of role transgression for the woman who chose career over marriage, and the dangers to the children of the poor working wife, were ideas that converged after 1920 to create a second era in the debate over women and work—a debate that was now acutely concerned with the social consequences of the employment of married women.

Wives, Mothers, and Work, 1920–1940

During the 1920s, married women edged onto center stage in the rhetoric over working women. Progressive reformers had noted the plight of the poverty-stricken woman with children and intended to restore her to her home. In a contrary direction, articulate feminists brought attention to their point of view, publishing in mass magazines and books. A spirited debate ensued, as the working wife of any class was seen by critics as a danger to long-hallowed ideals of family life, while feminists applauded the employment of women as a prerequisite for female independence.

The new controversy was reflected in a proliferation of newspaper and magazine articles, in surveys, in investigations, and in public-opinion polls. Whereas *Harper's Bazaar* in 1908 published a series of articles on self-supporting single women, *Harper's Magazine* in the mid-1920s devoted its pages to the discussion of working wives. And while a student-debate handbook in 1911 summarized the pros and cons of work for single women, a 1928 debate volume entitled *Jobs and Marriage?* questioned the results of employment for a married woman's health, her husband, her home, and her children.[10]

During the early period of the debate over working wives, the actual number of married women in the labor force was relatively small. We have seen that in 1920 only a fifth of the female labor force was married, and under a tenth of all wives worked. By 1940, 17 percent of wives worked, constituting just over a third of the female labor force.[11] Yet the emotional rhetoric of the debate over women's employment belied these statistics; the great majority of married women did not work, while the minority who did captured public attention. The employment of the married woman at this time touched a sensitive nerve in American culture. She was perceived by different factions as a symbol of the failure, or of the salvation, of the family and the social order.

There were two dominant viewpoints in the debate over working wives in this era. The first was the widely held conservative notion that the work of wives was dangerous for both moral and economic reasons. The married woman who left home to work was a "menace to the race" because she endangered the integrity of the family, the birthrate, the economic system— indeed, she threatened civilization itself. Proponents of this view contended that the ideal family should contain one wage earner—the husband. The wife should devote her time to caring for her children and spouse, and to maintaining the home. If a woman had to work because of financial need, her position was considered to be most unfortunate. If she chose to work for reasons other than survival, her decision was considered to be both selfish and immoral.

This perspective surfaced at the Women's Industrial Conference sponsored by the Department of Labor and the Women's Bureau in 1923. Labor Commissioner James Davis decried the employment of married women, stating that "we must see to it that we do not sacrifice motherhood upon the altar of greed for industrial production."[12] But a counter viewpoint was advanced by a minority group of feminists who argued that working wives were at the vanguard of women's emancipation, for they established "the greater personal freedom and financial independence of women."[13] The feminist position represented a challenge to traditional family life: either the family as commonly conceived would disappear, or it would be transformed as people other than the mother would share in child care and household duties.

Ironically, there was little discussion in either camp about why most married women were really motivated to seek employment, which was to contribute to family income in order to attain a higher standard of living. The Lynds, in *Middletown in Transition*, saw this factor as most important in the changing perspective of wives who began to work. Middletown residents attached great weight to the idea that a married woman's place was at home, the Lynds reported: "At every point this value is buttressed against change. The thing that is changing it most is not changes from within its own coherently knit ideologies—not changes in awareness of woman's individual differences, capacities, and propensities, not changes in the conception as to what "home" means or what the role of a "wife" or "mother" is—but the pressure from without of a culturally stimulated rising psychological standard of living."[14]

It was not the relative standard of living that framed the debate between proponents and opponents of working wives and mothers. Rather, the controversy focused on questions of how employment affected a woman's health in the context of prescribed social roles. Although the economic class of the working mother shaped the tenor of different aspects of this debate, in the end it was sex rather than class that characterized the social dogma of the times. The question was, What effect would work have on the physical and mental health of married women? Conservatives, focusing on poor women, warned that the activities of housework and employment constituted a "double burden" for women, while feminists countered that employment enhanced both physical and mental health. Several investigators argued that a wife who both worked and tended her household was left in a "shocking state of exhaustion" by day's end.[15] When critics pointed to the problems of the working wife, they cited cases of poor women whose health was threatened by insufficient medical care and years of unremitting toil as factory operatives and domestic workers. The ill health of working mothers was noted in a Children's Bureau study of Chicago women in 1922. Typical passages reported constant fatigue: "Mother complained of being tired all the time"; "Mother well and strong but very tired. Got up at 5 A.M. and left for work at 6"; "Mother . . . wearing out."[16]

The complaint of the employed working-class mother was one of physical debilitation—a result of work under oppressive conditions. It appears that many of these women did not suffer as much as did their middle-class counterparts from another complaint—that of psychological tension caused by role ambiguity. Rather, working-class mothers endorsed the ideology of domesticity. The New York working mothers surveyed by Katherine Anthony in 1914 approved of values opposed to the employment of women and aspired to leaving the labor force. "Not to work is a mark of the middle-class married woman," Anthony found, "and the ambitious West Side family covets that mark."[17] Nearly fifty years later, in 1962, Mirra Komarovsky in her study, *Blue-Collar Marriage*, similarly found little evidence of status frustration among working-class homemakers.[18]

But middle-class women in the 1920s were beginning to display a psychological tension when they confronted the dilemma between work and marriage. This tension, often termed the "problem with American women," has been cited repeatedly throughout the century. In 1926, Helen Glenn Tyson, a social scientist, outlined the mental conflict endured by the professional woman with a family:

> . . . on the one hand, a keen interest in her professional work, a real need of income, the fear of mental stagnation, and the restlessness that comes from filling all her day with petty things; on the other hand, new demands in child-care that were unknown even a decade ago; a supply of domestic helpers that is fast diminishing both in quality and quantity; and, like a cloud over all her activities, her own emotional conflict that is rooted deep in her maternity. . . . The feeling that the world is organized to her disadvantage alone is not conducive to resignation.[19]

Women attempting to fulfill two roles were often confounded; those choosing one role over the other were often dissatisfied. Women were repeatedly told they could not have it both ways. In a 1936 advice manual, for example, girls were cautioned that the attempt to work while married "detracts materially from success in both the home and in the business world because of the added physical and mental strain."[20]

Feminists were not convinced by these arguments. They contended that it was full-time housewifery, and not employment, that imperiled women's health. Feminists cited studies that hypothesized that the repression of mental abilities led to neurasthenia, fatigue, depression, and other ailments. Employment was suggested as a health remedy; some proponents suggested that by working married women could become "alert, brisk, hopeful" people rather than frustrated, thwarted individuals.[21]

The role of women as marriage partners was also under fire in this era, as the effect of employment on issues of dependence and independence were questioned. Some argued that if a woman worked outside the home, she undercut the status of her spouse. Others replied that working wives fulfilled important needs for self-expression and would as a result be better companions to their husbands.

Social scientist Ernest Groves maintained in 1926 that the average husband felt his place within the family to be endangered by a working wife. "In the past supremacy of the male in the family rested on his command of the family income and the prestige that has been his from being looked upon as the producer of the family funds," he wrote. "When the woman herself earns and her maintenance is not entirely at the mercy of her husband's will, diminishing masculine authority necessarily follows." This loss of authority, Groves added, was buttressed by a loss of social status, for public opinion opposed the work of wives and looked with suspicion on the competence of a husband whose wife earned a paycheck.[22]

Public opinion in 1929 tolerated the employment of only a few classes of married women, notably blacks, immigrants, women with grown children, and, occasionally, "women of rare talents." For the ordinary woman, housewifery was the expected pursuit, "the husband being sufficiently successful to assure a sufficient income to purchase all supplies and to accumulate some savings."[23] A survey of men in 1924 supported these findings; 65 percent of men in clerical, commercial, and professional occupations believed that married women should devote full time to family affairs. Another 31 percent believed that while it was acceptable for some wives to work, mothers of young children should stay at home.[24]

Working married women themselves were cognizant of the threat that their employment posed to their husbands. One woman wrote in the *Atlantic Monthly* in 1924 that the husband of a working wife was easily threatened. "He feels his crown as master of the household slipping," she noted. "He acquires an inferiority complex. . . . [I]t takes a steady hand to keep a marriage off the rocks at this period; . . . the husband wants to be the strong one in the family. . . . Really, he wants [his wife] to keep her place as the minor part of the family."[25] When a husband's self-esteem was threatened, critics warned, he might too easily lose his own drive for business success. A group of New York bankers declared that they would not hire married women. "A working wife," they stated, "often deadens ambition in a man. If he knows his wife is earning money just as he earns it, it encourages him to laziness. Her husband becomes a parasite without stamina or self-respect."[26] A social scientist, Anna Garlin Spencer, agreed with this opinion, stating that "the husband and the father is more easily tempted to shirk his family duties" when wives worked. She contended that in black families, where women were more likely to find jobs than were men, "the man grows flabby in character and lazy in habit because it is easy for him thus to depend upon his wife."[27]

Feminists countered these arguments by promoting the work of wives as the basis of egalitarian marriages. One woman writer proclaimed in 1927 that the working wife was a "feminist—new style" rather than the traditional homemaker or the militantly unmarried, grim, "old-style" feminist. The new feminist was a "full-fledged" individual who both worked and shared an egalitarian marriage.[28] Another writer suggested that a benefit of her job was a new comradeship—a sort of partnership—with her husband. "A working wife has a better chance of being friends with her husband than the stay-at-home wife. . . . She is no longer a dependent," the writer maintained. "She is an equal partner. The chances for domestic happiness seem greater than in the old-fashioned marriage where a woman could be nothing but what her husband made her."[29] A third woman agreed in 1926, stating in *Survey Graphic* magazine that "it is practically impossible to create a satisfactory relationship when one person is entirely dependent on the other, and that other is forced to carry the sole economic responsibility for the lives of both as well as of the family." Independence, these women argued, both enhanced their lives and improved their marriages.[30] But the feminist viewpoint was not widely shared. To many Americans before 1940, a working wife was a sign of a flawed marriage.

Another issue in the debate over married women workers was the effect of work on a woman's role as a mother. Two fears fueled this discussion: the possibility that employed wives consciously limited the size of their families, and the question of the impact of their employment on the health and upbringing of the offspring they did have.

The specter of "race suicide" had been raised earlier in the century; some feared that native-white and college-educated women were choosing to have fewer children than were immigrants, blacks, and poor women, and that the result would be a disastrous fall in "quality" in the American population.[31] Theodore Roosevelt led the charge of these critics, condemning women who deliberately avoided childbearing as "criminal against the race." One cause of the avoidance of childbirth, commentators warned, was the employment of women outside the home. In his study of the American family, for example, Arthur Calhoun suggested that to a working wife "children are an embarrassment and interfere with a career, hence the tendency to avoid maternity."[32]

In 1926, Paul Popenoe, a eugenicist, linked working women to forces that were destroying the family. He urged that only middle-aged and handicapped women, and, possibly, "geniuses" be encouraged to work. Young girls should not be allowed to work lest they be taught to find "all good things of life outside the scope of the home" and abandon marriage and motherhood. Young wives who had not yet had children should also be discouraged from employment, Popenoe maintained, for they might delay pregnancy, "and such postponement for more than a year is harmful, both mentally and physically."[33]

In fact, some studies found that college-educated women who were both married and working did have fewer children than did nonworking wives.[34] A 1927 study of Radcliffe graduates who were both married and employed showed that more than half of 243 women surveyed chose not to have any children. The average number of children for the group was 2.21 compared with from 3.35 to 4.32 for other college-educated mothers who did not work. The investigator concluded that these college-educated mothers who worked had fewer children than did other women of their class.[35]

Another contested issue was the impact of a woman's work on infant mortality and on the health of her children. Many people believed that women who worked before and after pregnancy damaged their health and so gave birth to fragile and sickly offspring. One Chamber of Commerce representative wrote in 1931 that married women in his city often chose to work in factories because of relatively higher wages. This was a cause, he suggested, "of the high infant mortality rate as the women work in the factories as long as possible prior to the birth of their children and return to the factory invariably within a month after the birth of a child and sometimes much sooner."[36]

The government conducted a number of studies examining the relationship of maternal employment to infant mortality in the 1910s. A Children's Bureau survey of Manchester, New Hampshire, in 1912 and 1913 revealed that the infant mortality rate—the number of infant deaths per thousand live births—rose when mothers worked during their pregnancy. The infant mortality rate for children of working mothers was 199.2 compared with 133.9 for unemployed mothers. Studies of Johnstown, Pennsylvania, and New Bedford, Massachusetts, found similar correlations.[37]

The Children's Bureau also argued that the employment of mothers after the birth of their children was linked to a higher death rate, and attributed this in part to the common practice of working mothers forgoing breast feeding in favor of nourishing their babies with infant formula or cow's milk. But the bureau cautioned that these correlations between employment and mortality did not necessarily imply causality. Equally important factors were the low wages of fathers and overcrowded, unsanitary housing conditions.[38] In these and other studies, the evidence mustered against the employment of mothers was drawn from studies of destitute and working-class women; the conditions of poverty that drove these women to the workplace were therefore the conditions under which their children died.

All classes of married women, however, were subject to questions about the child-rearing practices of employed women. The mother's role was changing. Whereas in the nineteenth century a mother's duty was to instill moral attributes of faith and "good character" into her progeny, now her duty was to shape the psychological well-being of her child.[39] In the progressive era there developed a new emphasis on efficiency and expertise in child rearing. An ideology of "educated motherhood" stressed the importance of scientific insight over maternal instinct in the nation's nurseries.[40] Child nurture became a topic of national import, as childhood development research centers and kindergartens proliferated, reflecting a recognition of the importance of the early years of life on later adult behavior.

The role of the mother in this era was to steer her children through the dangerous psychological shoals of infancy and childhood. Both proponents and opponents of the employment of married women acknowledged that childhood had become increasingly complex, with new needs for socialization and training. Anna Garlin Spencer's tally of a mother's duty held that a mother's role was to provide protection, care, shelter, and food for her offspring; to drill them in personal habits and in such skills as walking and talking; and to instill "preliminary training toward social order and social welfare."[41]

The standard text on child rearing in this era was John B. Watson's *Psychological Care of Infant and Child*, a behaviorist tract that advocated a rigorous regimen of activity for young children. Watson proposed strict schedules for care, discipline, and play: "Once a child's character has been spoiled by bad handling, which can be done in a few days, who can say that the damage is ever repaired?"[42] The mother, particularly if she worked, faced more demands on her time at home now than previously.

Those who discouraged wives from working believed that women could not possibly have time to both work and raise their children properly. The Children's Bureau contended that the children of working mothers suffered in various ways. These children, the bureau claimed, did less well in school than did their peers with mothers at home; these children had more behavior problems and sustained "the strain of the mother, the untidy homes, and the pressure of housework left to them to do."[43] Willystine Goodsell, a social scientist, noted that "a woman cannot be employed nine hours a day . . . and at the same time maintain a clean, well-ordered home and give intelligent care and oversight to her children."[44]

Although the conservative solution to the problem was for mothers to remain at home, feminists suggested that family structure should change to ease the burden of household responsibilities for women. And some, like

Goodsell, also suggested that a mother's absence from home could even be beneficial. Some psychologists in the 1920s warned against the formation of "mother-fixation" in children—a condition in which a mother, overly absorbed in the lives of her offspring, created spoiled children and made "the upbuilding in a child of an independent personality difficult, if not impossible."[45]

As the mother's role within the home had come to rest almost entirely on meeting the emotional needs of her family, her role had become double-edged. Her employment outside the home might result in the neglect of her children. On the other hand, by having an outside interest she might "relieve the child of the dangerous role of being the recipient of boundless love and anxiety."[46] As we shall see, this theme continued in the postwar period when the mother, whether working or not, was blamed for anything less than perfection in her children.

At issue also was not only a working wife's absence from the home but her presence in the marketplace. Feminists maintained that the lack of productive activity by housewives constituted a loss for society. In 1921, Elizabeth Kemper Adams, in a study for the Women's Educational and Industrial Union, reported a "deepening conviction" that "in order to bring up children to be intelligent citizens and workers, both parents alike must be intelligent citizens and workers themselves." A woman's obligation, she argued, was not only to her own children but also to the community at large.[47] In 1926, Willystine Goodsell asked, "Who can say that our tens of thousands of educated wives and mothers have nothing to offer by way of meeting . . . human needs; or that their work in managing a small household and rearing two or three children constitutes the full job of a lifetime, enlisting all their capabilities?"[48] No less a figure than Eleanor Roosevelt concurred. In 1933, Roosevelt argued that although a married woman's first duty was to her home, that did not "of necessity preclude her having another occupation" and contributing her talents to society. Full-time motherhood was enough for many women, she stated, but for others the sole role of "nurse and governess" was insufficient.[49]

But others were not convinced that the social benefits of the employment of married women outweighed the costs. Some argued that the work of wives took jobs from others who needed employment, including the by now acceptable self-supporting single women, and that since married women worked for "pin money," salaries were lowered.[50] Despite studies by the Women's Bureau, which earnestly attempted to disprove this thesis, business practice reflected the pin-money myth. Until 1917, no married women had been hired by the school board in Detroit. In 1921, the city of Highland Park, Michigan, discharged married women from city positions and barred the future hiring of single women, arguing that without the competition of cheap female labor, men's wages would rise and permit the establishment of a "family wage" for the married man. In 1924, more than three-fourths of Minneapolis firms surveyed preferred to hire only single women as clerical workers. In 1928, a nationwide survey found that 60 percent of school boards did not hire married women as teachers.[51]

Public sentiment against the employment of married women sharpened during the economic depression of the 1930s. In 1930 and 1931, a National Education Association poll of 1,500 cities found that 77 percent of the school boards questioned did not employ wives as teachers, and half of the boards fired women who married while on the job. In 1930, the Massachusetts Commission on Unemployment Relief recommended that industrial and government organizations fire married women who lived with husbands who supported them, and replace these women with men or with single women. The New England Telephone Company, as a result, dismissed their married women workers. From 1932 to 1937, the federal government barred more than one member of a family from working in civil service positions—a policy that effectively functioned to keep married women off government payrolls.[52]

Public opinion during the 1930s favored these policies. In 1937, an American Institute of Public Opinion poll found that only 18 percent of those surveyed believed that a woman should work if she "has a husband capable of supporting her." A *Fortune Magazine* poll the previous year found only 15 percent believed wives should work full time outside the home; 35 percent stated that "woman's place is in the home"; 36 percent thought working women took jobs that otherwise could be filled by men; 21 percent maintained that nonworking mothers had healthier children and a happier home life; and 7 percent believed that the working wife brought down the standard of living because of the lower wages she received.[53]

Supporters of restrictive employment policies justified their position by arguing that they hoped to decrease the unemployment of single women and of men and to strengthen the traditional values of home life at the same time. In 1934, a businessman reported, "We do not employ any married women nor do we believe in it. Their place is in the home!"[54] The organization of Women in the Naval Reserve resolved that "every married woman who is holding a job, who has a husband earning enough to keep the family, should give up her job for six months or so that men can take jobs to support their families."[55]

Those who believed that wives should work, on the other hand, argued that married women contributed an essential proportion of family income and that discrimination against any one class of worker threatened ideals of democracy. In 1932, the National Association of Working Women was founded to combat the movement against the employment of married women. Discrimination, they charged, was "only the beginning of an attempt to eliminate all women from the business and professional world" as well as a "sorry travesty upon freedom." In 1933, a proposal to eliminate all married women workers from the payroll of the Chesapeake and Ohio Railroad was dropped following protests from the National Business and Professional Women's Club.[56]

But during the depression, with its shortage of jobs, public opinion solidified against the employment of wives; most Americans firmly believed that the married woman should not work outside the home. This attitude persisted until 1940. A Women's Bureau investigation that year found that discrimination continued against married women in the work force of several large cities. In Los Angeles, banks and many business firms would not hire wives. In Kansas City, most oil and meat companies, as well as the public utilities, discriminated against married women. In Richmond, insurance offices, railroads, and wholesale establishments preferred hiring single women only, and one out of ten businesses surveyed summarily fired women if they married after they had been hired.[57]

The Working Mother during World War II

At the time that the United States entered World War II, the popular domestic ideology still prevailed over feminist proposals for social change. The Women's Bureau noted in 1941 that although the public recognized the need of paid work for widows and single women, it "still has to be convinced that married women have the right to work . . . and that they can work without harm being done to the home and to the working standards of men and women wage earners."[58] But the imperative need for labor caused by the military mobilization of the nation's men led the government to conduct a propaganda campaign aimed at convincing the public that wives could and should replace their husbands in factory and mill.[59] Yet even at the same time, this campaign appealed to those who valued women as preservers of the home, and although it eased the way for the employment of wives, it reinforced the ideology that mothers of young children should spurn employment.

Rosie the Riveter—the symbol of working women during the war years—appeared as a housewife in factory overalls in posters, magazine articles, and in such popular songs as "The Janes Who Make Planes," and "The Lady at Lockheed." She was expected to work for patriotic reasons and to support the war effort of the men in her life. She was just as strongly expected to gratefully trade in her factory goggles for an apron at war's end. The War Manpower Commission and the Office of War Information sold the idea of work to married women by casting Rosie the Riveter as a housewife who worked temporarily in order to preserve domestic values. One government publication declared that women's primary instinct "has been, and still is, to cherish their greater interest in the protection of the home, the family, and the community."[60]

Many books and magazines emphasized the new sanction of work for married women. Some authors, such as the grandniece of Susan B. Anthony, continued the earlier theme that a woman could be productive outside the domestic sphere; Susan B. Anthony II argued that "the key to Victory in this war is the extraction of women—all women—from the relative unproductivity of the kitchen, and the enrolling of them in the high productivity of factory, office, and field."[61]

The propaganda campaign paid off, both in expanding the numbers of wives who kept factory assembly lines rolling and in changing the attitudes of the public. Whereas 82 percent of those surveyed in 1936 had disapproved of married women working, only six years later, in 1942, 60 percent of the respondents in a National Opinion Research Center poll believed that married women should work in war industries. Other wartime surveys also found the objection to working wives eased during the 1940s.[62]

But the new social sanction of the employment of married women was limited. Although wives without young children were urged to work, official policy, as articulated by the Manpower Commission, mandated that mothers of young children stay at home. "The first responsibility of women with young children," the commission stated in 1942, "in war as in peace, is to give suitable care in their own homes to their children."[63] The old arguments were advanced once again that there was no substitute for a mother at home.

During the war, these arguments centered on the problem of "latch-key" children—youngsters expected to fend for themselves after school until their mothers returned from work. The National Association of Day Nurseries, one of the organizations concerned with the latch-key child, stated in 1941 that maternal employment would result in unsupervised, underfed children ripe for the "breeding grounds [of] delinquency." The Children's Bureau agreed, contending in 1943 that working mothers were "a hazard to the security of the child in his family."[64]

Many women undoubtedly worked for patriotic reasons, but economic necessity still impelled other women to seek employment. A 1944 Women's Bureau survey found that 80 percent of the women working in war-related industries wanted to continue working after the war's end. Sixty-one percent of employed women surveyed by the American Institute of Public Opinion in 1945 planned to continue working after the war.[65] But appeals made to women during the war foreshadowed the growth of the postwar "feminine mystique." "Because you are a wife as well as a working-woman you want something for the returning man as well as for yourself," the author of *So Your Husband's Gone to War!* reminded her readers in 1942. "And your most important job right now, you feel, is not necessarily entrenching your sex but keeping the home fires burning however you can."[66] The message was clear. The work of wives was a temporary necessity. When the soldiers came home, patriotism dictated that wives return their jobs to men and find in motherhood their major social role.

The Feminine Mystique, 1945–1960

In spite of this prescription, the employment rate of wives escalated dramatically in the years after the war. By 1950, we have seen, one in four married women worked. At the same time, the fertility rate was rising during the "baby boom" of the 1950s and 1960s. Hence the working wife was now more likely to be a working mother than previously. The rhetoric in the debate over women and work now occurred in a social context that had changed dramatically.

Proponents of the domestic ideology launched a virulent attack after the war, focusing on mothers who worked. In this foray, the battlefield was the nursery and the weapon psychological theory as sociologists and psychologists emphasized the relationship of a mother's employment to child neglect. The feminist voice was for the most part stilled, drowned out by the feminine mystique that grew to dominate popular opinion.[67] The working mother was roundly condemned for abandoning her place at home and for creating a nation of neurotic men and women.

A heightened emphasis on psychology after the war reflected the growth in the popularization of Freudian psychoanalytic theory in America.[68] Woman's transgression of her domestic role was viewed as a neurosis, a rejection of femininity. Earlier arguments that defended domesticity had been couched in the language of morality; now the language of psychology was put to work to defend the domestic prescription for women.

The popular dissemination of these psychological theories constituted what Betty Friedan has termed the "feminine mystique" of the postwar era. The mystique—a complex of popular attitudes about the feminine nature of women and the primacy of "nurturing maternal love"—was reflected in an outpouring of sentiment throughout American popular culture. As magazines, newspapers, books, and, later, television glorified the role of the housewife, the feminist perspective of earlier times was all but forgotten. "As swiftly as in a dream," Friedan observed, "the image of the American woman as a changing, growing individual in a changing world was shattered. . . . Her limitless world shrunk to the cozy walls of home."[69]

The most strident articulation of this mystique was Ferdinand Lundberg's and Marynia Farnham's notorious 1947 book, *Modern Woman: The Lost Sex*. This antifeminist tome went through six printings in one year and reached a wide audience through extensive publicity in newspapers, magazines, and textbooks. The authors contended that women, dissatisfied with their domestic role, were transmitting their confusion to their children, thus disrupting social order. Women had been unduly swayed by feminist proposals for careers, feminism being "at its core a deep illness" that encouraged women to assume the male traits of aggression, dominance, independence, and power. The "masculinization" of women, the authors warned, represented "enormously dangerous consequences to the home, the children . . . dependent on it, and to the ability of the woman, as well as her husband, to obtain sexual gratification." And if this were not enough, for the children of mothers who had rejected or were ambivalent about their domestic duties, a sense of confusion and abandonment was inevitable.[70]

The ideal woman, the authors proposed, was a "fully maternal" woman who "accepted her femininity" and understood that the phrase "independent woman" was a contradiction in terms. The working wife thus failed in her psychologically appointed task. Lundberg and Farnham cautioned that the masculinized strivings of women careerists should be minimized so that a woman's "femininity" would be available for the satisfaction of herself, her husband, and her children.[71]

The idea that "anatomy was destiny" and that gender roles were biologically determined was repeatedly advanced by social scientists in this period. Eric Dingwall, a British anthropologist, criticized those who claimed otherwise. "To maintain, as Margaret Mead does, that when women 'can act by choice rather than by necessity' they will be content, is to engage in that favorite feminine pastime of crying for the moon," he argued. "Indeed, it is precisely to the minimization of the biological factor of female life that we can ascribe so much of the growing lack of satisfaction among the women of so many lands, and above all of the United States."[72] This "growing lack of satisfaction" was often cited as a result of feminist proposals that offered women a choice of roles at a time when social conditions did not support that choice. When women were unhappy and ambivalent about their lives within the home, the possible result, critics claimed, was the overprotection of their children.[73]

Feminists in the 1920s had suggested that women confined to the domestic role might raise children with unhealthy "mother fixations." In the postwar period, charges of "momism" blamed women unhappy with their domestic duties for the neuroses of their children, particularly of their sons.[74] Dingwall maintained that American mothers were responsible for the demasculinization of their sons and for the creation of infantile "boys" rather than strong, independent men. The American mother, he commented, "is not at all anxious to see her sons exhibit too many of the male characteristics, which may remind her of her own deficiencies and thus tend to deflate her assertive personality."[75] Dingwall cited the findings of Dr. E. A. Strecker, a psychiatrist who consulted for the United States War Department. Strecker held that the large numbers of neurotic soldiers in the American army during the war stemmed from the behavior of mothers who had smothered their sons with too much love.[76] Lundberg and Farnham similarly censured mothers for being overaffectionate or domineering, claiming that these women played out tendencies of penis envy by thwarting the lives of their sons.[77]

At the same time, the working mother was presented as a source of disintegrating family life. In a well-known textbook on child development published in 1948, James Bossard placed his discussion of working mothers in a chapter entitled "Families under Stress." The social costs of a mother's decision to work, he claimed, included tired women and lonely, neglected, and unsupervised children. Other studies suggested that working mothers were more likely to have children who were delinquent because they were neglected and resentful, or because the children had fathers who were overly strict because of the mother's absence from home.[78]

Although the mother, and especially the working mother, was blamed on all sides for a variety of social ills, there was some recognition in this period that the antifeminist case was overstated. Some social scientists were beginning to question the imperative of biological determinism, finding that personality formation was shaped in part by the environment. Gender qualities were the result of social conditioning rather than of innate characteristics.[79] Mirra Komarovsky was one of those rejecting the thesis that a woman's discontent was the result of individual maladjustment. She argued instead that female role ambivalence resulted from the sharp conflicts caused by the differing expectations of education, career, and marriage.[80] Other researchers suggested that the question of the working mother was individual and dependent upon the needs of specific women and their children.[81] But the defense of the widening of "woman's sphere," and the relativistic view of qualities of gender, were overshadowed by the feminine mystique.

The mystique was reinforced by studies in the psychology of child development that stressed the importance of consistent mothering for infants and young children. These studies condemned working mothers for causing trauma in children left without maternal care for even a short part of the day. John Bowlby, in 1950, presented a seminal study to the World Health Organization on the subject of deprivation of maternal care in children. His investigation of young inmates in such institutions as hospitals and orphanages led him to conclude that "deprivation of mother-love in early childhood can have a far-reaching effect on the mental health and personality development of human beings." Bowlby stated that young children required a continuous relationship with one person—a mother or mother-substitute—for both the child's and the mother's well-being. He wrote, "The provision of constant attention day and night, seven days a week and 365 in the year, is possible only for a woman who derives profound satisfaction from seeing her child grow from babyhood . . . to become an independent man or woman, and knows that it is her care which has made this possible."[82] Bowlby enlisted as examples of family failure those families that were "broken up and therefore not functioning" because of the full-time employment of the mother. When the child did not have the full care of a mother, he or she was thus considered a victim of "maternal deprivation."[83]

Bowlby's findings of the trauma caused by extreme maternal deprivation were generalized by other scholars to include children who experienced "partial maternal deprivation" when their mothers worked. Subsequent studies suggested that a phenomenon of "attachment" of an infant to its mother required continuous interaction of mother and child. The regular removal of a mother from the home for even part of the day, critics claimed, interfered with the attachment process and snapped important bonds between mother and child that were crucial for the formation of trust, stability, and cognitive development.[84]

These arguments rose to dominate the debate about women and work at a time when more married women than ever before were working outside the home. The working mother was now labeled a neurotic or, worse, a cause of neurosis in her children. Public opinion again reflected the feminine mystique and turned to support the concept of a one wage-earner family and the domestic ideology.

The Resurgence of Feminism, 1960–1980

After 1960, a new wave of feminism reopened the case for the working mother. In 1963, Betty Friedan reminded the American public of the feminist position with her best-selling book, *The Feminine Mystique*: "We can no longer ignore that voice within women that says: 'I want something more than my husband, my children, and my home.' " Friedan insisted that employment was needed to insure fulfillment for women:

> Who knows what women can be when they are finally free to be themselves? . . . Who knows of the possibilities of love when men and women share not only children, home, and garden, not only the fulfillment of their biological roles, but the responsibilities and passions of the work that creates the human future and full human knowledge of who they are? It has barely begun, the search of women for themselves. But the time is at hand when the voices of the feminine mystique can no longer drown out the inner voice that is driving women on to become complete.[85]

Friedan's call for women's liberation from the ideology of domesticity was echoed in a surge of sentiment applauding the employment of women, whether married or single. The 1960s and 1970s saw the publication of hundreds of books in sociology, psychology, and other fields urging that women be given a full range of choices that included both marriage and career.[86]

Many scholars focused on the effect on family life of a wife's employment. A 1963 study, for example, found that when wives worked, husbands helped more with household tasks, and wives gained a stronger say in major economic decisions.[87] Social scientists also increasingly challenged concepts of masculinity and femininity, stating that social conditions, rather than innate sexual qualities, had the greater bearing on gender behavior.[88]

Several of the postwar studies proclaiming the damage done by a mother's employment were also questioned in this period. Bowlby's findings about the need for uninterrupted and exclusive mothering, for example, were challenged by scholars such as Margaret Mead, who suggested that "multiple mothering" was possible.[89] Others attacked the earlier studies on maternal deprivation for unsupported claims of causality. Lois Meek Stoltz, a psychologist, surveyed the literature on maternal employment and concluded that "one can say almost anything one desires about the children of employed mothers and support the statement by some research study."[90] The head of the Children's Bureau, Katherine Brownell Oettinger, similarly found that factors such as the temperament of mother and child, and the motivations for and conditions of a woman's work, were important considerations in the assessment of maternal employment. "Other things being equal," she stated, "we think few mothers with children under six, and fewer mothers with children under three, are able to carry a full-time job and also fill the needs of their children in these crucial and vulnerable early years. But other things are not always equal. Therefore the qualifications and the need to discuss them."[91] The fourth edition of Bossard's textbook on child development came out in 1966, and in it the earlier stance against the working mother was eased. The working mother was no longer portrayed as a symptom of family stress but as a possible benefit to family life. If wives worked, they and their husbands might "both have a greater appreciation of each other's roles," the textbook stated. "The children see them as a unity of parents with roles that are tightly interlocked."[92]

The feminist ideology reverberated throughout American society, influencing changes in government policy. In 1964, the United States Congress added the word "sex" to Title VII of the Civil Rights Bill, prohibiting discrimination in employment on the basis of race, color, religion, and national origin. Organizations such as the National Organization for Women, founded in 1966, and the Women's Equity Action League, founded in 1969, strove to combat employment discrimination against women.[93]

Public opinion had begun to reflect to some degree the changing work practices of women. In 1936, only 18 percent of those surveyed in a Gallup poll agreed that married women should work, but forty years later, in 1976, 68 percent approved of working women, even of those who had husbands who could support them.[94] However, this shift in values was tempered by a countermovement. Opponents of feminism were as insistent in their views as were feminists in theirs in the 1970s. A best-selling book of 1974, *The Total Woman*, was a tract advocating once again that the fulfillment of a woman could only be found in the wholehearted embrace of the role of wife and mother.[95]

Moreover, the 1970s witnessed a new twist in the class argument against working married women. In 1978, a *Wall Street Journal* article suggested that the increased work rate of middle- and upper-income wives was in part responsible for the widening of the gap between rich and poor. The *Journal* cited economist Lester Thurow's statement that "if males who earn high incomes are married to women who could earn high incomes in a perfectly fair and liberated world, then women's liberation will make the distribution of income more unequal." Once again, the class issue of women and work surfaced, as the work of married women who had to earn a salary to help support their families was contrasted with the work of women who chose employment for personal as well as economic reasons.[96]

In general, however, the debate in the 1970s narrowed to the troubling problem of employment for mothers of very young children. Psychologist Selma Fraiberg, in *Every Child's Birthright*, contended in 1977 that children under the age of three required uninterrupted caretaking from one person, preferably the mother, because human development rested on the quality of first attachments. The lack of adequate opportunities for day care, she implied, meant that most mothers of infants should not work outside the home. In 1978, Jerome Kagan, also a psychologist, countered that the early experience of childhood was not as important a factor in personality development as some persons believed; implicitly, then, a mother's duty to stay home during the infancy of her child was not as great an imperative.[97]

By the beginning of the 1980s, the changing social and economic behavior of women, and the changing ideological debate over female employment, had contributed to a widening of the idea of "woman's proper place." First single women, then wives, and then mothers of school-aged children were, in a sense, freed from social constraints against work outside the home. For each of these groups, wage labor was at one time controversial and debatable, but eventually employment became a socially acceptable—and even expected— act. But the mother of young children was left at the core of the debate over women and work. Whether her participation in the labor force would also become acceptable rather than problematic would depend on the success or failure of proposals for the care of her children.

Chapter 6
The Working Mother
and the Social Order

We have seen that the discovery of "respectable" single women workers in the late nineteenth century led to a heated debate over future motherhood, which in turn sparked a variety of reforms meant to extend domestic influences, improve the work environment, and control the impact of social change. At the same time, these reforms, by providing such services as housing, acknowledged de facto that the "place" of the single woman was now the labor force as well as the home, at least before marriage. The increased employment of married women in the twentieth century similarly provoked public controversy, this time about the nature of motherhood itself.

In contrast to the working-girl controversy, the working-mother controversy engendered by changing labor force demographics was not the primary motivator for social policy. Rather, policies enacted for the care of children of poor mothers before 1920 influenced later policies and reforms that arose because of the growing numbers of working mothers of all classes later in the twentieth century. As yet, society has remained ambivalent about the movement of mothers from home to work. The identification of day care as a class issue and the lack of quality day-care opportunities has combined with the retrenchment of the domestic ideology to insure that the working mother of young children still retains her controversial status.

The public consensus is that the full weight of child care should fall upon the shoulders of the mother alone, but it has been tempered by factors of class and race. That is, the exception to the rule that mothers not work outside the home has historically been the poor, unmarried, or widowed mother, whose employment has for the most part been seen as a preferable alternative to her economic dependency on the state. Hence a tension has developed in the philosophy of day care between the ideals of reluctant charity or social service.

Before discussing the public response to the working mother after 1920, then, we must first look back to those events during the "era of the working girl" which also concerned the working mother. In that time, child-care services first became defined as a charitable response to the needs of widows with dependent children rather than as a social service for parents who worked.

The Widow and Her "Half-Orphans" before 1920: Forerunners of Modern Policy

In the nineteenth and early twentieth centuries, the only working mothers who attracted public attention were widows or the desperately poor. "Respectable" single women were at the forefront of the debate over women and work, but still the older employed mother was also a beneficiary of the reform impulse. In sharp contrast to the single woman worker, however, what is most notable about this group of workers is their constancy over time. That is, although the proportion of single women in the female labor force rose markedly during the era of the working girl, and although the proportion of married women and mothers in the labor force similarly rose during the era of the working mother, the proportions of widowed and divorced women in the female labor force has remained relatively constant. Of all workers in the female labor force in 1890, 18 percent were widows, while 14 percent were widows in 1970. Moreover, while widows, like all groups of women, increased their relative numbers in the female labor force during the last century, still this increase has been at a much lower rate than that of both married and single women.

It was not, then, an increase in numbers that sparked the concern to reform conditions for working mothers. Rather, the social and cultural conditions that contributed to the public concern for working girls also contributed, at least in part, to a concern with their older and poorer sisters. But whereas the reforms for the working girl diminished as her dominance in the female labor force declined, the reforms for the working mother were maintained, even as the identity of the working mother was changing. In short, policies shaped by the early twentieth century which meant to help the destitute widow were still being used by mid-century—a time when the working mother was no longer a poor and minor segment of the female labor force but was instead a member of the fastest-growing group in the American labor force as a whole.

In the nineteenth century, the common response to the plight of the working mother was public charity. Reforms for widows were engineered not only to meet the moral and physical needs of dependent children, but also to meet the perceived moral needs of the women themselves.

The children of working mothers in the early twentieth century were cared for in a haphazard fashion at best. Most school-aged children received their primary care during the day from teachers; after school they looked after themselves, although occasionally working mothers sent their offspring to supervised programs at settlement houses, churches, and libraries. Generally, mothers believed that if children were old enough to dress themselves, make their own meals, and avoid being run over in the street, they were old enough to fend for themselves.

Despite the contention of middle-class reformers that even school-aged children required constant supervision for both physical and moral well-being, many working-class mothers believed otherwise. In 1918, for example, only 5 percent of the children of mothers who worked in the Chicago stockyards attended day nurseries; 40 percent received no care at all; and the rest were left to the "slight supervision" of night-working or disabled fathers, or neighbors. "The mothers of these children do not feel the need of a day nursery," the investigators concluded, "for as soon as a child can minister to his physical needs, he is considered fit to be left [alone]."[1]

Similarly, in Philadelphia in 1918, more than a third of the children aged from five to sixteen in the families of working mothers had no formal supervision after school. Infants and younger children were for the most part tended by relatives in their own homes, or watched over by neighbors. Some 82 percent of the young children of working mothers surveyed on the west side of New York City in 1914, and more than two-thirds of these children in Philadelphia in 1918, received this type of informal home day care.[2]

Occasionally a desperate mother would lock her children alone in the house as she left for work, sometimes asking a neighbor to "keep an eye" on them. These were the children whose condition most concerned reformers. Samuel Royce argued in 1877 that employment led the poor mother into such practices as "dosing the children with narcotic cordials . . . if not to shutting them up between cheerless walls, or converting them through this isolation . . . into semi-idiots."[3] In 1910, Jane Addams told the National Conference of Charities and Correction the story of a widowed scrubwoman, who locked three children in her tenement rooms as she left for work each day. When their constant wailing led to an eviction notice, Addams reported, the mother left the windows open, hoping the children would fall to their deaths.[4] Gwendolyn Hughes told the story of a Polish widow who left three children under the age of six locked up in her tenement home when she worked. The neighbor who sporadically checked up on the children could not prevent such tragedies as the scalding of the child who ignited a fire with coal oil.[5] Reformers, fearing for the safety of the children of working mothers, labeled these children "half-orphans" and considered them subject to public pity and public benevolence.

A common response to the plight of the widowed mother was the provision of limited "outdoor relief"—the donation of cords of wood, boxes of used clothing, and, occasionally, envelopes of money from philanthropists, churches, and city charity groups.[6] But the charity community agreed that too much help would demoralize the recipient and encourage the vice of pauperism. Oscar McCullogh, a minister, warned the 1888 gathering of charity workers that, at most, widows should receive loans, for "when the woman has tasted the bitter and poison bread of public relief, it is only the beginning of moral, physical, and intellectual death."[7]

CHILD REMOVAL

Removal of the child from the home was the most extreme remedy for the destitute mother, who faced no alternative but the starvation of her children. Many families relied on the help of kin, "putting out" their children with those relatives who were more able to care for them. Katherine Anthony reported that many women in her study of the west side of New York City claimed to have been raised by their aunts.[8] When family aid was unavailable, desperate mothers turned to the state.

In the early nineteenth century, destitute mothers sometimes committed their children to the local almshouse, where the children languished with a mix of other dependents, including the insane. Reformers argued that this proximity of innocent children to unstable adults would corrupt the children, and so they advocated the development of such specialized institutions as orphanages. By the latter part of the century, charity organizations or courts would commonly remand a dependent child to an orphanage, or pay the cost of support in a foster home.[9]

Many of the inmates in children's homes were "half-orphans"—the children of destitute, separated, divorced, or widowed parents. One charity worker reported as typical the case of Mary Morson, a stonecutter's widow, who supported seven children in New York City by scrubbing floors and doing piecework. When she failed to make ends meet in 1912, she turned four of her children over to the St. Rachel Orphan Asylum, and the city of New York paid $38.57 monthly for their upkeep.[10]

Thousands of "half-orphans" were cared for in this way through the early twentieth century. In Ohio, from 1867 to 1898, of 17,133 children resident in county children's homes, only six percent were orphans; the rest were the children of widowed, destitute, divorced, or otherwise incapacitated parents.[11] Nationally, in 1904, the Census Bureau found more than 3,000 children in orphan asylums, and another 50,000 in foster homes at state expense; many of these were the children of widows.[12] In New York in 1913, nearly 1,000 children were committed to orphanages because their widowed mothers were ill; an additional 2,716 were committed—like the children of Mary Morson—because of the poverty of their families.[13]

The institutionalization of the children of the married woman worker was much rarer. Of the New York mothers surveyed in 1914, only 7 percent "put away" their offspring—half were sent to institutions and half to relatives. In Philadelphia in 1918, 4 percent of the children of working mothers surveyed were cared for away from home.[14] Most working-class mothers abhorred the possibility that their children might be separated from them. As Anthony noted, their attitude was shaped by fear and suspicion, for, she asked, "What were they working for, if not to keep the home together?"[15]

Most reformers, too, decried the institutionalization of children, arguing that separation of mother and child was unnatural, that their upkeep was expensive to the public, and that separation made children unfit for their later roles as workers. Anthony cited the problems that institutionalized children experienced in later years when they were returned home. "Fresh from an environment which has deprived him of even a normal sense of property," she stated, "often the institution child doesn't know how to handle money or count change—he is thrust into industry and wage earning. The little autocratic world he has left did not train him in responsibility, but now he must suddenly assume it."[16]

Because institutional life was so criticized, many dependent children were sent instead to foster homes. Charles Loring Brace marshaled the movement of city children to country homes in the late nineteenth century; children were also sent to foster parents in cities. But this solution too was inadequate; often the children were little more than indentured servants, and reformers bewailed the lack of screening of foster parents. The secretary of the Minnesota State Board of Charities observed the placement of children sent to rural Minnesota by the New York Children's Aid Society from 1883 to 1885. He reported:

> The children arrived at about half-past three p.m. and were taken directly from the train to the Court House, where a large crowd was gathered. Mr. Matthews set the children, one by one, before the company, and in his stentorian voice gave a brief account of each. Applicants for children were then admitted in order behind the railing and rapidly made their selection. Then, if the child gave assent, the bargain was concluded on the spot. . . . I know that the Committee consented to some assignments against their better judgement.[17]

The separation of children from their mothers became controversial in the nineteenth century. However, another remedy was suggested that would partially solve the problem for the family faced with the separation dilemma. The subsidized day nursery, it was observed, would provide a family environment for the children of working-class mothers at the same time that it allowed the mother to retain primary responsibility for the upbringing and financial support of her children. It would do no less than stand "for the preservation and maintenance of the home."[18]

THE DAY NURSERY

Day nurseries were based on the models of the French *crèche* of the 1840s and on the infant school of early nineteenth-century America. Both institutions were intended to permit mothers to work while their children were being taught middle-class values. The first day nurseries were established before the Civil War. In Boston, a day nursery was formed in 1828; in New York, a children's hospital opened a day nursery for the children of wet nurses and former patients in 1854. But the growth of the day-nursery movement was slow; by 1880, only six were recorded in the United States.[19]

The concept of the day nursery gradually caught on, mostly in the large cities of the East Coast. The Chicago World's Fair of 1893 further spurred the acceptance of the day nursery, as some 10,000 children of visitors to the fair were cared for in a model day-nursery exhibit.[20] By 1897, there were 175 nurseries reported to the Census Bureau; by 1912, the National Federation of Day Nurseries had records for some 500 institutions.[21]

Advocates of the day nursery acknowledged that widowed mothers would often have to work. These reformers sought to provide an alternative to the institutionalization of children who would otherwise have no supervision during the day. The philosophy of the philanthropic day nursery was set forth by Josephine Jewell Dodge. She was related to Grace Hoadley Dodge, who had spearheaded many of the reforms for the single woman worker. Josephine Dodge established the Jewell Day Nursery in New York City in 1888, organized the first conference on day nurseries in 1892, and formed the National Federation of Day Nurseries in 1898. She was the archetypical moral entrepreneur, who believed that her mission was to bring middle-class values to the working class. The day nursery, as Josephine Dodge saw it, would be an instrument of moral nurture as well as of charity.[22]

According to Dodge, the day nursery would protect mothers from the evils of total dependency, protect children from the evils of neglect, and save society from unsupervised children who were a "serious menace to the state." It would provide an alternative to leaving the care of children in unsatisfactory hands, such as under the supervision of brothers and sisters, incapacitated fathers, or, worst of all, male lodgers whose "evil traits" might be "intensified by long periods of idleness." Dodge and her followers claimed the day nursery would be, in sum, a superior "second home" for children that would not only provide skillful care but would also save the state the costs of institutionalization. As Marjory Hall, of the National Federation of Day Nurseries, stated in about 1904, the advent of the day nursery meant that the cry "put away the children" was far less often heard.[23]

Early day nurseries were careful to screen their clients, preferring to serve the needs of destitute widows rather than married women. Most nurseries sent "friendly visitors" to investigate applicants to insure that home situations were of the most desperate kind. The proper case, one charity worker stated, was the child who was "necessarily homeless" during the day. "I say *necessarily* because I wish to exclude from my definition those cases where the mother works from a mere whim or the desire to have a little more in the way of dress or furniture or even money saved, or for any reason wishes to shirk the care of her children," she wrote. "This is to be condemned when it causes her to neglect her home duties. The mother's place is in the home, except in cases of absolute necessity."[24] Some nurseries required proof that the children had been born to married women. The nursery in Buffalo, New York, for example, claimed this was necessary because of the "sensitivity" of the mothers who patronized the nursery. Once a mother got past the friendly visitors, she was to pay a small fee, usually five cents a day, in order to "sustain . . . dignity and a sense of independence."[25]

Commonly the nurseries, set up in converted houses or brownstones, were open from seven in the morning until seven at night to children of all ages, including infants. Upon being dropped off at the nursery in the morning, the young children were usually bathed, fed, and dressed in clean clothes or nursery pinafores; older children arrived during lunch times or after school. Daily activities, supervised by a matron, included lessons in moral precepts, domestic training, religious instruction, singing, and play; a few of the more progressive nurseries taught "order and discipline" using the methods of the kindergarten pioneer Friedrich Froebel. In some nurseries, tickets were distributed for good behavior and punctuality, and redeemed for clothing.[26]

The child would be taught through these routines the virtues of cleanliness of body and spirit, according to day-nursery officials. In 1900, the National Federation of Day Nurseries stated, "If these children can be taught from infancy to be physically and morally clean, to eat proper food in an approved manner, to adopt our customs and our language, they will become a power for good; otherwise, like many who have developed under less favorable influences, they will fill up our hospitals, our homes for dependents, and our penal institutions."[27] The lessons learned, however, were strongly flavored with a dollop of class expectations. The federation noted that training should make children "useful and desirable" from an economic standpoint, and it suggested that children be given lessons in sewing and domestic service to "equip them for their station in life."[28]

Mothers, too, were to benefit from the largesse of the day-nursery workers. Nursery advocates were careful to stress that their charity did not absolve the mother of her "divinely appointed responsibility"; some nurseries guarded the "homemaking habit" by requiring that mothers stay home one day a week besides Sunday. On the other hand, many nurseries provided employment services, finding women jobs as scrubwomen or laundresses.[29]

The day nursery often tried to influence the mother in even more overt ways. At the Buffalo Fitch Creche, a mother was allowed to visit the nursery and absorb some of its influence only after a matron's investigation determined she was "clean." Many nurseries offered mothers classes in child care, thrift, sewing, and nutrition, hoping to teach them to "come to know something of the little decencies of life . . . [but] above all else . . . to be self-supporting, self-reliant, and self-respecting."[30]

Moreover, by visiting the nurseries, mothers came under the goodly influence of the matron, a personage who aspired to represent "all that is motherly and good" to children and "wisdom and power" to mothers. The nurseries also encouraged temperance; the Buffalo nursery, for example, offered tea to mothers picking up their children at night, hoping to discourage stops at the "grog shop" on the way home.[31]

The day nurseries did not have a large influence on the lives of working women in this era. Anthony found that only 3 percent of the mothers in her study used the nurseries in 1914; Hughes found that only 12 percent of the working mothers in Philadelphia in 1918 patronized them. There simply were not enough nurseries to meet the demand. Of the 166 day nurseries recorded by the Census Bureau in 1904, 113 were located in only four states—Massachusetts, New Jersey, New York, and Pennsylvania. The nurseries were overcrowded and understaffed. At the Kensington Day Nursery in Philadelphia in 1891, for instance, up to fifty children at a time were tended by a matron, nurse, cook, and housemaid.[32]

Furthermore, some mothers may have chosen not to use the nurseries because of rigid rules and regulations, or because they disliked being labeled as subjects for charity. Katherine Anthony reported a conflict between the mothers and the administrators of a New York nursery in 1914:

> The women regard the day nursery as a type of institution, and as such distrust it. It must be said that the attitude of the management too often shows the strain of autocracy with which we are prone to dilute our charity. At one nursery, the hotheaded Irish mothers were always getting their baby carriages mixed and then squabbling over them. Righteously indignant, the management finally forbade them to leave their go-carts at the nursery any longer. This severe ruling made it necessary for the mother either to carry a heavy child to the nursery in her arms or to let him walk too far on his unsteady legs, for it was impossible for her to return the go-cart to her home and get to work on time.[33]

Many mothers turned to a less formal kind of day care. Hughes noted in her Philadelphia study that many women took their children to neighbors and paid for their supervision. One widow, for instance, sent her two children to a neighbor and paid $3.00 weekly for their board. The neighbor claimed that this payment was inadequate for the price of food, but added, "We got to help each other."[34]

Less benevolent were the nurseries run by women for profit. The number of proprietary day nurseries is unknown, but charity workers often criticized the unhealthy conditions in which children were tended. According to historian Leslie Tentler, a Children's Bureau field-worker reported that in some nurseries in Cleveland in 1918, "one woman occupying four dark, poorly ventilated rooms was crowding into them thirty and forty children each day; another was caring for twelve children in equally bad surroundings; a third who had less than a tenth vision was caring for eight children whom she had the habit of shutting behind two locked doors on the second floor while she did her marketing. In all these places the food was sent by the mothers and was given cold."[35] Even in the charitable nurseries abuses were common. Critics cited unsanitary conditions, too few attendants for the number of children, and, occasionally, total lack of supervision.[36]

Other critics leveled further charges against day nurseries, claiming that their services encouraged married mothers, whose proper place was in the home, to work. Although widows were the desired group of clients, in practice other women also used nursery services. The New York Association of Day Nurseries found that nearly two-thirds of its clients were married women; only 17 percent were widows, and 20 percent were women whose husbands had deserted them.[37] For those dissatisfied with the remedies of the day nursery and the boarding out of children, another solution seemed more appropriate.

Instead of spending charitable and public funds on substitute care for children outside their homes, a growing number of charity workers endorsed the concept of "subsidized motherhood" through the meting out of mothers' pensions.

Charity workers had for some time argued that the goals of preserving the home were undercut when funds were paid to foster mothers, institutions, or day nurseries to care for children of mothers who worked because of destitution. They opposed the long-held view that a mother must work if no other family support was available. In 1888, one charity worker suggested that "benevolent individuals" take on the task of funding mothers to stay in their own homes; in 1910, the Jewish Charities of Chicago provided money to "board children" with their own mothers. Funding mothers to stay at home and care for their own children was increasingly proposed as a method to safeguard traditional family life.[38]

In 1909, President Theodore Roosevelt called the first Conference on the Care of Dependent Children, a gathering that resulted in the founding of the Children's Bureau of the Department of Labor and in the wholehearted advocacy of pensions for mothers. The National Congress of Mothers—later the National Congress of Parents and Teachers—took up the banner of subsidizing motherhood as an alternative to both the boarding out of children and the employment of mothers outside the home.[39] Missouri passed the first state pension law in 1911, providing cash assistance to qualified mothers in Jackson County, which included Kansas City. The idea spread rapidly. By 1915, twenty-three states adopted mothers' pension laws; by 1935, all but two states provided aid for dependent children.[40]

Most of the state pension laws specified that recipients be widowed or deserted women, or wives of men unable to work because of imprisonment or mental or physical disability. Children were considered to be dependent up to ages ranging from 14 to 18 and would under most state laws receive from $5.00 to $15.00 a month. In addition, most states had "suitable home" provisions; a mother was to be judged morally worthy before receiving state aid. In Kansas City, for example, the law stipulated that "the mother must, in the judgement of the juvenile court, be a proper person, morally, physically and mentally, for the bringing up of her children."[41] Pension officers could intervene in a family's private life to assure that a suitable home prevailed. Routine interviews with neighbors and relatives were meant to scout out such unacceptable behavior as the keeping of male boarders, sexual activity, or even "laziness." Besides immoral behavior, illness—particularly tuberculosis—and undesirable housing were also grounds for pension disqualification.[42]

In New York, the Commission on Relief for Widowed Mothers advocated the following principles as guidelines for a state pension law:

1. The mother is the best guardian of her children.
2. Poverty is too big a problem for private philanthropy.
3. No woman, save in exceptional circumstances, can be both the home-maker and the bread-winner of her family.
4. Preventive work, to be successful, must concern itself with the child and the home.
5. Normal family life is the foundation of the state, and its conservation an inherent duty of government.

The commission found that the work available to poor women "inevitably breaks down the physical, mental and moral strength" of the family by causing a low standard of living and parental neglect, which led to the delinquency and backwardness of children. Because other remedies for the problem of the working mother were thought to be failures, the commission recommended the immediate enactment of state aid for the dependent children of widowed mothers.[43]

Mothers' pensions were to be a panacea for delinquency of children deprived of a mother's care. Merrit Pinckney, a judge for the Chicago juvenile court, argued in 1912 that overworked and underpaid mothers were at best poor guardians for their children. "Many of these unfortunate children who never had a decent chance," he contended, "grow up into a depraved manhood and womanhood and drift naturally into that great and ever increasing army of criminals who are a menace to society."[44] Another reformer argued that the "lack of a mother's hand" led children to roam the streets and fall into bad company.[45] More affirmatively, some progressive reformers saw the mothers' aid movement as a way to rear useful citizens for the future.[46]

But mothers, too, were to profit from the pension system. Women were believed to be imperiled if their relationship with their children was inadequate. A judge in 1912 described the "otherwise fit" mother who worked because of poverty and was forced to board her children away from home. She was, he said, heartbroken and alone, "her children widely separated, not only from her but from each other. . . . [W]eakened now, mentally and physically and morally, by the ruthless tearing of maternal heart-strings, where will her footsteps tend to lead . . . ? Will she survive the test and continue to lead an honest, upright life, or will she drift along the line of least resistance, ending in the brothel or in the madhouse?"[47] A similar view was expressed by charity workers concerned with the fate of unmarried mothers. The Boston Society for Helping Destitute Mothers and Infants stated in 1912 that unwed mothers should receive a pension, for "one who retains the personal charge of her baby has a wholesome occupation for her mind and heart, and a constant incentive to an upright, industrious life."[48]

Still another argument suggested that pensions for mothers were justified on the grounds of social justice. William Hard, for one, suggested that mothers' pensions be seen not as charity but as payment for public service. Judge Ben Lindsey similarly noted that pensions for mothers were a right, like soldiers' pensions. He wrote, "As justice due mothers whose work in rearing their children is a work for the state as much as that of the soldier, . . . it is a recognition for the first time by society that the state is responsible in a measure for the plight of the mother, and acknowledges its responsibility by sharing the burden of her poverty that it created largely by the conditions that the state permits to exist."[49] And at the First International Congress of Working Women, held in 1919, delegates proposed the idea of "maternity aid" for women regardless of financial need, as well as the idea of maternity insurance, so that motherhood would be a "joy and not a burden."[50] Finally, some argued that pensions were financially more sound than public support of children in institutions.[51]

But opponents of mothers' pensions were equally vehement. Some argued that pensions would increase the desertion of fathers, or at least encourage working-class families to falsely claim that the father had deserted. Others argued that pensions would increase public expenditures and relieve families of "wholesome responsibilities for the assistance of unfortunate relatives." Some claimed, too, that if the state entered the business of social welfare, private charity would be doomed. Finally, some critics argued that mothers' pensions treated the symptom rather than the cause of impoverished widowhood by not remedying the preventable deaths of husbands in dangerous occupations or the low wages paid to women workers.[52]

The ideological underpinnings of the mothers' pension movement prescribed that a mother's place was in a home suitable for the rearing of proper citizens. But to what degree was the administration of the pension laws coincident with this prescription? In practice, the mothers' pension laws rarely achieved their goals of subsidizing motherhood. Rather, they promoted the employment of women in the marginal labor market outside the home. There were two reasons for the failure of the mothers' pension movement: pension laws excluded too many potential recipients, and, for those who did qualify, assistance was too limited to support the family without additional income.

Qualifications for pension eligibility varied from state to state. In general, by 1919, self-supporting mothers could apply for pensions if they had little in the way of savings, insurance, equity, or personal property. In nine states, only widows could qualify; in others, deserted wives and wives of prisoners, hospital patients, or disabled men were also eligible for assistance. In only three places—Hawaii, Michigan, and Nebraska—could unmarried mothers apply for relief.[53]

But additional standards were also enforced. In Philadelphia, up to two-thirds of the women who were financially entitled to pensions were rejected for other reasons. In Pennsylvania in general, mothers' aid applicants had to prove they had lived at least two years in the state. Other restrictions, in various states, included the disqualification of women whose children were adopted, who were pregnant at the time of their husband's death, and who had only one child.[54] Black women were implicitly ineligible because of their color. A 1931 Children's Bureau study of eighteen states found that 96 percent of mothers' pensions beneficiaries were white, even in districts where nearly half of the population was black.[55]

Even when a woman met the eligibility requirements, the process of application for relief was slow and discouraging. In Cook County, Illinois, a widow applying for a pension through the juvenile court faced a waiting period of from four to six months while a social worker scrutinized her financial and moral fitness. In New York, after the pension law passed in 1915, less than half of the 12,000 initial applicants had been processed by the end of the first year. In 1931, the Children's Bureau estimated that less than a third of those eligible for pensions nationally had received any assistance.[56]

Once a woman was accepted for a pension, her financial security was not assured. In most cases, mothers' pensions were inadequate. In 1919, pensions ranged from an $8 maximum monthly allowance per child in Iowa and Vermont to a $25 maximum monthly allowance per child in Nevada. Additional children in a family received smaller grants. Observers agreed that, in general, a pension alone would not support a family. In Pennsylvania, for example, investigators said of the maximum monthly grants of $20 for the first child and $10 for each additional child that between one-third and one-fourth of the families dependent upon state support could not survive on the income supplied by the pension.[57]

Yet despite the financial inadequacy of the pensions, most states did not permit welfare recipients to work, thus reflecting the prevailing ideology that a mother's place was in the home. Whereas some welfare workers continued to support the idea of part-time work for widows, all agreed that the employment of a mother should be secondary to the needs of her children. In eighteen states, in 1919, a woman could not work "regularly" away from home and remain eligible for public funds; in other states, she could not work more than one to three days a week away from home. Some pension advocates further suggested that fit work for women would be domestic service, waitressing, and the care of women and children boarders.[58]

Despite these restrictions on employment, a high proportion of women who received mothers' pensions worked "regularly." Reliable statistics are difficult, if not impossible, to obtain, because many women who worked would not report employment to the officials who might then cut off their funding. But there is ample evidence that pension recipients worked. In Chicago, more than a fourth of the pensioned women worked full time by 1920, and Illinois was one of the states prohibiting "regular" work outside the home. In 1922, at least 20 percent of the mothers receiving assistance in Boston, and 40 percent of the pension recipients in New York, were employed.[59]

Some self-supporting women preferred employment to public relief. In Philadelphia, of 237 widows studied in 1921, only 38 had applied for pensions.[60] In 1910, Boston charity workers observed that a certain kind of widow felt that it was "unnatural, in her eyes and those of her neighbors, to earn nothing" even after pension laws were established.[61] In 1931, the Children's Bureau found that of some 7,000 women who had been disqualified from pension eligibility, only 44 percent had remarried. More often, women were declared ineligible because they preferred to work for a higher income for their families than the pensions allowed.[62]

Though limited by qualification restrictions and inadequate budgeting, mothers' pensions reshaped the welfare process in the United States. By 1921, the Census Bureau estimated that some 121,000 children in 45,000 families were at least partially supported by public funds and that thousands of these children might otherwise have been committed to institutions because of the poverty of their families.[63] Pensions, moreover, proved to be a less expensive means of welfare than were institutions. In 1922, the city of New York supported 27,000 children in their own homes for about half of the cost of institutional care.[64]

The spread of the mothers' pension movement affected other forms of aid for working women. Most important, it retarded the growth of the day-nursery movement. In Kansas City, for example, the United Jewish Charities abandoned their day nursery for a pension program by 1911.[65] Furthermore, as widows were widely believed to be taken care of by state aid, the day nurseries that survived were forced to redefine their admissions policies to favor the children of working mothers who were married.

Day-Care Policy and Practice, 1920–1960

As the 1920s began, public pensions for widows were seen by many as the solution to the problem of the working mother. The home was preserved; the mother had been reinstated in her proper place. But by this time, more married women had entered the labor force, including an articulate class of middle-income women. How did they care for their children?

Middle-income women who worked came up with their own solutions to the child-care dilemma. Those who could afford the cost hired servants to care for their sons and daughters during the day. A "wage-earning wife" told readers of the *Woman's Home Companion* in 1925, for example, that she relied on "Mrs. Maguire, our incredibly neat, competent, amiable cook-housekeeper" to solve her career-family problem.[66] A 1927 survey of women who had graduated from Radcliffe found that almost three out of four of those both married and working had hired household help.[67] The option of hiring servants, however, was becoming less feasible for working wives both because of the decreasing availability of domestic servants and because many more married women who worked could not so easily afford to hire household help.

There is evidence that some middle-class mothers had approached the philanthropic day nurseries for child-care services. The secretary of the National Federation of Day Nurseries reported "numerous requests for nursery care for the children of business and professional women who were able and willing to pay the full cost for such service."[68] But these women were turned down by most nurseries because of the belief that the day nursery was meant as a last resort for poor women rather than as a service for women who worked.

Middle-income women relied instead on the growing nursery school movement, on proprietary day care, and on relatives and neighbors. By this time, nursery schools did not promise mere custodial care for children but rather promoted the educational enrichment of their students. In 1929, one writer argued that nursery schools would "give the child an eminently safe and hygienic environment during his mother's working hours, and furnish him with the physical, mental and moral nourishment that he needs. . . . Perhaps it is not too much to say that such an institution can give the child better care, physically and psychologically, than most mothers, with their limited knowledge of the far-reaching sciences that contribute to the welfare of the child, could hope to give."[69] Nursery schools began to slowly increase in the 1920s, growing from a recorded 16 schools in 1923 to 108 by 1928. Some day nurseries evolved into nursery schools in order to meet the new expectations of clients; the Chicago Hull-House Day Nursery, for example, became the Mary Crane Nursery School in 1925.[70]

The philanthropic day nursery itself was changing in the 1920s. The impact of the widow's pension caused a shift in the day-nursery movement; if the widow was the expected client before 1920, now it was the employed married woman, especially if she was seen as coming from an "economically handicapped" family.[71] The professionalization of social work also had an effect, as new standards of nutrition, health, and education were proposed. What had once been a service for poor working mothers was becoming more of a social welfare agency for women defined as "problem cases." Nursery school teachers and social workers replaced matrons and nurses, with the result that infants were gradually excluded from day-nursery eligibility. Mothers of very young children, social workers deemed, should not work. Those who did were less visible than previously. The most destitute of mothers—widows—had been taken care of through the pension system, and so the mother who came to the day nursery was viewed as having another problem—a social-psychological problem subject to the expert remedies of the caseworker.

Many working married women defined their situation quite differently. They saw the interest of social workers in their lives not as helpful inquiry but as intrusion. A social worker at the Leila Day Nursery in New Haven, Connecticut, noted with some surprise the hostile attitude of families to the intrusion of social workers into their homes: "In most of the families the parents' attitude is that the Nursery is a community resource, such as the public school, and it is, therefore, for them to use as they wish. Families find it difficult to see the need of discussing financial, social and personal factors affecting their lives, as in their minds these facts are not related to nursery care."[72] Other observers noted the struggle that went on between parent and social worker over the admission of children to a nursery. One woman, for example, sputtered after an interview, "I guess I know my own business best. She can refuse my baby if she wants to. But telling me to stay at home is too much!"[73]

By the early 1930s, the day-nursery movement was marginal at best and suspect as a welfare agency for troubled families. In 1935, federal funds were appropriated for the first time for day care in the form of nursery schools for the children of poor mothers. The Works Project Administration provided money for rapid expansion, and by 1935, 1,900 WPA nurseries, as they were called, tended some 75,000 children. But these nurseries were not geared toward the needs of mothers who worked or toward the educational and psychological needs of children. Rather, their avowed function was to provide employment for teachers, nurses, nutritionists, cooks, janitors, and clerical workers. With the end of the New Deal, the WPA nurseries lost their federal funding and began to close.[74]

But this decline was temporary. During World War II, day nurseries once again revived, this time to free mothers for work in the wartime labor force. Although mothers of young children were not officially encouraged to work, still mothers as a group were the reserve of labor identified as necessary for the success of wartime production. The care of their children was therefore seen as a function of the government defense program. "Good care for the children of working mothers," the federal Office of Education argued, "means more planes and armaments for our fighting men, and victory *sooner*." The Office of Education suggested that public school hours be extended to provide day care for children of working mothers.[75] Others suggested the expansion of services in the day nursery. The National Association of Day Nurseries argued the need for stemming the tide of "latch-key children of war industry mothers": "This is the day nursery part in the Home Defense program—in order to see to it that as little damage as possible is done to family life and childhood by the present upheavals and to conserve human values for the period of reconstruction when the crisis is past."[76]

In 1941, Congress passed the Community Facilities Act, also known as the Lanham Act, to meet on a fifty-fifty basis the social service needs of communities affected by the war. In 1942, the Lanham Act was interpreted as being applicable to day-care centers. By July 1944, there were over 3,000 centers servicing 129,000 children. By 1945, nearly $50 million had been spent to support day-care facilities for more than 1.5 million children.[77]

Private industry, too, experimented with funding day-care centers during the war. The best-known of these was the Kaiser shipbuilding business in Oregon. The Kaiser firm established centers open to its workers twenty-four hours daily, providing not only child care for children as young as eighteen months, but also medical care, and hot meals that could be picked up along with the children and taken home.[78]

It is important to note that even at that time day care was limited. Most mothers relied on the old methods—using relatives, friends, and neighbors to watch their children. Federally funded day care remained insufficient—there were no services for the care of infants, for example, and the centers open to older children met less than 10 percent of the need.[79]

But some mothers did support the idea of government-funded care for their children—an idea that was threatened when the Lanham funds were cut off after the war. In 1945, the Child Care Center Parents' Association of New York organized to battle for the survival of the day-care centers as well as for free public nursery schools, free hot lunches in schools, and equal pay for equal work. Day care, they argued, was a right, not a charitable gift:

We working mothers have been holding down three full-time jobs, as mothers, housewives, and wage earners. 24 hours a day gives us barely enough time to get everything done. And yet we do it. . . . Super-women? No! Just women who love their children and want to keep their families together. That's why we are going to take on a fourth full-time job! That of convincing our government . . . that investing in our children is not a philanthropic enterprise! It is a privilege! For when they invest in our children, they will reap the kind of profits that pay dividends in good, healthy, well-adjusted useful citizens![80]

When the state of New York discontinued its day-care program, these mothers picketed the residence of Governor Thomas Dewey, who promptly labeled them Communists.

But the day-care mothers persisted, fighting to shake off the welfare label and to get the recognition and approval of middle-class mothers. The Child Care Center Parents' Association recorded the struggle, for example, to get PTA meetings held at night, after work, rather than during the day.[81] This battle was aided by the Child Welfare League of America, which proposed that Congress consider a bill to fund locally administered day-care centers. "It is hardly American," the league argued, "to leave a mother, too often poorly paid for her work, to shift for her child without some minimum guarantee of community service and some subsidy for the child's care."[82]

Generally, however, the end of the war signaled the closing of hundreds of day-care centers; the official need for working mothers had ended. By 1946, only 1,504 centers for some 40,000 children were still in operation. Centers closed because of money problems and "changing needs." The Brightside Day Nursery, for example, which had opened in 1894 to serve the community on New York's Lower East Side, shut down in 1948.[83]

Ironically, as the day-care movement was once again in eclipse, the number of working mothers was in its greatest acceleration. In 1953, as we have seen, more than 2 million women with children under the age of six were working outside the home.[84] But the feminine mystique continued to define the problems of the working mother as individual and not social. Old attitudes persisted; one community-chest worker wrote in 1952 that children in day nurseries were "day-time orphans whose mothers must work to pay the rent and buy the groceries."[85]

Most children in this era continued to be cared for by relatives and neighbors. In 1958, a Children's Bureau study found that of children of mothers working full time, 80 percent of the children under the age of twelve were cared for at home, most by a father, grandparent, sibling, friend, or neighbor.

Eight percent of these children had no supervision at all. Only 2 percent of the children of working mothers were in day care or nursery school.[86] Hidden within these figures, of course, were proprietary day-care businesses—neighborhood women who took in children for a fee.

Some social workers pushed for the transformation of the day-care ideal. Gertrude Binder argued in 1953 that day care should adapt to the changing employment practices of mothers, "to promote the well being of an expanding circle of human beings rather than merely to mitigate the ill-being of the exceptionally unfortunate." Day care, she concluded, should shift from an emergency resource only for poor women to a community-based educational resource for children.[87]

1960 to 1980

Day care resurfaced as a vital social issue in the 1960s. In this period, the movement to define day care as a normal rather than as an exceptional service gained strength; increasing numbers of people saw day care not as a charity, or as a welfare function, but as a community service for normal families, similar to public education or public transportation.

But this trend was tempered by the resurgence of the link between publicly supported day care and the needs of dependent children. State-supported mothers' pensions had, by 1935, become Aid to Dependent Children, a federal program under the Social Security Act.[88] In 1962, as Aid and Services to Needy Families with Children, the pension movement had come full circle, as interest in the preservation of family life had given way to fears that "welfare mothers" were taking advantage of public support. As a result, a requirement for aid in many cases was that recipients had to work.[89] This in turn led to assumptions about day care. If poor mothers were expected to work, then provisions were needed for the care of their children. In 1967, Congress amended the Social Security Act to provide funds for day care, intending to meet the needs of mothers on public assistance. But the lack of adequate child care led to the failure of governmental efforts to get welfare mothers into the workplace.[90]

In 1970, the White House Conference on Children deemed day care the most serious problem confronting American families and urged the massive infusion of federal funds to meet the growing need. The Comprehensive Child Development Act of 1971 recommended that the government provide day care for all children. In Senate hearings, day-care advocates proposed that child care would not only free mothers to work but would also bring the children of various races and classes together, facilitate community control of public services, and enhance health care. To some advocates, too, federally funded day care would also "invest in the development of the next generation and thereby . . . begin to break the terrible, dehumanizing cycle of poverty." Secretary of Health, Education, and Welfare Elliot Richardson told the Senate Committee on Finance:

> Many parents are unable to give their offspring the experiences necessary to achieve success in our fast-paced society. They themselves often lack experience and schooling and are ill-prepared to assure the full development their children need to compete in a highly technological world. . . . If we fail to invest in these children now . . . we are likely to find them on the welfare rolls as parents 15 years from now. In short, there is a great need for child care programs which contribute to the development of the child as well as provide a safe place for the child while the mother is working.[91]

Other day-care proponents, debating standards of care and priorities of clients, questioned whether middle-income families required services as desperately as did welfare mothers.[92] But the idea of federal funding for day care, particularly the national network of centers proposed in the child-development centers sponsored by the Senate, was defeated by the veto of President Richard Nixon, who maintained that government's involvement in child care should be kept "to an absolute minimum" and that "family-centered" rather than "communal" care should be supported.[93] With Nixon's veto, the idea of federally funded day care—begun as a response to the dependency of poor mothers— was again submerged. Once again, child care was to be sanctioned only in terms of the dependent mother and not because it was needed by working mothers of every class.

But some parents spoke out for continued subsidized day care. In New York City in 1972, for example, some 350 parents, children, and day-care workers took over a government office to oppose a state order limiting eligibility for government-financed day care.[94]

A related trend was the growth in programs for early education for children. From 1967 to 1979, there was a dramatic rise in the proportion of children aged three to five enrolled in preschool programs. Whereas 6.8 percent of all three-year-olds were registered for preschool in 1967, by 1979 25 percent of this group spent at least part of the day in educational activities. Of all children aged three to five, excluding five-year-olds enrolled in elementary school, 51 percent were reported to be in preschool in 1979. In part this trend was spurred by federal programs such as Head Start, which attempted to compensate for the "cultural deprivation" of poor children, and in part by the growth of nursery and preschool programs for the middle class.[95]

By the mid-1970s, there were still far too few day-care centers to meet the needs of working mothers. In 1973, there were 700,000 day-care slots for the 6 million preschoolers whose mothers worked. Child-care programs were of diverse sponsorship, ranging from profit-making franchises, which critics labeled "Kentucky-Fried Children" centers for their emphasis on quantity care, and nonprofit centers run by church groups, welfare organizations, educational institutions, and other community associations. Some corporations, including Polaroid and the John Hancock Company, also sponsored day-care centers for the children of employees.[96] Most children, however, continued to be cared for at home. In 1974 and 1975, of children aged three to six with working mothers, 81 percent received primary care in their own homes, 13 percent in someone else's home, and only 2 percent in day-care centers.[97]

By the end of the decade, there appeared to be increased support for the idea of day care as a social service for average families. The Tax Reform Act of 1976 and the Revenue Act of 1978 established tax credits for parents who purchased day-care services for their children.[98] Social critics proposed a range of improvements in the child-care system, including more business-sponsored day care at the workplace, state-supported neighborhood child-care centers, increased foster-home care for infants, and the extension of school services for preschoolers. Reformers suggested that a diversity of day-care opportunities would allow parents to choose the best arrangements for their families and would also benefit business by reducing the absenteeism of mothers.[99]

Increased recognition was now also given to the adjustment of work hours to allow parents to work and yet tend their own children. Mothers had for decades attempted to adjust their work hours by working odd hours, part-time, or on split shifts. The Working Family Project, a study of lower-middle-income families in the Boston area, reported in 1975 that parents in one-third of the dual-income families surveyed worked staggered hours in order to meet child-care needs. Case studies illustrate this practice. The Project reported, for example, that "Mr. Henry works from 8 a.m. to 4 p.m., except for two evenings a week. . . . Mrs. Henry works a 4 p.m. to 11 p.m. shift. Because of their commuting time, there is an hour each day when they must use a child-care arrangement; also there is an occasional evening to be covered when Mr. Henry works overtime. To cover these hours, the Henrys exchange child care with one of their neighbors."[100] The practice of exchanging child care was also found in more formal baby-sitting cooperatives, where parents relied on friends and neighbors for a consistent sharing of child care.[101]

Reformers in the 1970s urged that part-time work be upgraded by securing benefits for part-time workers, by widening part-time opportunities, and by encouraging job-sharing programs. Still, part-time workers remained a surprisingly constant segment of the labor force, given the remarkable growth in the numbers of mothers of young children at work. From 1965 to 1980, the proportion of women workers employed part-time (less than thirty-five hours a week) remained steady, ranging from 19 to 21 percent of all working women over the age of twenty.

More recently, the idea of "flexitime" has been brought to public attention. Flexitime would allow workers to put in a full eight-hour day on a staggered schedule, such as from 6 A.M. to 2 P.M., or by squeezing a full work week into four long days. In 1973, an amendment to the Comprehensive Employment and Training Act targeted funds for research on flexitime arrangements; by the end of the decade many civil service and corporation offices provided this opportunity for their workers. By 1980, some 12 percent of all workers surveyed worked on flexible schedules; the largest proportions of flexitime workers were salespersons (26.5 percent), managers and administrators (20.2 percent) and federal workers (20.2 percent).[102]

By 1980, only about 27 percent of American families reflected the idealized image of the home, where the father worked while the mother did not.[103] But still working mothers were caught between the traditional definition of woman's sphere, the association of day care with welfare, and changing economic roles. Despite their rapidly growing numbers and despite more than a half century of public discussion, working mothers remain defined as a social problem. The continued failure of American society to reconcile the reality of women's work patterns with the ideology of domesticity has reinforced the identification of working mothers as an unresolved issue on the national agenda.

Conclusion

The historical debate about women, work, and social order continues in the 1980s. In the nineteenth century, the entrance of young single women into the labor force generated a controversy over the "working girl" that contributed to both meliorative reform and structural change in the workplace. By the turn of the century, young single women had become well established in the American labor force and were no longer thought of as problematic. But in the twentieth century, there was a startling transformation in the composition of the female labor force, as first wives and then mothers rapidly increased their numbers among the employed. Because social responses to twentieth-century working mothers remain mired in nineteenth-century concepts of domesticity and dependency, American society has not yet implemented policies necessary for the full and equitable integration of women into the economic structure.

The disjuncture between the work of mothers of young children and the domestic ideology remains powerful and may even deepen. The Bureau of Labor Statistics predicts that, by 1990, up to two-thirds of women aged 25 to 54 will be in the work force, as the demand for female labor continues to grow. Moreover, by 1990, mothers may be more likely to work full time continuously rather than part-time and intermittently.[1]

Two themes persist in the debate about working women. One is the problem of day care for very young children; the other is the question of structural change in the workplace.

If present trends continue, the expansion of the American labor force will mean the rising work participation of mothers of very young children. By March 1981, 8.2 million children under the age of six had working mothers. As of March 1982, nearly half of married women with preschool-aged children were employed and more than half of unmarried mothers with preschool children were also working.

Day care for children over the age of three seems to have become an accepted practice in the United States. But 45 percent of married women with children under the age of three were working by 1982 as well.[2] It is the care for these younger children that must be addressed by policymakers and parents. Most very young children of working mothers are cared for in family or home day-care situations, but there has been a movement to provide more institutional day-care facilities for these infants. Yet child-care provisions remain underfunded and understudied. Recent scholarship suggests that, for children under the age of two, group day care outside the home *may* "put at risk" their future cognitive and emotional development. Although studies are preliminary, and in the main focused on lower-income children in proprietary day-care situations, for many young children it is clear that present day-care opportunities are often not in their best interests.[3]

In *The Erosion of Childhood*, Valerie Polakow Suransky presents case studies of different types of day care to illustrate the lack of child-centered arrangements for the children of working mothers. Suransky maintains that it is ironic that the movement for women's liberation may too often rely on the dialectical antithesis of the "containment of children"—that humanistic freedom for one group endorses the early and anti-humanistic institutionalization of the other. Suransky suggests that the "current call for free and universal daycare should not be viewed as a progressive or radical answer to the social needs of women in society entering the work force seeking equalization of opportunity; rather, the daycare phenomenon merely extends and exacerbates the corporate paradigm, thereby contributing to the *maintenance*, not the *transformation* of the social order."[4] For example, if day care has become too often an industry supporting such franchised centers as the Mary Moppets of the Southwest or the Universal Education Corporation of the East Coast, questions must surely be raised about how the growing *business* of child care affects the very nature of childhood. With an emphasis on profit rather than on human development, day care as it is available for many people to some degree abrogates the freedom and rights of children.[5]

Suransky has joined that group of Americans who urge alternative forms of day care for the children of working mothers. In particular, she calls for the deinstitutionalization of early childhood through a variety of measures. These measures range from a form of income redistribution—perhaps through a type of government subsidy like the mothers' pensions, which would allow parents to choose whether or not to work when their children were very young—to the spread of cooperative day-care centers. These latter cooperatives would be small and community-based, and they would rely on the support of society and employers to help parents take an active role in the daily lives of their young children. Other possible reforms might include more liberal policies for maternity and paternity leaves, especially during the first year of parenthood, increased tax benefits for parents, and expanded child-care facilities at the work site. Mothers are working, and will continue to work, and the availability of good quality, affordable day care has become an increasingly critical problem.

As Alison Clarke-Stewart has pointed out, day care is now a fact of life and no longer a debatable issue.[6]

What remains debatable is the structure of work in American society. As the entrance of young single women into the labor force in the nineteenth century contributed to a movement for legislation shortening the hours of work and setting a minimum wage, so the entrance of mothers into the labor force has spurred the still-nascent movement for flexible hours of work, job-sharing arrangements, and a more fluid approach to the boundaries of work and home. This new posture is reflected in the efforts of mothers to keep their babies with or near them in the workplace, and in the efforts of other parents who choose to work, via remote computer terminal or telephone, at least part of the time in their own homes.

It will be a combination of child care and work reforms that, in the end, will protect and benefit not only the rights of mothers and their children but all members of society. These changes will require a transformation of the domestic ideology. The current undervaluation of women's work, characterized by the two-tiered labor force with its sexual divisions of status and pay, must give way to economic and social equity. As long as the worlds of men and women are separated by differing prescriptions for family and economic roles, and as long as economic need is seen as a determinant in the acceptance or rejection of work for women, the employment of mothers outside the home will remain defined as a problem. Working mothers will continue to be condemned, explained, and justified until the right to work is recognized as being within the normal range of experience for women just as it is for men.

Notes

Abbreviations

CWLA Child Welfare League of America
JAMC Jane Addams Memorial Collection
TA Travelers' Aid
WCA Woman's Christian Association
WEIU Women's Educational and Industrial Union
YWCA Young Women's Christian Association

Introduction

1. See, for instance, Kreps, *Sex in the Marketplace*; Kessler-Harris, "Stratifying by Sex."
2. Examples of recent scholarship include Wandersee, *Women's Work*; Walsh, *Doctors Wanted*; Yans-McLaughlin, *Family and Community*. A more recent work that takes a broad view of the integration of women into wage labor is Kessler-Harris, *Out to Work*.
3. The phrase "working girl" will be used throughout to label those young—and not so young—women who were so designated by their contemporary culture. For a discussion of the regulation of female behavior by labeling, see Fox, " 'Nice Girl.' "
4. This interaction of ideology and reality is also considered in Kessler-Harris, "Women's Wage Work."
5. The analysis of the intent and function of reform movements and social policy has generated a debate among historians. For a summary of this controversy, see Grob, "Reflections on the History of Social Policy in America."
6. For an extensive discussion of the changing composition of the female labor force, see Oppenheimer, *Female Labor Force*.
7. Examples of problems with longitudinal comparisons of census data include differing instructions to enumerators about what constitutes work, and different times of the year during which enumeration took place. See Oppenheimer, *Female Labor Force*, pp. 2–6; Conk, "Accuracy, Efficiency, and Bias," pp. 65–72.
8. The attempt to make industrial life more "domestic," both for nineteenth-century self-supporting women and for twentieth-century working mothers, illustrates an interweaving of "family time" and "social time." Tamara Haraven has argued that the family life-cycle should be seen as dynamic rather than static; this would lead to an analysis of boarding and lodging, for example, as a function both of life-cycle and economic needs. See Haraven, "Family as Process."

Chapter 1

1. For a discussion of antebellum migrations of women, see Hobson, "Seduced and Abandoned."
2. Self-supporting women in Philadelphia in the 1820s are depicted in Carey, *Miscellaneous Essays*, pp. 267–71.

3. Demos, *A Little Commonwealth*, p. 78.

4. For a discussion of urban housing practices, see Wolfe, *Lodging House Problem*.

5. Salmon, *Domestic Service*, chap. 3.

6. Ibid., pp. 54–55.

7. Abbott, *Women in Industry*, p. 32.

8. Salmon, *Domestic Service*, pp. 71–73; Scott and Tilly, "Women's Work and the Family," pp. 52–53. Faye Dudden views this shift as a redefinition of household workers from "hired girls" or "help" to "domestics" or "servants." See Dudden, *Serving Women*, pp. 5–8.

9. Glasco, "Life Cycles and Household Structure," pp. 122–43.

10. Abbott, *Women in Industry*, chap. 3; Meserve, *Lowell*, chap. 6.

11. Meserve, *Lowell*, p. 61. See also Dublin, *Women at Work*.

12. Miles, *Lowell*, p. 128.

13. Ware, *Industrial Worker*, p. 107.

14. Meserve, *Lowell*, p. 61.

15. Robinson, *Loom and Spindle*, pp. 80–91. See also Bushman, "*A Good Poor Man's Wife.*"

16. Scoresby, *American Factories*, p. 16.

17. Engle, "Story of the Mercer Expeditions," pp. 225–37.

18. Abbott, *Women in Industry*, pp. 138–39; Lerner, "Lady and the Mill Girl," pp. 5–14.

19. Lerner, "Lady and the Mill Girl."

20. Dublin, *Women at Work*, pp. 35–40. A fascinating glimpse of the lives of these women through the perspective of their letters home is offered in Dublin's *Farm to Factory*.

21. U.S. Department of Labor, Commissioner of Labor, *Working Women in Large Cities*, p. 64; Wright, *Working Girls of Boston*; U.S. Department of Labor, *Boarding Homes and Clubs*, p. 142.

22. For a discussion of supply-and-demand factors in the shaping of the female labor force, see Oppenheimer, *Female Labor Force*, chap. 5.

23. Maclean, *Women Workers and Society*, pp. 88–89.

24. U.S. Bureau of the Census, *Women at Work*.

25. Ibid., p. 28. Louise Tilly cautions against the common assumption that industrialization alone might cause an increase in the employment of women. Her study of Milan, Italy, found no link between industrialization and the feminization of the work force. See Tilly, "Urban Growth," pp. 467–84.

26. For statistics on the distribution of women in the population and in the labor force at the turn of the century, see U.S. Bureau of the Census, *Women at Work*, pp. 132–33, table 2, p. 146, table 9.

27. Ibid., pp. 260–62, table 28, pp. 298–300.

28. In Boston, New York, and Philadelphia, native-born white women of foreign parentage were 14, 15, and 17 percent of women boarders respectively. In Minneapolis and St. Paul, they were 40 and 44 percent. See ibid., p. 224, table 28, pp. 266, 280–84.

29. Taeuber and Taeuber, *Changing Population*, p. 53, table 11, p. 68.

30. Ibid.; Hvidt, *Flight to America*, p. 92, table 9.1.

31. One study of immigrant women in Philadelphia found that two out of five crossed the ocean alone. U.S. Department of Labor, Women's Bureau, *Immigrant Woman and Her Job*. See also "Immigrant Women and Girls in Boston," 1907, typewritten, Women's Educational and Industrial Union Papers, Box 7; Kowaleska, "Conditions of Work for Immigrant Girls," pp. 51–59.

32. Sarah Beaulieu, "A Farm Girl's Diary," in *Women in the American Economy*, ed. Brownlee and Brownlee, p. 130.

33. Garland, *Rose of Dutcher's Coolly*, pp. 148–49.

34. Edith H. to Women's Department, Minnesota Bureau of Labor, 7 July 1909, Minnesota Labor and Industry Department Records, Employment Correspondence. The full names of cor-

respondents to the Bureau of Labor are not given in the text and notes in keeping with current privacy regulations.

35. This is by no means a universal law of migration. A review of the literature shows a diversity of sex-selectivity by time and place. It appears, however, that rural-urban migrants were more likely to be women, while urban-rural migrants were more likely to be men. One estimate made in the United States suggested that the rural-urban migration of women exceeded that of men by about 22 percent between 1920 and 1930. See Jansen, *Sociology of Migration*, pp. 18–19; Sorokin and Zimmerman, *Principles of Rural-Urban Sociology*, chap. 24; Zimmerman, "Migration to Towns and Cities," pp. 450–55; Williams, "Rural Youth Studies," pp. 166–78.

36. U.S. Bureau of the Census, *Women at Work*, p. 18, table XI.

37. Ibid., pp. 198–207, table 26.

38. Taeuber and Taeuber, *Changing Population*, pp. 15, 152–55, 249.

39. Oppenheimer, *Female Labor Force*, p. 27.

40. Calhoun, *Social History of the American Family*, 1:67–69; 3:107.

41. U.S. Bureau of the Census, *Women at Work*, pp. 9–11; Smuts, *Women and Work in America*, chap. 2.

42. Van Vorst and Van Vorst, *Woman Who Toils*, p. 82.

43. "Girl Who Comes to the City," July 1908, p. 694; December 1908, p. 1228.

44. Ibid., March 1908, p. 277; May 1908, p. 595; December 1908, p. 1226; Smuts, *Women and Work*, chap. 2.

45. Smuts, *Women and Work*, chap. 3. For a comparison of men's and women's wages, see U.S. Bureau of the Census, *Earnings of Factory Workers*, pp. 394–95.

46. U.S. Department of Labor, *Working Women in Large Cities*, p. 625, table XXXII, p. 532, table XXXI.

47. Minnesota Bureau of Labor, *Ninth Biennial Report of . . . 1903–04*, 1:129.

48. For a comprehensive survey of local and national studies of working women, see U.S. Department of Labor, Women's Bureau, *Women Workers and Their Dependents*, pt. 2.

49. U.S. Bureau of the Census, *Women at Work*, p. 10.

50. Ibid., p. 198, table 26.

51. U.S. Department of Labor, Women's Bureau, *Family Status of Breadwinning Women*; U.S. Department of Labor, Women's Bureau, *Share of Wage-Earning Women in Family Support*.

52. Brownlee and Brownlee, *Women in the American Economy*, pp. 20–23.

53. Oppenheimer, *Female Labor Force*, chap. 1.

54. See Kessler-Harris, "Stratifying by Sex."

55. U.S. Bureau of the Census, *Women at Work*, p. 31.

56. The next highest nativity group for urban servants was Hungarians (42 percent) followed by Austrians (36 percent), Irish (31 percent), and Germans (31 percent). In the country as a whole, however, only 28 percent of domestic servants were immigrants. Ibid., p. 41, table XXXIV, p. 47.

57. Katzman, *Seven Days a Week*, p. 268. See also Sutherland, *Americans and Their Servants*, and Dudden, *Serving Women*, for the history of domestic service in the United States.

58. Bliven, *Wonderful Writing Machine*; Davies, "Woman's Place Is at the Typewriter," pp. 1–28.

59. U.S. Department of Labor, Bureau of Labor Statistics, *Summary of Report on Condition of Woman and Child Wage-Earners*, p. 296. For a discussion of the emerging culture of sales work for women, see Benson, "Customers Ain't God," pp. 185–211.

60. Rayne, *What Can a Woman Do?*, p. 123. See also Candee, *How Women May Earn a Living*.

Chapter 2

1. U.S. Congress, Senate, *Report on Condition*, 9:17.
2. Hamilton, "Report on Manufactures," 1:87. Hamilton also thought that children could be usefully employed by manufacturing establishments. For a discussion of the promotion of female factory labor as an antidote to dependency, see Nash, "Failure of Female Factory Labor," pp. 165–88.
3. Marx, *Machine in the Garden*, p. 159; Abbott, *Women in Industry*, p. 57.
4. Benson, *Women in Eighteenth-Century America*, chap. 6.
5. Cott, *Bonds of Womanhood*; Sklar, *Catharine Beecher*, chap. 6; Kraditor, *Up from the Pedestal*, pp. 12–13.
6. Cott, *Bonds of Womanhood*, p. 199.
7. Bloch, "American Feminine Ideals in Transition," pp. 101–26.
8. Gordon, *Woman's Body, Woman's Right*, pp. 10–11.
9. Beecher, *Evils Suffered*, p. 11.
10. Brownlee and Brownlee, *Women in the American Economy*, p. 135.
11. *New York Daily Tribune*, 19 August 1845, quoted in U.S. Congress, *Report on Condition*, 9:22.
12. Beecher, *Evils Suffered*, p. 12.
13. Cited in U.S. Congress, Senate, *Report on Condition*, 9:131–33.
14. Ibid., pp. 234–35.
15. Penny, *Think and Act*, p. 25.
16. Beecher, *Evils Suffered*, p. 12.
17. Julianna, "Factory Life as It Is, By an Operative," in *America's Working Women*, ed. Baxandall, Gordon, and Reverby, p. 67.
18. *Voice of Industry*, 4 September 1846, cited in Ware, *Industrial Worker*, p. 53.
19. National Trades Union, "Report of the Committee on Female Labor," in *Documentary History of American Industrial Society*, ed. Commons et al., 6:281.
20. Adapted from Herbert Blumer, quoted in Douglas, *Defining America's Social Problems*, pp. 106–8.
21. See, for example, "Report of the Committee on Vagrancy," p. 244.
22. For a discussion of male social status, see Thernstrom, *Poverty and Progress*.
23. Rhine, "Women in Industry," pp. 287–88. For a discussion of the rise of feature journalism as a function of urban culture, see Hofstadter, *Age of Reform*, pp. 188–90.
24. Campbell, *Prisoners of Poverty*.
25. Eva McDonald Valesh, writing under the pen name "Eva Gay," published her articles in the Minneapolis Sunday edition of the *St. Paul Globe* from 26 March 1888 through 3 August 1891. Valesh was later an organizer for the American Federation of Labor. I am grateful to Rhoda Gilman, of the Minnesota Historical Society, for bringing the "Eva Gay" articles to my attention.
26. Rhine, "Women in Industry," pp. 302–3.
27. Wisconsin Bureau of Labor Statistics, *First Biennial Report of . . . 1883 and 1884*, p. 109.
28. *Report and Testimony*, 1:3–4; U.S. Department of Labor, *Working Women in Large Cities*; U.S. Department of Labor, Bureau of Labor Statistics, *Summary of Report*; Bullock, *Employment of Women*.
29. Van Vorst and Van Vorst, *Woman Who Toils*, p. 11; Parker, *Working with the Working Woman*.
30. Richardson, *The Long Day*; *Four Years in the Underbrush*; "Girl Who Comes to the City." The expression of similar themes in fiction can be found in such novels as Theodore Dreiser's *Sister Carrie* (1900) and Sinclair Lewis's *The Job* (1917).

31. For a discussion of this idea, see Smith-Rosenberg and Rosenberg, "Female Animal," p. 338.
32. Mary Sidney, "The Ideal Farm Girl," *Farm Journal*, March 1903, reprinted in *So Sweet to Labor*, ed. Juster, p. 65.
33. Juster, *So Sweet to Labor*, pp. 140–78.
34. Van Vorst and Van Vorst, *Woman Who Toils*, pp. 80–82; 160–62.
35. Flora McDonald Thompson, "Truth about Women in Industry," *North American Review*, May 1904, reprinted in Bullock, *Employment of Women*, p. 107.
36. Hall, *Adolescence*, 2:609; Calhoun, *History of the American Family*, 3:92–93.
37. Hall, *Adolescence*, 2:630. See also Hyde, *College Man and the College Woman*.
38. Richardson, "Difficulties and Dangers," pp. 624–26.
39. Henry T. Finck, "Employments Unsuitable for Women," *Independent*, 11 April 1901, portions reprinted in Bullock, *Employment of Women*, pp. 76–78, and in Minnesota Bureau of Labor, *Eighth Biennial Report of . . . 1901–02*, pp. 335–41.
40. Finck, in Bullock, *Employment of Women*, p. 77.
41. Ibid., p. 78.
42. Mary Abigail Dodge, *A New Atmosphere*, p. 27.
43. Ibid., pp. 31–32.
44. Gordon, "Wherein Should the Education of a Woman Differ," pp. 790–91.
45. Ida Husted Harper, "Women Ought to Work," *Independent*, 16 May 1901, reprinted in Bullock, *Employment of Women*, pp. 63–70.
46. A listing of some of the progressive-era studies of working women is presented in U.S. Department of Labor, Women's Bureau, *Women Workers and Their Dependents*, pt. 2.
47. May, *Protestant Churches and Industrial America*; Dorn, *Washington Gladden*.
48. Dorn, *Gladden*, p. 303.
49. Rauschenbusch, *Christianizing the Social Order*, pp. 14–15.
50. May, *Protestant Churches*, pp. 225–31.
51. Wiebe, *Search for Order*, p. 169.
52. Minnesota Bureau of Labor, *Twelfth Biennial Report of . . . 1909–10*, p. 625.
53. MacLean, *Women and Industry*, p. 103.
54. Bullock, *Employment of Women*, p. 4.
55. U.S. Congress, Senate, *Report on Condition*, 13:169.
56. Rauschenbusch, *Christianizing the Social Order*, p. 414.
57. Brandeis and Goldmark, *Women in Industry*, appendix.
58. Penny, *Think and Act*, p. 64; U.S. Congress, Senate, *Report on Condition*, 15:114.
59. Wright, *Working Girls*, p. 128.
60. The commission's report is summarized in Illinois General Assembly, Senate, *Report of the Senate Vice Committee*, p. 26. Hull House reformer Louise DeKoven Bowen found department store work to be especially dangerous. She argued that salesgirls not only worked "surrounded by . . . the luxuries which they all crave" but also exposed to a constant flow of strangers, some of them procurers or otherwise immoral. Bowen, *Department Store Girl*.
61. Klapp, "Relation of Social Vice to Industry," pp. 147–52.
62. Ibid. For the concurring opinion of working-class women that factory work meant low status, see Anthony, *Mothers Who Must Earn*, pp. 51–52.
63. Addams, *A New Conscience*, pp. 91–92.

Chapter 3

1. "Poor Nelly—A Life Sketch," *Household*, 1892, quoted in Juster, *So Sweet to Labor*, pp. 71–72.
2. Pivar, *Purity Crusade*.
3. Rosen and Davidson, eds., *Maimie Papers*, p. xxvii. This estimate may be too high. Prostitutes testifying before the Illinois Vice Commission earned relatively high wages, but paid a good proportion of this money to their madams. See Illinois General Assembly, Senate, *Report of the Senate Vice Committee*, pp. 153, 164, 211, and 215.
4. Valesh, *St. Paul Globe*, 2 September 1888, p. 1. For a discussion of prostitution and the culture of the working class, see Stansell, "Women of the Laboring Poor," chap. 5. Prostitution in the progressive era is examined in Rosen, *Lost Sisterhood*.
5. Anonymous, "My Experiences in New York."
6. Sanger, *History of Prostitution*. See also Ellington, *Women of New York*, p. 589.
7. Bell, *Fighting the Traffic*, p. 68.
8. Pivar, *Purity Crusade*; Wagner, "Virtue against Vice."
9. Minneapolis WCA, *1886 Report*, p. 13, Minneapolis WCA Papers.
10. For another perspective on the issue of reform and its relationship to class, see Berg, *Remembered Gate*.
11. "100-Year Travelers' Aid Calendar," n.d., typewritten, TA Records, Box 2. See also Bertha McCall, "Historical Résumé of Bryan Mullanphy Fund," 1949, typewritten, TA Records, Box 2.
12. Quoted in "Early History of Selected Travelers' Aid Societies and Events in the History of the National Travelers' Aid Association 1917–1918 with Exhibits Compiled by Bertha McCall," n.d., typewritten, p. 4, TA Records, Box 2.
13. "Early History," TA Records, Box 2. See also Weiner, "Our Sisters' Keepers," pp. 193–95, and Chicago YWCA, *1893 Report*, p. 31, Chicago YWCA Records, Box 3.
14. Minneapolis WCA, "Minutes of Meetings of the Travelers' Aid Committee, 1909–1915," typewritten notebook; Minneapolis WCA *1942 Report*, p. 19, Minneapolis WCA Papers.
15. "Early History," p. 41, TA Records, Box 2; Graham, *Grace H. Dodge*, pp. 221–26.
16. "Early History," p. 24, TA Records, Box 2; Baker, *Travelers' Aid Society in America*, p. 20.
17. Russell, *Girl's Fight for a Living*, p. 146.
18. "100-Year Calendar," p. 2, TA Records, Box 2.
19. U.S. Department of Labor, *Working Women in Large Cities*, p. 64; Wolfe, *Lodging House Problem*, pp. 44–50; U.S. Department of Labor, *Summary of Report*, p. 219.
20. Ellington, *Women of New York*, p. 640. See also Hendee, *Growth and Development*, p. 25; Valesh, "Search for Homes," *St. Paul Globe*, 5 August 1888, p. 1; Van Vorst and Van Vorst, *Woman Who Toils*, p. 30. In a novel published in 1863, the heroine, Madge, has a hard time finding respectable lodgings in a New England mill town. When she finally sets up a cottage for herself and a cousin, public opinion is stirred. According to the author, neighbors opine that "'tis very odd and strange for a young lady to commence housekeeping before she is married." Talcott, *Madge*, p. 358.
21. Post, *Etiquette*, p. 288.
22. U.S. Department of Labor, *Working Women in Large Cities*, p. 31.
23. Ibid., p. 32; U.S. Department of Labor, *Boarding Homes and Clubs*, p. 142; Dorothy Richardson, *Long Day*, pp. 287–88.
24. Penny, *Think and Act*, p. 215; Wolfe, *Lodging House Problem*, pp. 145–49. See also Chicago YWCA, *Report 1892–93*, p. 32.
25. The confusion of identity for these early boarding homes is reflected by the difficulties of the Minneapolis Woman's Boarding Home, which reported in 1874 that it had to overcome the "common notion" that it was a rescue home for prostitutes. See *Minneapolis Tribune*, 3

May 1874. This confusion was long-lived. In its 1910 survey of welfare institutions, the U.S. Census Bureau included working women's homes among its tally of homes for dependents, immigrants, prostitutes, the aged, and veterans. See U.S. Bureau of the Census, *Benevolent Institutions*, table III.

26. U.S. Department of Labor, *Working Women in Large Cities*, p. 32.
27. Richmond, *New York*, p. 468. The first temporary home for "respectable women" was the Philadelphia Temporary Home Association, founded in 1849. See U.S. Department of Labor, *Boarding Homes and Clubs*, p. 186.
28. U.S. Department of Labor, *Boarding Homes and Clubs*, pp. 186–88; Richmond, *New York*, pp.470–71; Gardner, "Hotel Is Not a Home."
29. Calculated from U.S. Department of Labor, *Boarding Homes and Clubs*, pp. 190–91, table III.
30. Ibid., p. 152; Tolman and Hemstreet, *Better New York*, p. 139.
31. Bosworth, "Living Wage," p. 29.
32. U.S. Department of Labor, *Boarding Homes and Clubs*, pp. 188–89, table II, pp. 190–91, table III; U.S. Department of Labor, *Working Women in Large Cities*, chap. 2; Gardner, "Hotel Is Not a Home," p. 3; Humphries, "Working Women," pp. 49–52.
33. Chicago YWCA, *1883 Report*, p. 10, Chicago YWCA Records.
34. Minneapolis WCA, *1898 Report*, p. 34, Minneapolis WCA Papers.
35. Richmond, *New York*, pp. 468–69.
36. U.S. Department of Labor, *Boarding Homes and Clubs*, p. 183.
37. Ibid., pp. 194–96, table V.
38. Ibid., pp. 144–45; Kellor, "Immigrant Woman," p. 406.
39. Providence YWCA, *1876 Report*, quoted in Hyman, "Young Women's Christian Association," p. 12; Minneapolis WCA, *1881 Report*, p. 22, Minneapolis WCA Papers.
40. Providence YWCA, *1893 Report*, quoted in Hyman, "Young Women's Christian Association," p. 12; U.S. Department of Labor, *Working Women in Large Cities*, chap. 2.
41. U.S. Department of Labor, *Boarding Homes and Clubs*, p. 156. In the Philadelphia Clinton Street Boarding House, additional restrictions included the exclusion of women from their bedrooms from 7 to 9 P.M., in order to "insure fresh, pure air for sleeping." Board of Commissioners of Public Charities of the Commonwealth of Pennsylvania, *Twenty-second Annual Report* (1892), p. 118.
42. Bosworth, "Living Wage," p. 28; Laughlin, *Work-a-Day Girl*, pp. 137–38.
43. Bosworth, "Living Wage," p. 28; U.S. Department of Labor, *Boarding Homes and Clubs*, pp. 90–91; U.S. Department of Labor, *Working Women in Large Cities*, chap. 2.
44. Minutes of the Woman's Boarding Home, 1879, handwritten, Minneapolis WCA Papers.
45. For a discussion of police station lodging for women who were not criminals, see Barney, "Care of the Criminal," pp. 368–69, and Devoll, "Results of Employment," p. 311.
46. "Miss Hayseed's Adventures," reprinted in Chicago YWCA, *1887–88 Report*, pp. 57–63, Chicago YWCA Papers.
47. Minneapolis WCA, *1888 Report*, p. 14, Minneapolis WCA Papers.
48. U.S. Department of Labor, *Boarding Homes and Clubs*, chap. 2.
49. "Limping Alone," *Annals of No Man's Land*, October 1924, p. 11, Minneapolis WCA Papers. See also Bosworth, "Living Wage," p. 30.
50. Providence YWCA, *1890 Report*, quoted in Hyman, "Young Women's Christian Association," p. 12.
51. U.S. Department of Labor, *Boarding Homes and Clubs*, pp. 146–47.
52. Minneapolis WCA, Minutes of the Woman's Boarding Home, 5 June 1888; May 1887, Minneapolis WCA Records; New York Bureau of Social Hygiene, *Housing Conditions*, p. 66.
53. Bosworth, "Living Wage," p. 30.
54. Campbell, *Problem of the Poor*, p. 225.

55. Rosen, *Maimie Papers*, p. 155.
56. Laughlin, *Work-a-Day Girl*, p. 132. See also Butler, *Women and the Trades*, p. 322.
57. New York Bureau of Social Hygiene, *Housing Conditions*, p. 7.
58. De Graffenried, "Needs of Self-Supporting Women," p. 8.
59. U.S. Department of Labor, *Boarding Homes and Clubs*, p. 145; *Four Years in the Underbrush*, p. 14; Spencer, "What Machine-Dominated Industry Means," p. 208; Nathan, "Women Who Work and Women Who Spend," pp. 648–50.
60. Bosworth, "Living Wage," p. 30; "Girl Who Comes to the City," February 1908, p. 71; December 1908, p. 1226; Donovan, *Saleslady*, p. 176.
61. "Girl Who Comes to the City," February 1908, p. 170; May 1908, p. 593.
62. Minnesota Bureau of Labor Statistics, *First Biennial Report of . . . 1887–88*, pp. 188–89. Another solution to the problem was for women to divide work and housekeeping tasks among themselves. In 1890, for example, five Irish flaxmill operatives rented an apartment and appointed one of their number to stay home and keep house for the group. See De Graffenried, "Needs of Self-Supporting Women," p. 6, and also Anna Steese Richardson, *Girl Who Earns Her Own Living*, pp. 278–81.
63. U.S. Department of Labor, *Boarding Homes and Clubs*, p. 170; McLean, "Eleanor Clubs," pp. 60–61; New York Bureau of Social Hygiene, *Housing Conditions*, pp. 65–76.
64. "The Jane Club," *Inter-Ocean* (July 1892), found in Hull House Scrapbook, 1:15, JAMC. The Jane Club, connected to Hull House, was named for Jane Addams.
65. Marguerite Wells, "Report of the Sub-Committee on Homes for Working Girls," 1917, typewritten, p. 6, Minneapolis WCA Papers.
66. New York Bureau of Social Hygiene, *Housing Conditions*, p. 108. For further discussion of cooperative housekeeping in this period, see Hayden, *Grand Domestic Revolution*, pp. 167–70.
67. Addams, *Spirit of Youth*, p. 15.
68. Addams, *Plea for More Pay*, p. 5.
69. U.S. Congress, Senate, *Report on Condition*, 15:91–92.
70. Bowen, *Road to Destruction*. See also Erenberg, *Steppin' Out*, chap. 3, and Addams, "Why Girls Go Wrong."
71. For the history of the YWCA, see Simms, *Natural History*, and Wilson, *Fifty Years of Association Work*. For a comparison of the efforts of the YWCA to protect young women with the parallel movement of the YMCA to protect young men, see Boyer, *Urban Masses and Moral Order*, pp. 112–20.
72. Massachusetts League of Girls Clubs, leaflet, n.d., Niles Papers, Box 1, folder 7.
73. Graham, *Grace H. Dodge*, pp. 67–68, 103–4; U.S. Department of Labor, *Working Women in Large Cities*, p. 39; National League of Women Workers and Association of Working Girl's Societies, *1890 Report*; *1894 Report*; *1897 Report*; *1901 Report*.
74. National League of Women Workers, leaflet, n.d., Niles Papers, Box 1, folder 2; National League of Girls Clubs, *History of the National League*, pp. 5–36.
75. Grace Hoadley Dodge, "Sunny Spots for Working Girls," p. 8.
76. Ferris, *Girls Clubs*, pp. 155–58.
77. U.S. Department of Labor, *Working Women in Large Cities*, p. 39; Blackwell, "Responsibility of Women," p. 79.
78. Croly, *Thrown on Her Own Resources*, p. 142.
79. Stokes, "Condition of Working Women," pp. 627–37.
80. Ibid., p. 628.
81. "Girl Who Comes to the City," February 1908, p. 172.
82. "The Working Girls Clubs of Chicago," March 1896, clipping, Hull House Scrapbook, 3:69–70, JAMC.

83. Julia Ward Howe, "A Symposium—Domestic Service," *Chatauquan*, February 1891, clipping, Howe Papers, scrapbook vol. 5, p. 6.
84. Minnesota Bureau of Labor, *Eighth Biennial Report of . . . 1901–02*, p. 304.
85. Quoted in Wisconsin Bureau of Labor Statistics, *First Biennial Report of . . . 1883 and 1884*, p. 112.
86. Salmon, *Domestic Service*, chaps. 10–15; Klink, "Housekeeper's Responsibility," pp. 372–81; "Household Labor," *Union Signal*, 4 February 1892, Hull House Scrapbook, 1:13, JAMC.
87. Salmon, *Domestic Service*, p. 133.
88. Ibid., chaps. 8–9; Minnesota Bureau of Labor Statistics, *First Biennial Report of . . . 1887–88*, pp. 149–53; Klink, "Put Yourself in Her Place," p. 16.
89. Herrick, *Expert Maid-Servant*, pp. 125–33. See also Katzman, *Seven Days a Week*, pp. 120–24.
90. Minnesota Bureau of Labor Statistics, *First Biennial Report of . . . 1887–88*, p. 149; Wisconsin Bureau of Labor and Industrial Statistics, *Tenth Biennial Report of . . . 1900–1901*, p. 677; Klink, "Put Yourself in Her Place," p. 16.
91. Minnesota Bureau of Labor Statistics, *First Biennial Report of . . . 1887–88*, pp. 149–51.
92. Salmon, *Domestic Service*, p. 153.
93. Mary Gove Smith, "Immigration as a Source of Supply for Domestic Workers," n.d., typewritten, p. 9, WEIU Papers, Box 7.
94. Ibid., p. 10; Wald, "Immigrant Young Girl," p. 264.
95. This committee was composed of representatives of the Boston Women's Educational and Industrial Union, the New York Association of Household Research, the Philadelphia Civic Club and Housekeeper's Alliance, the College Settlements Association, and the Association of Collegiate Alumnae. See *Bulletin of the Inter-Municipal Committee*, November 1904; Kellor, "Inter-Municipal Research Committee," pp. 193–200.
96. Burrington, "Immigrant in Household Employment," p. 6.
97. Wald, "Immigrant Young Girl," p. 263; Kellor, *Out of Work*, chap. 7; Kellor, "Rights of Patrons," pp. 6–7.
98. Kellor, "Southern Colored Girls," pp. 5–6.
99. Huggins, *Protestants against Poverty*, p. 88; Campbell, *Prisoners of Poverty*, p. 234.
100. Kneeland, *Commercialized Prostitution*, p. 212, table X; U.S. Department of Labor, *Working Women in Large Cities*, pp. 64–75, 625; U.S. Congress, Senate, *Report on Condition*, 15:114.
101. U.S. Congress, Senate, *Report on Condition*, 10:89–91.
102. Dorothy Richardson, "Trades-Unions in Petticoats," p. 489.
103. Raybeck, *History of American Labor*, p. 259; Chafe, *American Woman*, p. 68. For a discussion of the historically low level of unionization among clerical workers, see Feldberg, "Union Fever."
104. Agnes Donham, "History of the Women's Educational and Industrial Union," n.d., typewritten, p. 6, WEIU Papers, vol. 1; Rhine, "Women in Industry," pp. 291–92.
105. For the history of the Consumer's League, see Stewart, *Philanthropic Work*, chap. 16; Nathan, *Story of an Epoch-making Movement*.
106. U.S. Congress, Senate, *Report on Condition*, 10:157–59; U.S. Department of Labor, Women's Bureau, *Towards Better Working Conditions for Women*, pp. 3–5; Clark and Wyatt, *Making Both Ends Meet*, p. 187, n. 1. In 1919, the Women's Trade Union League convened the International Federation of Working Women, a group that met three times between 1919 and 1923 to promote the worldwide organization of women workers. See "International Federation of Working Women," pamphlet, ca. 1919, International Federation of Working Women Papers. For a discussion of the cross-class organization processes

of the Women's Trade Union League, see Moore, "Life and Labor."

107. For a recent examination of labor legislation history, see Baer, *Chains of Protection*.
108. Ibid.; Hutchinson, "Women's Wages," chap. 5. The Women's Bureau cautioned that protective legislation might exclude women from labor that was really less taxing than work at home, adding that "safe standards of work for women must come to be safe standards of work for men also if women are to have an equal chance in industry." U.S. Department of Labor, Women's Bureau, *Employment of Women*, p. 8.
109. Ames, *Sex in Industry*, pp. 151, 141–44.
110. Connecticut Special Commission to Investigate Conditions of Wage-Earning Women and Minors, *1913 Report*, quoted in Brandeis and Goldmark, *Case against Nightwork*, p. 223.
111. John Quincy Ames, *Cooperation*, p. 43.
112. Goldmark, *Fatigue and Efficiency*, pt. 2, pp. 1–26. This volume contains the material submitted in four briefs to the supreme courts of the United States, Illinois, and Ohio between 1908 and 1912 in defense of hours laws for women.
113. U.S. Congress, Senate, *Report on Condition*, 9:62–73; Elizabeth Brandeis, "Women's Hour Legislation," in *History of Labor*, ed. Commons et al., 3:461; Hutchinson, "Women's Wages," p. 147.
114. Brandeis, "Women's Hour Legislation," p. 462.
115. Baer, *Chains of Protection*, pp. 53–54.
116. Brandeis and Goldmark, *Women in Industry*; Brandeis, "Women's Hour Legislation," pp. 474–75.
117. Brandeis, "Women's Hour Legislation," p. 472; U.S. Department of Labor, Women's Bureau, *Employment of Women at Night*, p. 16.
118. U.S. Department of Labor, Women's Bureau, *State Laws Affecting Working Women*, pp. 5–9.
119. De Graffenried, "Needs of Self-Supporting Women," p. 1.
120. Rayback, *History of American Labor*, p. 265; Brandeis, "Hours Laws for Men," in *History of Labor*, ed. Commons et al., 3:540–63.
121. These reports are cited in Goldmark, *Fatigue and Efficiency*, pt. 2, pp. 267–68.
122. Brandeis and Goldmark, *Women in Industry*, p. 47; Brandeis and Goldmark, *Case against Nightwork*, p. 209.
123. Baer, *Chains of Protection*, pp. 79–80.
124. *Muller* v. *Oregon*, p. 7, in Brandeis and Goldmark, *Women in Industry*, appendix.
125. Brandeis and Goldmark, *Case against Nightwork*, pp. 426–27.
126. Ibid., pp. 187–208; Baer, *Chains of Protection*, p. 84; U.S. Department of Labor, Women's Bureau, *Employment of Women at Night*, p. 57.
127. U.S. Department of Labor, Women's Bureau, *Effects of Legislation*, p. 15; U.S. Department of Labor, Women's Bureau, *Effects of Labor Legislation*, p. 105.
128. U.S. Department of Labor, Women's Bureau, *Summary: Effects of Labor Regulation*; Chafe, *American Woman*, pp. 124–25; Rothman, *Woman's Proper Place*, p. 163; *Chicago Tribune*, 3 August 1911, p. 1.
129. U.S. Department of Labor, Women's Bureau, *Development of Minimum Wage Laws*.
130. Kauffman, *House of Bondage*, cited in Bremner, *From the Depths*, p. 239.
131. U.S. Department of Labor, Women's Bureau, *History of Labor Legislation*, p. 130.
132. Russell, *Girl's Fight for a Living*, p. 29.
133. Illinois General Assembly, Senate, *Report of the Senate Vice Committee*, p. 178; Hutchinson, "Women's Wages," pp. 90–92; U.S. Department of Labor, Women's Bureau, *Development of Minimum-Wage Laws*, p. 75. Department store owners had long taken the stand that their saleswomen were not self-supporting. In 1895, a representative of Lord and Taylor's argued that they never hired self-supporting saleswomen because they could not afford to pay wages sufficient for women to live on. See *Report and Testimony*, p. 91.

134. U.S. Department of Labor, Women's Bureau, *History of Labor Legislation*, p. 130.
135. Elizabeth Brandeis, "Minimum Wage Legislation," in *History of Labor*, ed. Commons et al., 3:525; U.S. Department of Labor, Women's Bureau, *Development of Minimum-Wage Laws*, pp. 80–81, table 19.
136. Brandeis, "Minimum Wage Legislation," p. 526.
137. Minnesota Minimum Wage Commission, *First Biennial Report, 1913–1914*, p. 43.
138. Ibid., pp. 32–34, table IX.
139. Brandeis, "Minimum Wage Legislation," p. 525.
140. For example, see Clark and Wyatt, *Making Ends Meet*.
141. Naomi M. to chairman of Minnesota Minimum Wage Commission, 10 November 1920, Minnesota Labor and Industry Department Records, Minimum Wage Correspondence, Box 15.
142. Ibid.; Minnesota Minimum Wage Commission, *Report*; Brandeis, "Minimum Wage Legislation," p. 529.
143. U.S. Department of Labor, Women's Bureau, *Development of Minimum-Wage Laws*, pp. 880–81.
144. U.S. Department of Labor, Women's Bureau, *Proceedings of the Women's Industrial Conference*, p. 139.
145. Hutchinson, "Women's Wages," pp. 129–40.
146. Ibid., p. 136.
147. Ibid., p. 134; Brandeis, "Minimum Wage Legislation," p. 536; Chafe, *American Woman*, p. 125; U.S. Department of Labor, Women's Bureau, *Development of Minimum-Wage Laws*, p. 370.
148. U.S. Department of Labor, Women's Bureau, *Development of Minimum-Wage Laws*, pp. 323–25; Brandeis, "Minimum Wage Legislation," pp. 688–89; Chafe, *American Woman*, p. 81; Wandersee, *Women's Work*, p. 95.
149. "Early History," TA Records, Box 2.
150. See, for example, Hyman, "Young Women's Christian Association," p. 53.
151. U.S. Bureau of the Census, *Women in Gainful Occupations*, pp. 140–47.
152. Katzman, *Seven Days a Week*, pp. 87–91; Stigler, *Domestic Servants*. See also Sutherland, *Americans and Their Servants*, chap. 10.
153. Information Bureau on Women's Work, *Floating World*, p. 11.
154. U.S. Department of Labor, Women's Bureau, *Proceedings of the Women's Industrial Conference*, p. 4.

Chapter 4

1. See, for example, Bancroft, *American Labor Force*; Durand, *Labor Force in the U.S.*
2. U.S. Bureau of the Census, *Women at Work*, p. 15.
3. Tentler, *Wage-Earning Women*, p. 39; U.S. Department of Labor, *Summary of Report*, p. 18. A study of Italian women in New York from 1900 to 1950 observes that married Italian women viewed employment as a component of their strategy for family maintenance. See Cohen, "Workshop to Office," p. 198.
4. Anthony, *Mothers Who Must Earn*, pp. 128–29.
5. Hughes, *Mothers in Industry*, pp. 107–9.
6. Long, *Labor Force under Changing Income and Employment*, pp. 92–93.
7. U.S. Bureau of the Census, *Comparative Occupation Statistics*, p. 92, table XV.
8. Fraundorf, "Labor Force Participation," pp. 401–18.
9. *Report and Testimony*, 1:604.
10. U.S. Department of Labor, *Summary of Report*, pp. 106–7.

11. Hughes, *Mothers in Industry*, pp. 111–13.
12. Untitled MS (ca. 1918), McDowell Papers, Box 4.
13. U.S. Bureau of the Census, *Women in Gainful Occupations*, pp. 73–74.
14. U.S. Department of Labor, Women's Bureau, *Immigrant Woman and Her Job*, p. 17.
15. Wandersee, *Women's Work*, p. 3.
16. U.S. Department of Labor, *Summary of Report*, p. 410; U.S. Bureau of the Census, *Women at Work*, p. 170, table 21.
17. Anthony, *Mothers Who Must Earn*, p. 58; Tentler, *Wage-Earning Women*, p. 47; Hughes, *Mothers in Industry*, p. 143.
18. U.S. Bureau of the Census, *Women in Gainful Occupations*, pp. 80–81.
19. For a discussion of home work, see U.S. Department of Labor, Women's Bureau, *Homework in Bridgeport, Connecticut*, Bulletin 9.
20. Campbell, *Prisoners of Poverty*, p. 201.
21. Butler, *Women and the Trades*, pp. 136–37.
22. U.S. Congress, Senate, *Report on Condition*, 5:57.
23. U.S. Department of Labor, Commissioner of Labor, *Eighteenth Annual Report*, pp. 63, 260, 368.
24. Smuts, *Women and Work*, p. 14; U.S. Department of Labor, Women's Bureau, *Immigrant Woman and Her Job*, p. 62; U.S. Bureau of the Census, *Comparative Occupation Statistics*, p. 30.
25. Brownlee, "Household Values," pp. 199–209.
26. U.S. Department of Labor, Women's Bureau, *Immigrant Woman and Her Job*, p. 13.
27. Schiffman, "Marital and Family Characteristics," p. 13.
28. See, for instance, Ivan Nye and Lois Hoffman, "The Socio-Cultural Setting," in Nye and Hoffman, *Employed Mother in America*, chap. 1; Kreps, *Sex in the Marketplace*, p. 49; Bancroft, *American Labor Force*, pp. 28–29.
29. Oppenheimer, *Female Labor Force*, pp. 39–52; Sum, "Women in the Labor Force," p. 19.
30. Bancroft, *American Labor Force*, p. 29.
31. See table 2, above.
32. National Bureau of Economic Research, *Aspects of Labor Economics*, pp. 98–99. For a discussion of the history of birth control, see Gordon, *Woman's Body, Woman's Right*.
33. Wilson H. Grabill et al., "A Long View," in *American Family in Social-Historical Perspective*, ed. Gordon, pp. 374–76.
34. U.S. Department of Labor, Bureau of Labor Statistics, *Working Women: A Databook*, p. 26, table 26.
35. U.S. Bureau of the Census, *Nineteenth Census of the U.S., 1970*, vol. 1, pt. 1, pp. 688–89, table 216.
36. U.S. Bureau of the Census, *Historical Statistics*, pp. 13–25, table D; U.S. Bureau of the Census, *Nineteenth Census . . . , 1970*, vol. 1, pt. 1, p. 688, table 216; Oppenheimer, *Female Labor Force*, p. 11, table 1.4.
37. See U.S. Bureau of the Census, *Farm Population of the U.S.*, chap. 2.
38. U.S. Bureau of the Census, *Women at Work*, p. 17, table X.
39. Bancroft, *American Labor Force*, p. 54.
40. Sweet, *Women in the Labor Force*, pp. 199–200.
41. Kreps, *Sex in the Marketplace*, p. 49.
42. National Bureau of Economic Research, *Aspects of Labor Economics*, p. 101.
43. Ibid., p. 91.
44. Durand, *Labor Force in the U.S.*, p. 21.
45. Jacob Mincer, "Labor Force Participation," in National Bureau of Economic Research, *Aspects of Labor Economics*, pp. 63–64.
46. Ibid., p. 67.

47. See, for example, Nye and Hoffman, *Employed Mother*, p. 35.
48. Oppenheimer, *Female Labor Force*, pp. 30–35.
49. Cowen, "Case Study of Technological and Social Change," pp. 245–53; Vanek, "Time Spent in Housework," pp. 116–21.
50. U.S. Bureau of the Census, *Occupations of the Twelfth Census*, p. cxlvii.
51. U.S. Bureau of the Census, *Comparative Occupation Statistics*, p. 92, table XV.
52. For a discussion of the child-labor movement, see Trattner, *Crusade for the Children*; Clark, *Child Labor and the Social Conscience*.
53. For an economist's interpretation of why this did not happen, see Mincer, "Labor Force Participation," in National Bureau of Economic Research, *Aspects of Labor Economics*.
54. Schiffman, "Marital and Family Characteristics," p. 363; Kreps, *Sex in the Marketplace*, p. 23, table 2.2.
55. U.S. Department of Labor, Women's Bureau, *Women Workers and Their Dependents*, pp. 12, 40.
56. Dowsall, "Structural and Attitudinal Factors," pp. 121–30.
57. Chafe, *American Woman*, pp. 183–84.
58. Rupp, *Mobilizing Women for War*, p. 177.
59. Oppenheimer, *Female Labor Force*, chap. 3.
60. Bancroft, *American Labor Force*, p. 209, table D-2; Oppenheimer, *Female Labor Force*, p. 47, table 5.3.
61. U.S. Bureau of the Census, *U.S. Census of Population, 1960*, pp. 97–98, table 5.
62. Chafe, *American Woman*, pp. 135–45.
63. Ibid., p. 52.
64. Ibid., p. 141. See also Clive, "Women Workers in World War II," pp. 44–72.
65. Durand, *Labor Force in the U.S.*, p. 26.
66. U.S. Department of Labor, Employment Standards Administration, Women's Bureau, *Minority Women Workers*, p. 9, table 8, p. 6, table 5. See also U.S. Department of Labor, Bureau of Labor Statistics, *Perspectives on Working Women*, p. 102, table 100.
67. Bednarzik and Klein, "Labor Force Trends," p. 3; U.S. Department of Labor, Bureau of Labor Statistics, *Marital and Family Characteristics*, p. 49; U.S. Department of Labor, Bureau of Labor Statistics, *Perspectives*, p. 9, table 10.
68. U.S. Department of Labor, Employment Standards Administration, Women's Bureau, *1975 Handbook on Women Workers*, p. 23; David Ignatius, "Women at Work: The Rich Get Richer as Well-to-do Wives Enter the Labor Force," *Wall Street Journal*, 8 September 1978, p. 1; U.S. Department of Labor, Bureau of Labor Statistics, *Marital and Family Characteristics*, p. A-28, table G.
69. U.S. Department of Labor, Bureau of Labor Statistics, *Perspectives*, p. 26, table 25.
70. Waldman et al., "Working Mothers," pp. 45–48.
71. U.S. Department of Labor, Bureau of Labor Statistics, *Marital and Family Characteristics*, p. A-23, table F; U.S. Department of Labor, Bureau of Labor Statistics, *Perspectives*, p. 27, table 26; Grossman, "Children of Working Mothers," p. 32; Oppenheimer, "Demographic Influence," p. 185.
72. "Census Shows 30% of Mothers with Children under One Held Jobs in '78," *Minneapolis Tribune*, 14 November 1979, p. 8B; Waldman, "Working Mothers," p. 43.

Chapter 5

1. Helen Glenn Tyson, introduction to Hughes, *Mothers in Industry*, p. xiii.
2. Lynd and Lynd, *Middletown in Transition*, p. 182.
3. The decline of family production is evidenced by the increase in commercial food services.

From 1914 to 1925, the production of bakeries increased 60 percent; in the same period, there was growth in the canned goods, delicatessen, and restaurant industries. See LaFollette, *Married Women Homemakers*, p. 27; U.S. Department of Labor, Children's Bureau, *Children of Working Mothers in Philadelphia*; Ogburn, "Family and Its Functions," pp. 664–66.

4. Ogburn, "Family and Its Functions," p. 661.

5. Massachusetts Bureau of Statistics of Labor, *Sixth Annual Report (1875)*, cited in Baker, *Technology and Women's Work*, p. 84.

6. U.S. Industrial Commission, *Report*, vol. 19 (1902), cited in Goldmark, *Fatigue and Efficiency*, p. 285.

7. Gilman believed that children were better off in the hands of experts than in the care of their mothers. She wrote that "a newborn baby leads a far happier, healthier, more peaceful existence in the hands of the good trained nurse, than it does when those skilled hands are gone, and it is left on the trembling knees of the young, untrained mother." See Gilman, *Home*, p. 340; *Women and Economics*.

8. Terhune, "Counting Room," p. 340.

9. "American Woman in the Marketplace," p. 19. For a fuller discussion of the debate over marriage and career in this period, see Masteller, "Marriage or Career, 1880–1914."

10. See, for example, Bromley, "Feminist—New Style," pp. 552–60; Mativity, "Wife, the Home, and the Job," pp. 189–99; Hansel, "What about the Children?," pp. 220–27. See also Coyle, *Jobs and Marriage?*

11. See table 2, above.

12. U.S. Department of Labor, Women's Bureau, *Proceedings of the Women's Industrial Conference*, p. 5.

13. Hughes, *Mothers in Industry*, p. 1.

14. Lynd and Lynd, *Middletown in Transition*, p. 181.

15. Goodsell, *Problems of the Family*, pp. 169–70. For an expression of the idea that women were handicapped in employment pursuits because of "maternal function and periodic illness," see Macy, "Equality of Woman with Man," pp. 705–10.

16. U.S. Department of Labor, Children's Bureau, *Children of Wage-Earning Mothers*, p. 49, quoted in Tentler, *Wage-earning Women*, p. 152.

17. Anthony, *Mothers Who Must Earn*, pp. 15–16.

18. Komarovsky, *Blue-Collar Marriage*.

19. Tyson, "Professional Woman's Baby," p. 192.

20. Van Duzer, *Everyday Living*, pp. 233–34.

21. Coyle, *Jobs and Marriage?*, pp. 53–55.

22. Groves, "Psychology of the Woman Who Works," pp. 94–96.

23. Peters, *Status of the Married Woman Teacher*, pp. 21–22.

24. Pruette, *Women and Leisure*.

25. Littell, "Meditations of a Wage-Earning Wife," pp. 732–33.

26. Coyle, *Jobs and Marriage?*, p. 83.

27. Spencer, *Women's Share in Social Culture*, pp. 165–66.

28. Bromley, "Feminist—New Style."

29. Littell, "Meditations of a Wage-Earning Wife," p. 734.

30. Hinkle, "Changing Marriage," p. 288.

31. For an overview of the "race-suicide" issue, see Gordon, *Woman's Body, Woman's Right*, chap. 7.

32. Calhoun, *Social History of the American Family*, 3:250–52.

33. Popenoe, *Conservation of the Family*, pp. 231–32.

34. Coyle, *Jobs and Marriage?*, pp. 40–41; LaFollette, *Married Women Homemakers*, pp. 54–56.

35. Anna Byrd Kennon, "College Wives Who Work," quoted in Coyle, *Jobs and Marriage?*, p. 40; Kennon, "Gainful Employment of Former Radcliffe Students Who Are Married," 1927, typewritten, WEIU Papers.

36. LaFollette, *Married Women Homemakers*, p. 14; Coyle, *Jobs and Marriage?*, pp. 52–53.

37. U.S. Department of Labor, Children's Bureau, *Infant Mortality*.

38. Ibid. See also Goodsell, *Problems of the Family*, pp. 157–65.

39. Wishy, *Child and the Republic*.

40. Rothman, *Woman's Proper Place*, chap. 3; Greenblatt, *Responsibility for Child Care*, pp. 41–44.

41. Spencer, *Family and Its Members*, chap. 11.

42. Watson, *Psychological Care of Infant and Child*, p. 3. One historian cautions that the expert's advice to mothers does not necessarily reflect common child-rearing practice. See Mechling, "Advice to Historians," pp. 44–63.

43. U.S. Department of Labor, Children's Bureau, *Children of Wage-Earning Mothers*, quoted in Coyle, *Jobs and Marriage?*, p. 50.

44. Goodsell, *Problems of the Family*, pp. 166–67.

45. Ibid., pp. 313, 426.

46. Groves, "Psychology of the Woman Who Works," p. 96.

47. Adams, *Women Professional Workers*, p. 32.

48. Goodsell, *Problems of the American Family*, p. 286.

49. Eleanor Roosevelt, *It's Up to the Women*, pp. 145–50.

50. Peters, *Status of the Teacher*, p. 6.

51. Ibid., p. 23; Hughes, *Mothers Who Must Earn*, pp. 15–16; Elmer, *A Study of Women*. A summary of arguments for and against the employment of married teachers is presented in Lewis, *Personnel Problems*, pp. 185–88.

52. Pruette, *Women Workers through the Depression*, p. 104; Peters, *Status of the Teacher*, p. 9.

53. Gallup, *Gallup Poll*, 1:39; Cantril, *Public Opinion*, p. 1044.

54. LaFollette, *Married Women Homemakers*, p. 15.

55. Peters, *Status of the Teacher*, pp. 10–11.

56. For a summary of these views during the 1930s, see ibid., pp. 11–12; Wandersee, *Women's Work*, chap. 4; and Chafe, *American Woman*, chap. 4.

57. U.S. Department of Labor, Women's Bureau, *Office Work and Office Workers in 1940*.

58. U.S. Department of Labor, Women's Bureau, *Women Workers in Their Family Environment*, p. 1.

59. Rupp, *Mobilizing Women for War*; Straub, "United States Government Policy," pp. 240–54.

60. Rupp, *Mobilizing Women for War*, p. 139; Straub, "United States Government Policy," pp. 241–42.

61. Susan B. Anthony, *Out of the Kitchen*, p. 5.

62. Cantril, *Public Opinion*, p. 1045.

63. Susan B. Anthony, *Out of the Kitchen*, p. 130.

64. Ibid., pp. 6–8; "A Statement from the National Association of Day Nurseries," 15 July 1941, typewritten, CWLA Records, Box 46, folder 8. The National Association of Day Nurseries, formed in 1938, merged with the CWLA in 1942.

65. U.S. Department of Labor, Women's Bureau, *Women Workers in Ten Production Areas*; Cantril, *Public Opinion*, p. 1047.

66. Gorham, *So Your Husband's Gone to War!*, p. 38.

67. One notable exception was the publication in the U.S. of Simone de Beauvoir's *The Second Sex*.

68. Harris, *Beyond Her Sphere*, chap. 6.

69. Friedan, *Feminine Mystique*, p. 38.

70. Friedan notes that *Modern Woman* was "paraphrased ad nauseam in the magazines and in

marriage courses, until most of its statements became a part of the conventional, accepted truth of our time." Ibid., p. 111. See also Lundberg and Farnham, *Modern Woman*, chaps. 7 and 12.

71. Lundberg and Farnham, *Modern Woman*, chap. 12.
72. Dingwall, *American Woman*, p. 273.
73. For a discussion of role confusion, see Craven, *American Family*, pp. 19–20.
74. The popularization of this idea came with the publication of Philip Wylie's *Generation of Vipers* in 1942.
75. Dingwall, *American Woman*, pp. 137–38.
76. Ibid., pp. 138–39.
77. Lundberg and Farnham, *Modern Woman*, chap. 12.
78. Bossard, *Sociology of Child Development*, pp. 380–83. For a review of the experimental literature on maternal employment, see Stoltz, "Effects of Maternal Employment," pp. 749–82.
79. See Schaffer, *Mothering*, pp. 95–100.
80. Komarovsky, *Women in the Modern World*.
81. Josselyn and Goldman, "Should Mothers Work?," pp. 74–87.
82. Bowlby, *Maternal Care*, pp. 15, 67. Bowlby was first published by the World Health Organization in 1951.
83. Ibid., pp. 73, 11.
84. For a critical discussion of Bowlby's theories, see Bowlby, *Maternal Care*, pt. 2; Ainsworth et al., *Deprivation of Maternal Care*; Galinsky and Hooks, *New Extended Family*, pp. 16–17.
85. Friedan, *Feminine Mystique*, pp. 27, 364.
86. For a summary of contemporary feminist writings, see Yates, *What Women Want*.
87. Robert O. Blood, Jr., "The Husband-Wife Relationship," in Hoffman and Nye, *Employed Mother in America*, chap. 20.
88. Callahan, *Working Mother*, p. 20; Benton, *American Male*, chap. 2.
89. Margaret Mead, "A Cultural Anthropologist's Approach to Maternal Deprivation," in Ainsworth et al., *Maternal Deprivation*, pp. 237–54.
90. Stoltz, "Evidence from Research," pp. 722–23.
91. Oettinger, "Maternal Employment," p. 135.
92. Bossard and Boll, *Sociology of Child Development*, p. 277.
93. Yates, *What Women Want*, pp. 3–13.
94. Gallup, *Gallup Poll*, 2:702.
95. Morgan, *Total Woman*.
96. Ignatius, "Women at Work," pp. 1, 18.
97. Fraiberg, *Every Child's Birthright*; Kagan, *Growth of the Child*.

Chapter 6

1. Untitled MS (ca. 1918), McDowell Papers, Box 4.
2. Anthony, *Mothers Who Must Earn*, pp. 151–52; Hughes, *Mothers in Industry*, pp. 194–98.
3. Quoted in Calhoun, *History of the American Family*, 3:73.
4. Addams, "Charity and Social Justice," p. 7.
5. Hughes, *Mothers in Industry*, p. 197.
6. See Bennett, *Woman's Work among the Lowly*.
7. McCullogh, "Poor Widows with Dependent Children," p. 419.
8. Anthony, *Mothers Who Must Earn*, p.154.
9. Thurston, *Dependent Child*; Huggins, *Protestants against Poverty*, pp. 83–94.

10. William Hard, "Motherless Children of Living Mothers," *Delineator* (January 1903), quoted in Bullock, *Mothers' Pensions*, pp. 108–14.

11. Ohio Board of State Charities, *Twenty-third Annual Report*, p. 17.

12. U.S. Bureau of the Census, *Benevolent Institutions* (1904).

13. Bullock, *Mothers' Pensions*, p. 33.

14. Anthony, *Mothers Who Must Earn*, p. 153; Hughes, *Mothers in Industry*, p. 193.

15. Anthony, *Mothers Who Must Earn*, p. 53.

16. Ibid., p. 153.

17. Thurston, *Dependent Child*, pp. 115–16. See also Schneider, "In the Web of Class," chap. 2.

18. Marjory Hall, "For What Does the Day Nursery Stand?," National Federation of Day Nurseries, leaflet no. 5 (ca. 1904), p. 3, Day Care Subject File.

19. "Development of Day Nurseries in Charity Work," n.d. but ca. 1900, typewritten, CWLA Records, Box 21, folder 9; "Origins of Day Nursery Work," 1940, typewritten, CWLA Records, Box 21, folder 9; Beer, *Working Mothers*, p. 35; Steinfels, *Who's Minding the Children?*, p. 36.

20. "The Association of the Day Nurseries of New York City," leaflet, n.d. but ca. 1908, p. 4, Day Care Subject File.

21. "Origins of Day Nursery Work," CWLA Records, Box 21, folder 9; Josephine J. Dodge, "Neighborhood Work," pp. 113–18; U.S. Department of Labor, Women's Bureau, *Employed Mothers*.

22. For a biography of Dodge, see James et al., eds., *Notable American Women*, 1:492–93.

23. "Development of Day Nurseries," p. 2, CWLA Records, Box 21, folder 9; Untitled MS, n.d. but ca. 1910, typewritten, CWLA Records, Box 21, folder 9; Mulry, "Care of Children," p. 170; Hall, "For What Does the Day Nursery Stand?," p. 14; Josephine J. Dodge, "Neighborhood Work," p. 113.

24. Burgess, "Day Nursery Work," p. 424.

25. Rosenau, "Schemes for Self-Help," pp. 179–80.

26. "Historical Sketch of the Day Nursery Movement," 1940, typewritten, pp. 3–7, CWLA Records, Box 21, folder 9; Steinfels, *Who's Minding the Children?*, p. 48; Greenblatt, *Responsibility for Child Care*, pp. 24–27; Burgess, "Day Nursery Work," pp. 426–27.

27. "Development of Day Nurseries," p. 12, CWLA Records, Box 21, folder 9.

28. "Historical Sketch," p. 3, CWLA Records, Box 21, folder 9.

29. Rosenau, "Schemes for Self-Help," p. 181; Higgins and Windom, "Helping Widows," p. 141.

30. Rosenau, "Day Nurseries," p. 337; "Development of Day Nurseries," p. 5.

31. Rosenau, "Day Nurseries," pp. 333–40; "Duties of a Matron," leaflet no. 7, n.d., p. 7, CWLA Records, Box 46, folder 13.

32. Anthony, *Mothers Who Must Earn*, p. 152; Hughes, *Mothers in Industry*, p. 194; U.S. Bureau of the Census, *Benevolent Institutions, 1904*, pp. 30–32; Board of Commissioners of Public Charities of the Commonwealth of Pennsylvania, *Twenty-second Annual Report*, pp. 136–38.

33. Anthony, *Mothers Who Must Earn*, p. 152.

34. Hughes, *Mothers in Industry*, p. 197.

35. Quoted in Tentler, *Wage-Earning Women*, p. 162.

36. Ibid.

37. Steinfels, *Who's Minding the Children?*, p. 52; E. H. Lewinski-Corwin, "Day Nurseries in New York City," in Association of Day Nurseries of New York City, *1924 Report*, CWLA Records, Box 21, folder 9.

38. Addams, "Charity and Social Justice," p. 7; Wolcott, "Discussion," p. 423.

39. C. C. Carstens, "Social Security through Aid for Dependent Children in their Own Homes,"

n.d., typewritten, Carstens Papers, Box 1.

40. U.S. Department of Labor, Children's Bureau, *Laws Relating to Mothers' Pensions.*

41. L. A. Halbert, "The Widows' Allowance Act in Kansas City," *Survey*, 28 February 1914, pp. 675–76, quoted in Bullock, *Mothers' Pensions*, p. 9.

42. U.S. Department of Labor, Children's Bureau, *Administration of Mothers' Aid*; U.S. Department of Labor, Children's Bureau, *Laws Relating to Mothers' Pensions*, pp. 12–16; Hall, *Mothers' Assistance in Philadelphia*, p. 2.

43. New York Commission on Relief for Widowed Mothers, *1914 Report*, quoted in Bullock, *Mothers' Pensions*, pp. 32–34.

44. Merrit W. Pinckney, "Public Pensions to Widows," *Child*, July 1912, quoted in Bullock, *Mothers' Pensions*, p. 150.

45. "The Needy Mother and the Neglected Child," *Outlook*, 7 June 1913, quoted in Bullock, *Mothers' Pensions*, p. 28; New York Conference of Charities and Correction, *Proceedings, 1912*, p. 77.

46. I would like to thank Blanche D. Coll for sharing with me her ideas about mothers' pensions and the progressives.

47. William Hard, "Motherless Children of Living Mothers," *Delineator*, January 1913, quoted in Bullock, *Mothers' Pensions*, p. 113.

48. Boston Society for Helping Destitute Mothers and Infants, *1912 Report*, Schlesinger Library, Radcliffe College, Cambridge, Mass.

49. Ben B. Lindsey, "The Mothers' Compensation Law of Colorado," *Survey*, 15 February 1913, quoted in Bullock, *Mothers' Pensions*, p. 23.

50. *Life and Labor*, December 1919, pp. 307–10; "Working Women and the World," leaflet, 1919, International Federation of Working Women Papers.

51. C. C. Carstens, "Recent Trends in Child Care," 21 June 1932, typewritten, Carstens Papers, Box 1.

52. Bullock, *Mothers' Pensions*, p. x; New York Conference of Charities and Correction, *Proceedings, 1912*, pp. 93–94; Bremner, *From the Depths*, pp. 222–23.

53. U.S. Department of Labor, *Laws Relating to Mothers' Pensions*, pp. 12–14.

54. Bogue, "Problems in Administration," p. 352; U.S. Department of Labor, *Laws Relating to Mothers' Pensions*, p. 14; Hall, *Mothers' Assistance in Philadelphia*, pp. 2–11.

55. U.S. Department of Labor, Children's Bureau, *Mothers' Aid 1931*, pp. 13–14.

56. Travis, "Origins of Mothers' Pensions," pp. 422–43; "Widows' Pension Legislation," p. v.; Lundberg, "Aid to Mothers," p. 101.

57. U.S. Department of Labor, *Laws Relating to Mothers' Pensions*, pp. 15–16; U.S. Department of Labor, *Administration of Mothers' Aid*, p. 43.

58. U.S. Department of Labor, *Laws Relating to Mothers' Pensions*, p. 15; "Widows' Pension Legislation," p. 73; Tyson, "The Fatherless Family," p. 86.

59. U.S. Department of Labor, *Children of Wage-Earning Mothers*, p. 81; U.S. Congress, Senate, *Proceedings of the Conference on the Care of Dependent Children*, p. 35; Bogue, "Problems in Administration," p. 354.

60. Helen Tyson, Foreword to Hughes, *Mothers in Industry*, p. xiv.

61. Richmond and Hall, *Study of Nine Hundred and Eighty-Five Widows*, p. 21.

62. Lundberg, "Aid to Mothers," p. 101.

63. U.S. Bureau of the Census, *Children under Institutional Care, 1923*, p. 14, table 1, p. 29, table 9; U.S. Congress, Senate, *Mothers' Aid in the District of Columbia*, p. 35.

64. U.S. Congress, Senate, *Mothers' Aid in the District of Columbia*, p. 34.

65. Halbert, "Widows' Allowance Act," quoted in Bullock, *Mothers' Pensions*, p. 8. See also Lewinski-Corwin, "Day Nurseries in New York City."

66. Anonymous, "We Both Had Jobs," *Woman's Home Companion*, August 1925, quoted in Coyle, *Jobs and Marriage?*, p. 34.

67. See Kennon, "Gainful Employment of Radcliffe Students."
68. Greenblatt, *Responsibility for Child Care*, p. 49.
69. Chambers, "Plea for Teachers," p. 574.
70. Greenblatt, *Responsibility for Child Care*, p. 53; Lois Hayden Meek, "Minimum Essentials for Nursery School Education," 1929, typescript, CWLA Records, Box 21, folder 9.
71. Greenblatt, *Responsibility for Child Care*, p. 48.
72. Steinfels, *Who's Minding the Children?*, p. 63.
73. Ibid., p. 64.
74. Ibid., p. 767; Marion S. Newcombe, "Nursery Education in New York City," n.d., typewritten, CWLA Records, Box 46, folder 14; U.S. Department of Labor, Women's Bureau, *Employed Mothers and Child Care*, p. 15.
75. U.S. Office of Education, "School Services," p. 6.
76. "A Statement from the National Association of Day Nurseries," 15 July 1941, typewritten, p. 3, CWLA Records, Box 46, folder 8.
77. Emma O. Lundberg, "A Community Program of Day Care for Children of Mothers Employed in Defense Areas," December 1941, typewritten, CWLA Records, Box 22, folder 1; Steinfels, *Who's Minding the Children?*, p. 67.
78. Susan B. Anthony II, *Out of the Kitchen*, p. 134; Goodlad et al., *Early Schooling*, pp. 6–7.
79. "Day Care of Children in Post-War United States," May 1945, typewritten, p. 2, CWLA Records, Box 22, folder 1; Rothman, *Woman's Proper Place*, p. 223.
80. Child Care Center Parents' Association of New York, *1948 Report*, p. 4, Child Care Center Parents' Association of New York Records, Box 1, folder 2.
81. Child Care Center Parents' Association of New York, untitled MS, n.d., Child Care Center Parents' Association of New York Records, Box 2, folder 11; Greenblatt, *Responsibility for Child Care*, p. 64.
82. "Day Care of Children in Post-War United States," CWLA Records, p. 4.
83. "History of Brightside Day Nursery," 1948, typewritten, p. 9, CWLA Records, Box 22, folder 1.
84. U.S. Department of Labor, Women's Bureau, *Employed Mothers and Child Care*.
85. Cited in Binder, "Affirmative Day Care," p. 24.
86. Steinfels, *Who's Minding the Children?*, p. 72.
87. Binder, "Affirmative Day Care," pp. 24–28.
88. For a general history of government aid to mothers, see Bell, *Aid to Dependent Children*.
89. Steinfels, *Who's Minding the Children?*, pp. 81–82; Greenblatt, *Responsibility for Child Care*, p. 134.
90. Greenblatt, *Responsibility for Child Care*, pp. 267–69; Bane et al., "Child-Care Arrangements," p. 52.
91. U.S. Congress, Senate, *Hearings . . . before the Committee on Finance*, p. 93.
92. For the details of this debate, see ibid.; Rothman, *Woman's Proper Place*, pp. 267–81. See also Clarke-Stewart, *Daycare*.
93. See U.S. Congress, Senate, *Veto Message*.
94. Michael T. Kaufman, "Day-Care Truce Ends Sit-In at Lindsay Center," *New York Times*, 20 January 1972, p. 41.
95. Steinfels, *Who's Minding the Children?*, p. 197; Levitan and Alderman, *Child Care*, p. 3; U.S. Bureau of the Census, *Statistical Abstract, . . . 1980*, p. 147, table 234; Bane, "Child-Care Arrangements," p. 52.
96. Featherstone, "Kentucky-Fried Children," pp. 12–16; Thomas J. Bray, "Mother's Helper," *Wall Street Journal*, 10 April 1970, p. 1.
97. U.S. Department of Labor, *Working Women*, p. 25, table 25.
98. Waldman, "Working Mothers in the 1970s," pp. 39–40; Grossman, "Children of Working Mothers," p. 32.

99. Levitan and Alderman, *Child Care*, pp. 110–11; Nona Glazer et al., "The Homemaker, the Family, and Employment," in *Women in the U.S. Labor Force*, ed. Cahn, pp. 155–69.
100. Bane, "Child-Care Arrangements," p. 51.
101. For a comparison with European day-care policies, see Alice H. Cook, "Working Women: European Experience and American Need," in *Women in the U.S. Labor Force*, ed. Cahn, pp. 271–306.
102. Carol S. Greenwald, "Part-Time Work," in *Women in the U.S. Labor Force*, ed. Cahn, pp. 182–94; Waldman, "Working Mothers in the 1970s," p. 40. See also U.S. Bureau of the Census, *Statistical Abstract, . . . 1981*, p. 384, table 642, p. 389, table 657.
103. Giraldo, *Public Policy*, p. 29.

Conclusion

1. U.S. Department of Labor, Bureau of Labor Statistics, *Working Women*, p. 15; Masnick and Bane, *Nation's Families*, chap. 3.
2. U.S. Department of Labor, Bureau of Labor Statistics, *Children of Working Mothers*, p. 1; Shreve, "Careers and the Lure of Motherhood," p. 39.
3. I am grateful to Patsy L. Chronis, director of the Circle Children's Center, University of Illinois at Chicago, and Brian Vaughn, Psychology Department, University of Illinois at Chicago, for sharing with me their ideas about current issues in child-care policy. For a recent discussion of the literature on maternal employment, see Shreve, "Careers and the Lure of Motherhood," pp. 48–50.
4. Suransky, *Erosion of Childhood*, p. 185.
5. Ibid.; Featherstone, "Kentucky-Fried Children," p. 15. For another point of view, see Clarke-Stewart, *Daycare*.
6. Clarke-Stewart, *Daycare*, p. 136; Suransky, *Erosion of Childhood*, pp. 200–203.

Bibliography

Manuscript Sources

Cambridge, Massachusetts
  Schlesinger Library, Radcliffe College
    Child Care Center Parents' Association of New York Records.
    Day Care Subject File.
    Julia Ward Howe Papers.
    International Federation of Working Women Papers.
    Marion H. Niles Papers.
    Women's Educational and Industrial Union Papers.
Chicago, Illinois
  Chicago Historical Society
    Mary McDowell Papers.
  The University Library, University of Illinois at Chicago
    Jane Addams Memorial Collection.
    Young Women's Christian Association of Metropolitan Chicago Records.
Minneapolis, Minnesota
  Minneapolis Woman's Christian Association
    Minneapolis Woman's Christian Association Papers.
  Social Welfare History Archives, University of Minnesota
    Christian Carl Carstens Papers.
    Child Welfare League of America Records.
    Travelers' Aid Association of America Records.
St. Paul, Minnesota
  Minnesota State Archives, Minnesota Historical Society
    Minnesota Labor and Industry Department Records.

Government Publications

U.S. Bureau of the Census. *Benevolent Institutions*. Washington, D.C.: GPO, 1904.
_____. *Benevolent Institutions*. Washington, D.C.: GPO, 1910.
_____. *Children under Institutional Care, 1923*. Washington, D.C.: GPO, 1927.
_____. *Comparative Occupation Statistics for the United States, 1870–1940*, by Alba M. Edwards. Washington, D.C.: GPO, 1943.
_____. *Earnings of Factory Workers, 1899 to 1927*, by Paul F. Brissenden. Washington, D.C.: GPO, 1929.
_____. *Farm Population of the United States*, by Leon E. Truesdell. Washington, D.C.: GPO, 1926.
_____. *Historical Statistics of the United States*. Washington, D.C.: GPO, 1960.
_____. *Nineteenth Census of the U.S., 1970: U.S. Summary*. Vol. 1. Washington, D.C.: GPO, 1971.
_____. *Occupations of the Twelfth Census*. Washington, D.C.: GPO, 1904.
_____. *Statistical Abstract of the United States, 1980*. 101 ed. Washington, D.C.: GPO, 1980.

————. *Statistical Abstract of the United States, 1981.* 102 ed. Washington, D.C.: GPO, 1981.

————. *Statistics of Women at Work.* Washington, D.C.: GPO, 1907.

————. *U.S. Census of Population, 1960: Subject Reports: Marital Status.* Final Report PC(2)-4E. Washington, D.C.: GPO, 1966.

————. *Women in Gainful Occupations, 1870–1920,* by Joseph Hill. Washington, D.C.: GPO, 1929.

U.S. Congress. Senate. *Hearings on S. 2003, before the Committee on Finance,* 92d Cong., 1st sess., 1971.

————. *Mothers' Aid in the District of Columbia: Hearings on S. 120 and S. 129.* 69th Cong., 1st sess., 1926.

————. *Proceedings of the Conference on the Care of Dependent Children.* 60th Cong., 2d sess., 1909. S. Doc. 721.

————. *Report on Condition of Woman and Child Wage-Earners in the United States.* Vol. 5: *Wage-Earning Women in Stores and Factories.* 61st Cong., 2d sess., 1910. S. Doc. 645.

————. *Report on Condition of Woman and Child Wage-Earners in the United States.* Vol. 9: *History of Women in Industry in the United States,* by Helen L. Sumner. 61st Cong., 2d sess., 1910. S. Doc. 645.

————. *Report on Condition of Woman and Child Wage-Earners in the United States.* Vol. 10: *History of Women in Trade Unions,* by John B. Andrews and W. D. P. Bliss. 61st Cong., 2d sess., 1910. S. Doc. 645.

————. *Report on Condition of Woman and Child Wage-Earners in the United States.* Vol. 13: *Infant Mortality and Its Relation to the Employment of Mothers.* 61st Cong., 2d sess., 1912. S. Doc. 645.

————. *Report on Condition of Woman and Child Wage-Earners in the United States.* Vol. 15: *Relation between Occupation and Criminality of Women,* by Mary Conyington. 61st Cong., 2d sess., 1912. S. Doc. 645.

————. *Veto Message—Economic Opportunity Amendments of 1971.* 120th Cong., 1st sess., 1971. S. Doc. 92-48.

U.S. Department of Labor. *Boarding Homes and Clubs for Working Women,* by Mary S. Fergusson. Department of Labor Bulletin no. 15. Washington, D.C.: GPO, 1898.

U.S. Department of Labor. Bureau of Labor Statistics. *Children of Working Mothers.* Bulletin 2158. Washington, D.C.: GPO, 1983.

————. *Children of Working Mothers, March 1977.* Special Labor Force Report no. 217. Washington, D.C.: GPO, 1977.

————. *Families and the Rise of Working Wives: An Overview.* Special Labor Force Report no. 189. Washington, D.C.: GPO, 1979.

————. *Handbook of Labor Statistics, 1978.* Bulletin 2000. Washington, D.C.: GPO, 1979.

————. *Marital and Family Characteristics of Workers, 1970–1978.* Special Labor Force Report no. 219. Washington, D.C.: GPO, 1979.

————. *Marital and Family Patterns of Workers: An Update.* Bulletin 2163. Washington, D.C.: GPO, 1983.

————. *Perspectives on Working Women: A Databook.* Bulletin 7080. Washington, D.C.: GPO, 1980.

————. *Summary of the Report on Condition of Woman and Child Wage-Earners in the United States.* Women in Industry Series no. 5. Bulletin of the Bureau of Labor Statistics no. 175. Washington, D.C.: GPO, 1916.

————. *Working Women: A Databook.* Bulletin 1977. Washington, D.C.: GPO, 1977.

U.S. Department of Labor. Children's Bureau. *Administration of Mothers' Aid in Ten Localities,* by Mary F. Bogue. Publication no. 184. Washington, D.C.: GPO, 1928.

————. *Children of Wage-Earning Mothers: A Study of a Selected Group in Chicago.* Publication no. 102. Washington, D.C.: GPO, 1922.

_____. *Children of Working Mothers in Philadelphia*, by Clara M. Beyer. Publication no. 204. Washington, D.C.: GPO, 1931.

_____. *Infant Mortality: Results of a Field Study in New Bedford, Mass.* Publication no. 68. Washington, D.C.: GPO, 1920.

_____. *Laws Relating to "Mothers' Pensions" in the United States, Denmark, and New Zealand.* Publication no. 7. Washington, D.C.: GPO, 1914.

_____. *Mothers' Aid 1931.* Publication no. 220. Washington, D.C.: GPO, 1933.

U.S. Department of Labor. Commissioner of Labor. *Eighteenth Annual Report: Cost of Living and Retail Prices of Food.* Washington, D.C.: GPO, 1904.

_____. *Fourth Annual Report: Working Women in Large Cities.* Washington, D.C.: GPO, 1889.

U.S. Department of Labor. Employment Standards Administration. *Minority Women Workers: A Statistical Overview.* Rev. ed. Washington, D.C.: GPO, 1977.

_____. *1975 Handbook on Women Workers.* Bulletin no. 297. Washington, D.C.: GPO, 1975.

U.S. Department of Labor. Women's Bureau. *The Development of Minimum-Wage Laws in the United States, 1912 to 1927.* Bulletin no. 61. Washington, D.C.: GPO, 1927.

_____. *The Effects of Labor Legislation on the Employment Opportunities for Women.* Bulletin no. 65. Washington, D.C.: GPO, 1928.

_____. *Employed Mothers and Child Care.* Bulletin no. 246. Washington, D.C.: GPO, 1953.

_____. *The Employment of Women at Night*, by Mary D. Hopkins. Bulletin no. 64. Washington, D.C.: GPO, 1928.

_____. *The Employment of Women in Hazardous Industries in the United States.* Bulletin no. 6. Washington, D.C.: GPO, 1920.

_____. *The Family Status of Breadwinning Women: A Study of Material in the Census Schedules of a Selected Locality.* Bulletin no. 23. Washington, D.C.: GPO, 1922.

_____. *History of Labor Legislation for Women in Three States*, by Clara M. Beyer, and *Chronological Development of Labor Legislation for Women in the United States*, by Florence Smith. Bulletin no. 66. Washington, D.C.: GPO, 1929.

_____. *Homework in Bridgeport, Connecticut.* Bulletin no. 9. Washington, D.C.: GPO, 1920.

_____. *The Immigrant Woman and Her Job*, by Caroline Manning. Bulletin no. 74. Washington, D.C.: GPO, 1930.

_____. *Office Work and Office Workers in 1940.* Bulletin no. 188. Washington, D.C.: GPO, 1942.

_____. *Proceedings of the Women's Industrial Conference.* Bulletin no. 33. Washington, D.C.: GPO, 1923.

_____. *The Share of Wage-Earning Women in Family Support.* Bulletin no. 30. Washington, D.C.: GPO, 1923.

_____. *Some Effects of Legislation Limiting Hours of Work for Women.* Bulletin no. 15. Washington, D.C.: GPO, 1921.

_____. *State Laws Affecting Working Women: Hours, Minimum Wage, Home Work.* Bulletin no. 63. Washington, D.C.: GPO, 1927.

_____. *Summary: The Effects of Labor Regulation on the Employment Opportunities of Women.* Bulletin no. 68. Washington, D.C.: GPO, 1928.

_____. *Towards Better Working Conditions for Women.* Bulletin no. 352. Washington, D.C.: GPO, 1953.

_____. *Women Workers and Their Dependents*, by Mary-Elizabeth Pidgeon. Bulletin no. 239. Washington, D.C.: GPO, 1951.

_____. *Women Workers in Ten Production Areas and Their Postwar Production Plans.* Bulletin no. 209. Washington, D.C.: GPO, 1946.

_____. *Women Workers in Their Family Environment.* Bulletin no. 183. Washington, D.C.: GPO, 1941.

U.S. Office of Education. *School Services for Children of Working Mothers*. School Children and the War Leaflet no. 1. Washington, D.C.: GPO, 1943.

Books and Articles

Abbott, Edith. *Women in Industry: A Study in American Economic History*. New York: D. Appleton and Company, 1910.

Adams, Elizabeth Kemper. *Women Professional Workers: A Study Made for the Women's Educational and Industrial Union*. New York: Macmillan, 1921.

Addams, Jane. "Charity and Social Justice." *Proceedings of the National Conference of Charities and Correction, 37th Annual Meeting*. Fort Wayne, Ind.: Archer Publishing, 1910.

————. *A New Conscience and an Ancient Evil*. New York: Macmillan, 1912.

————. *A Plea for More Play, More Pay, and More Education for Our Factory Girls and Boys*. Chicago: Chicago Association of Commerce, [1914?].

————. *The Spirit of Youth and the City Streets*. New York: Macmillan, 1909.

————. "Why Girls Go Wrong." *Ladies' Home Journal*, September 1907, pp. 13–14.

Ainsworth, Mary D. *Deprivation of Maternal Care: A Reassessment of Its Effects*. New York: Schocken, 1966. Part 2 of *Maternal Care and Mental Health: A Report Prepared on Behalf of the World Health Organization as a Contribution to the United Nations Programme for the Welfare of Homeless Children*, by John Bowlby. 1951. Reprint. New York: Schocken, 1966.

"The American Woman in the Marketplace." *Ladies' Home Journal*, April 1900.

Ames, Azel, Jr. *Sex in Industry: A Plea for the Working-Girl*. Boston: James R. Osgood and Co., 1875.

Ames, John Quincy, comp. *Co-operation between the Young Women's and the Young Men's Christian Associations*. Chicago: Young Men's Christian Association College, 1929.

Anthony, Katherine. *Mothers Who Must Earn*. New York: Survey Associates, 1914.

Anthony, Susan Brownell, II. *Out of the Kitchen—Into the War*. New York: Stephan Daye, 1943.

Baer, Judith A. *The Chains of Protection: The Judicial Response to Women's Labor Legislation*. Contributions to Women's Studies no. 1. Westport, Conn.: Greenwood Press, 1978.

Baker, Elizabeth Faulkner. *Technology and Woman's Work*. New York: Columbia University Press, 1964.

Baker, Orin C. *Travelers' Aid Society in America: Protection from Danger and Prevention of Crime for Travelers, Especially Young Women, Girls, and Boys Travelling Alone*. New York: Funk and Wagnalls, 1917.

Bancroft, Gertrude. *The American Labor Force: Its Growth and Changing Composition*. New York: John Wiley and Sons, 1958.

Bane, Mary Jo, et al. "Child-Care Arrangements of Working Parents." *Monthly Labor Review* 102 (October 1979): 50–56.

Barney, Susan Hammond. "Care of the Criminal." In *Woman's Work in America*, edited by Annie Nathan Meyer, pp. 359–72. New York: Henry Holt, 1891.

Baxandall, Rosalyn; Gordon, Linda; and Reverby, Susan, eds. *America's Working Women: A Documentary History 1600 to the Present*. New York: Vintage Books, 1976.

Beauvoir, Simone de. *The Second Sex*. New York: Alfred A. Knopf, 1952.

Bednarzik, Robert W., and Klein, Deborah P. "Labor Force Trends: A Synthesis and Analysis." *Monthly Labor Review* 100 (October 1977): 3–11.

Beecher, Catharine E. *The Evils Suffered by American Women and Children: The Causes and the Remedy*. New York: Harper and Brothers, 1846.

Beer, Ethel S. *Working Mothers and the Day Nursery*. New York: Whiteside, Inc., and William Morrow and Co., 1957.

Bell, Ernest. *Fighting the Traffic in Young Girls, Or War on the White Slave Trade*. N.p.: 1910.

Bell, Winifred. *Aid to Dependent Children*. New York: Columbia University Press, 1965.

Bennett, Sarah R. I. *Woman's Work among the Lowly: Memorial Volume of the First Forty Years of the American Female Guardian Society and Home for the Friendless*. New York: American Female Guardian Society, 1877.

Benson, Mary Sumner. *Women in Eighteenth-Century America: A Study of Opinion and Social Usage*. Columbia University Studies in History, Economics and Public Law no. 405. New York: Columbia University Press, 1935.

Benson, Susan Porter. " 'The Customers Ain't God': The Work Culture of Department-Store Saleswomen, 1890–1940." In *Working-Class America: Essays on Labor, Community, and American Society*, edited by Michael H. Frisch and Daniel J. Walkowitz, pp. 185–211. Urbana, Ill.: University of Illinois Press, 1983.

Berg, Barbara J. *The Remembered Gate: Origins of American Feminism*. New York: Oxford University Press, 1978.

Binder, Gertrude. "Affirmative Day Care." *Social Work Journal* 34 (January 1953): 24–28.

Blackwell, Emily. "The Responsibility of Women in Regard to Questions Concerning Public Morality." In *The National Purity Congress*, edited by Aaron M. Powell. New York: American Purity Alliance, 1896.

Bliven, Bruce, Jr. *The Wonderful Writing Machine*. New York: Random House, 1954.

Bloch, Ruth H. "American Feminine Ideals in Transition: The Rise of the Moral Mother, 1785–1815." *Feminist Studies* 4 (June 1978): 101–26.

Board of Commissioners of Public Charities of the Commonwealth of Pennsylvania. *Twenty-second Annual Report*. Harrisburg, Pa.: Edwin K. Meyers, 1892.

Bogue, Mary. "Problems in the Administration of Mothers' Aid." *Proceedings of the National Conference of Charities and Correction, 45th Annual Meeting*. Chicago: Rogers and Hall, 1918.

Bossard, James H. S. *The Sociology of Child Development*. New York: Harper and Row, 1948.

––––––, and Boll, Eleanor Stokes. *The Sociology of Child Development*. 4th ed. New York: Harper and Row, 1966.

Bosworth, Louise Marion. "The Living Wage of Women Workers: A Study of Incomes and Expenditures of Four Hundred and Fifty Women Workers in the City of Boston." Supplement to the *Annals of the American Academy of Political and Social Science* 37 (May 1911): 1–90.

Bowen, Louise DeKoven. *The Department Store Girl: Based upon Interviews with 200 Girls*. Chicago: Juvenile Protective Association, 1911.

––––––. *The Road to Destruction Made Easy in Chicago*. Chicago: Hale-Crossley Printing, 1916.

Bowlby, John. *Maternal Care and Mental Health: A Report Prepared on Behalf of the World Health Organization as a Contribution to the United Nations Programme for the Welfare of Homeless Children*. Part 1. 1951. Reprint. New York: Schocken, 1966.

Boyer, Paul. *Urban Masses and Moral Order in America*. Cambridge, Mass.: Harvard University Press, 1975.

Brandeis, Louis D., and Goldmark, Josephine. *The Case against Nightwork for Women; The People of the State of New York, Respondent, against Charles Schweinler Press, A Corporation, Defendant-Appellant*. 1914. Rev. ed. New York: National Consumers' League, 1914.

––––––. *Women in Industry; Decision of the United States Supreme Court in Curt Muller vs. State of Oregon Upholding the Constitutionality of the Oregon Ten-Hour Law for Women, and Brief for the State of Oregon*. New York: National Consumers' League, [1908]. Reprint. New York: Arno Press, 1969.

Bremner, Robert. *From the Depths: The Discovery of Poverty in the United States*. New York: New York University Press, 1956.

Brenton, Myron. *The American Male*. Greenwich, Conn.: Fawcett Publications, 1966.

Bromley, Dorothy Dunbar. "Feminist—New Style." *Harper's Monthly Magazine*, October 1927, pp. 552–60.

Brownlee, W. Elliot. "Household Values, Women's Work, and Economic Growth, 1880–1930." *Journal of Economic History* 39 (March 1979): 199–209.

————, and Brownlee, Mary M., eds. *Women in the American Economy: A Documentary History, 1675 to 1929*. New Haven: Yale University Press, 1976.

Bullock, Edna, comp. *Selected Articles on the Employment of Women*. Debaters' Handbook Series. Minneapolis: H. W. Wilson, 1911.

————. *Selected Articles on Mothers' Pensions*. Debaters' Handbook Series. New York: H. W. Wilson, 1915.

Burgess, M. H. "Day Nursery Work." *Proceedings of the National Conference of Charities and Correction, 19th Annual Meeting*. Boston: Geo. H. Ellis, 1892.

Burrington, Venila S. "The Immigrant in Household Employment." *Bulletin of the Inter-Municipal Committee on Household Research*, February 1905, pp. 5–8.

Bushman, Claudia L. *"A Good Poor Man's Wife": Being a Chronicle of Harriet Hanson Robinson and Her Family in Nineteenth-Century New England*. Hanover, N.H.: University Press of New England, 1981.

Butler, Elizabeth Beardsley. *Women and the Trades: Pittsburgh, 1907–1908*. Volume 1 of the Pittsburgh Survey, edited by Paul Underwood Kellogg. New York: Charities Publication Committee, 1909.

Cahn, Anne Foote, ed. *Women in the U.S. Labor Force*. New York: Praeger Publishers, 1979.

Calhoun, Arthur Wallace. *A Social History of the American Family from Colonial Times to the Present*. 3 vols. Cleveland: Arthur H. Clark, 1917–19.

Callahan, Sidney Cornelia. *The Working Mother*. New York: Macmillan, 1971.

Campbell, Helen. *Prisoners of Poverty: Women Wage-Workers, Their Trades and Their Lives*. Boston: Roberts Brothers, 1887.

————. *The Problem of the Poor: A Record of Quiet Work in Unquiet Places*. New York: Fords, Howard and Hulbert, 1882.

Candee, Helen Churchill. *How Women May Earn a Living*. New York: Macmillan, 1900.

Cantril, Hadley. *Public Opinion, 1935–1946*. Princeton, N.J.: Princeton University Press, 1951.

Carey, Matthew. *Miscellaneous Essays*. Philadelphia: Carey and Hart, 1830.

Chafe, William H. *The American Woman: Her Changing Social, Economic, and Political Roles, 1920–1970*. New York: Oxford University Press, 1972.

Chambers, M. M. "A Plea for Married Women Teachers." *School and Society* 30 (26 October 1919): 572–75.

Clark, Davis Wasgatt. *Child Labor and the Social Conscience*. New York: Abingdon Press, 1924.

Clark, Sue Ainslie, and Wyatt, Edith. *Making Both Ends Meet: The Income and Outlay of New York Working Girls*. New York: Macmillan, 1911.

Clarke-Stewart, Alison. *Daycare*. Cambridge, Mass.: Harvard University Press, 1982.

Clive, Alan. "Women Workers in World War II: Michigan as a Test Case." *Labor History* 20 (Winter 1979): 44–72.

Cohen, Miriam Judith. "From Workshop to Office: Italian Women and Family Strategies in New York City, 1900–1950." Ph.D. dissertation, University of Michigan, 1978.

Commons, John Roger, et al., eds. *A Documentary History of American Industrial Society*. Vol. 6. New York: Russell and Russell, 1958.

————. *History of Labor in the United States*. Vol. 3. New York: Macmillan, 1918–35.

Conk, Margo A. "Accuracy, Efficiency, and Bias: The Interpretation of Women's Work in the U.S. Census of Occupations, 1890–1940." *Historical Methods* 14 (Spring 1981): 65–72.

Cott, Nancy F. *The Bonds of Womanhood: "Woman's Sphere" in New England, 1780–1835*. New Haven: Yale University Press, 1977.

Cowan, Ruth Schwartz. "A Case Study of Technological and Social Change: The Washing Machine and the Working Wife." In *Clio's Consciousness Raised: New Perspectives on the History of Women*, edited by Mary S. Hartman and Lois W. Banner, pp. 245–53. New York: Harper and Row, Harper Colophon Books, 1974.

Coyle, Grace L. *Jobs and Marriage? Outlines for the Discussion of the Married Woman in Business*. New York: Woman's Press, 1928.

Craven, Ruth Shonle. *The American Family*. New York: Thomas Y. Crowell, 1956.

Croly, Jane C. *Thrown on Her Own Resources: Or, What Girls Can Do*. New York: Thomas Y. Crowell, 1891.

Davies, Margery. "Woman's Place Is at the Typewriter: The Feminization of the Clerical Labor Force." *Radical America* 8 (July–August 1974): 1–28.

De Graffenried, Clare. "The Needs of Self-Supporting Women." *Johns Hopkins University Studies in Historical and Political Science, Supplementary Notes No. 1* 10 (1890).

Demos, John. *A Little Commonwealth: Family Life in Plymouth Colony*. New York: Oxford University Press, 1970.

Devoll, Sarah W. "The Results of the Employment of a Police Matron in the City of Portland, Maine." *Proceedings of the National Conference of Charities and Correction, 8th Annual Meeting*. Boston: Geo. H. Ellis, 1881.

Dingwall, Eric John. *The American Woman*. New York: Rinehart and Co., 1957.

Dodge, Grace Hoadley. "Sunny Spots for Working Girls." *Ladies' Home Journal*, January 1892.

Dodge, Josephine Jewell. "Neighborhood Work and Day Nurseries." In *Proceedings of the National Conference of Charities and Correction, 39th Annual Meeting*. Fort Wayne, Ind.: Fort Wayne Printing Co., 1912.

Dodge, Mary Abigail [Gail Hamilton, pseud.]. *A New Atmosphere*. Boston: Ticknor and Fields, 1865.

Donovan, Frances R. *The Saleslady*. Chicago: University of Chicago Press, 1929.

Dorn, Jacob Henry. *Washington Gladden: Prophet of the Social Gospel*. Columbus, Ohio: Ohio State University Press, 1967.

Douglas, Jack D. *Defining America's Social Problems*. Englewood Cliffs, N.J.: Prentice-Hall, 1974.

Dowsall, Jean. "Structural and Attitudinal Factors Associated with Female Labor Force Participation." *Social Science Quarterly* 55 (June 1974): 121–30.

Dublin, Thomas. *Farm to Factory: Women's Letters, 1830–1860*. New York: Columbia University Press, 1981.

————. *Women at Work: The Transformation of Work and Community in Lowell, Massachusetts, 1826–1860*. New York: Columbia University Press, 1979.

Dudden, Faye E. *Serving Women: Household Service in Nineteenth-Century America*. Middletown, Conn.: Wesleyan University Press, 1983.

Durand, John D. *The Labor Force in the United States, 1890–1960*. New York: Social Science Research Council, 1948.

Ellington, George. *The Women of New York: Or, the Underworld of the Great City*. New York: New York Book Co., 1869.

Elmer, M. C. *A Study of Women in Clerical and Secretarial Work in Minneapolis, Minn.* Minneapolis: Woman's Occupational Bureau, 1925.

Engle, Flora A. P. "The Story of the Mercer Expeditions." *Washington Historical Quarterly* 6 (October 1915): 225–37.

Erenberg, Lewis A. *Steppin' Out: New York Nightlife and the Transformation of American Culture, 1890–1930*. Contributions in American Studies, no. 50. Westport, Conn.: Greenwood Press, 1981.

Featherstone, Joseph. "Kentucky-Fried Children." *New Republic*, 5 September 1970, pp. 12–16.

Feldberg, Roslyn L. "Union Fever: Organizing among Clerical Workers, 1900–1930." *Radical*

America 14 (May–June 1980): 53–67.

Ferris, Helen. *Girls Clubs, Their Organization and Management: A Manual for Workers.* New York: E. P. Dutton, 1918.

Four Years in the Underbrush: Adventures of a Working Woman in New York City. New York: Charles Scribner's Sons, 1921.

Fox, Greer Litton. " 'Nice Girl': Social Control of Women through a Value Construct." *Signs* 2 (Summer 1977): 805–17.

Fraiberg, Selma. *Every Child's Birthright: In Defense of Mothering.* New York: Basic Books, 1977.

Fraundorf, Martha Norby. "The Labor Force Participation of Turn-of-the-Century Married Women." *Journal of Economic History* 34 (June 1979): 401–18.

Friedan, Betty. *The Feminine Mystique.* New York: Dell Publishing Co., 1964.

Galinsky, Ellen, and Hooks, William H. *The New Extended Family: Day Care That Works.* Boston: Houghton Mifflin, 1972.

Gallup, George H. *The Gallup Poll: Public Opinion, 1935–1971.* 3 vols. New York: Random House, 1972.

Gardner, Deborah S. "A Hotel Is Not a Home: Architecture Too Splendid for the Working Women of New York." Paper presented at the Second Conference on the History of Women, St. Paul, Minn., October 1977.

Garland, Hamlin. *Rose of Dutcher's Coolly.* 1895, 1899. Reprint of 1899 ed. New York: AMS Press, 1969.

Gilman, Charlotte Perkins. *The Home.* New York: McClure, Phillips and Co., 1903.

————. *Women and Economics.* Boston: Small, Maynard and Co., 1898.

Giraldo, E. I. *Public Policy and the Family.* Lexington, Mass.: D. C. Heath and Co., Lexington Books, 1980.

"The Girl Who Comes to the City: A Symposium." *Harper's Bazaar*, January 1908–January 1909.

Glasco, Laurence A. "The Life Cycles and Household Structures of American Ethnic Groups: Irish, German, and Native-born Whites in Buffalo, New York, 1855." In *Family and Kin in Urban Communities, 1700–1930*, edited by Tamara K. Haraven, pp. 122–43. New York: New Viewpoints, 1977.

Goldmark, Josephine. *Fatigue and Efficiency: A Study in Industry.* New York: Charities Publication Committee, 1912.

Goodlad, John I.; Klein, Frances M.; and Novotney, Jerrold M. *Early Schooling in the United States.* New York: McGraw-Hill, 1973.

Goodsell, Willystine. *Problems of the Family.* New York: Century Co., 1928.

Gordon, Kate. "Wherein Should the Education of a Woman Differ from That of a Man." *School Review* 13 (1905): 789–94.

Gordon, Linda. *Woman's Body, Woman's Right: A Social History of Birth Control in America.* New York: Grossman Publishers, 1976.

Gordon, Michael, ed. *The American Family in Social-Historical Perspective.* New York: St. Martin's Press, 1973.

Gorham, Ethel. *So Your Husband's Gone to War!* New York: Doubleday, Doran and Co., 1942.

Graham, Abbie. *Grace H. Dodge: Merchant of Dreams.* New York: Women's Press, 1926.

Greenblatt, Bernard. *Responsibility for Child Care.* San Francisco: Jossey-Bass, 1977.

Greenwald, Maurine Weiner. *Women, War, and Work: The Impact of World War I on Women Workers in the United States.* Westport, Conn.: Greenwood Press, 1980.

Grob, Gerald N. "Reflections on the History of Social Policy in America." *Reviews in American History* 7 (September 1979): 293–306.

Grossman, Allyson Sherman. "Children of Working Mothers, March 1977." *Monthly Labor Review* 101 (January 1978): 30–33.

Groves, Ernest R. "The Psychology of the Woman Who Works." *Family* (May 1927): 92–97.

Hall, Elizabeth L. *Mothers' Assistance in Philadelphia: Actual and Potential Costs.* Hanover, N.H.: Sociological Press, 1933.

Hall, G. Stanley. *Adolescence.* 2 vols. New York: D. Appleton and Co., 1904.

Hamilton, Alexander. "Report on Manufactures." In *Reports of the Secretary of the Treasury of the United States*, vol. 1. Washington, D.C.: Duff, Green, 1828.

Hansel, Harriet. "What about the Children?" *Harper's Monthly Magazine*, January 1927, pp. 220–27.

Haraven, Tamara K. "The Family as Process: The Historical Study of the Family Cycle." *Journal of Social History* 7 (Spring 1974): 322–29.

Harris, Barbara J. *Beyond Her Sphere: Women and the Professions in American History.* Contributions in Women's Studies no. 4. Westport, Conn.: Greenwood Press, 1978.

Harris, Louis, and Associates. *The 1970 Virginia Slims American Women's Opinion Poll.* Vol. 1. N.p., n.d.

Hayden, Dolores. *The Grand Domestic Revolution: A History of Feminist Designs for American Homes, Neighborhoods, and Cities.* Cambridge, Mass.: MIT Press, 1982.

Hendee, Elizabeth Russell. *The Growth and Development of the Young Women's Christian Association.* New York: Women's Press, 1930.

Herrick, Christine Terhune. *The Expert Maid-Servant.* New York: Harper and Brothers, 1904.

Higgins, Alice L., and Windom, Florence. "Helping Widows to Bring Up Citizens." *Proceedings of the National Conference of Charities and Correction, 37th Annual Meeting.* Fort Wayne, Ind.: Archer Publishing, 1910.

Hinkle, Beatrice M. "Changing Marriage." *Survey Graphic*, December 1926.

Hobson, Barbara M. "Seduced and Abandoned—A Tale of the Wicked City: The Response to Prostitution in Boston, 1820–1850." Paper presented at the Fourth Berkshire Conference on the History of Women, Mt. Holyoke, Mass., August 1978.

Hofstadter, Richard. *The Age of Reform.* New York: Vintage Books, 1955.

Huggins, Nathan I. *Protestants against Poverty: Boston's Charities, 1820–1900.* Contributions in American History no. 9. Westport, Conn.: Greenwood Press, 1971.

Hughes, Gwendolyn Salisbury. *Mothers in Industry: Wage-Earning Mothers in Philadelphia.* New York: New Republic, 1925.

Humphries, Elizabeth Jeanne. "Working Women in Chicago Factories and Department Stores, 1870–95." Master's thesis, University of Chicago, 1943.

Hutchinson, Emilie Josephine. "Women's Wages: A Study of the Wages of Industrial Women and Measures Suggested to Increase Them." Ph.D. dissertation, Columbia University, 1919.

Hvidt, Kristian. *Flight to America: The Social Background of 300,000 Danish Emigrants.* New York: Academic Press, 1975.

Hyde, William Dewitt. *The College Man and the College Woman.* Boston: Houghton Mifflin, 1906.

Hyman, Colette A. "The Young Women's Christian Association and the Women's City Missionary Society: Models of Feminine Behavior, 1868–1920." Senior thesis, Brown University, 1979.

Illinois. General Assembly. Senate. *Report of the Senate Vice Committee Created under the Authority of the Senate of the Forty-Ninth General Assembly as a Continuation of the Committee Created under the Authority of the Senate of the Forty-Eighth General Assembly, State of Illinois.* Chicago, 1916.

Information Bureau on Women's Work. *The Floating World.* Toledo, Ohio: Information Bureau on Women's Work, 1927.

James, Edward T., et al., eds. *Notable American Women, 1607–1950: A Biographical Dictionary.* 3 vols. Cambridge, Mass.: Harvard University Press, 1971.

Jansen, C. J. *Readings in the Sociology of Migration.* Oxford: Pergamon Press, 1970.

Josselyn, Irene M., and Goldman, Ruth Schley. "Should Mothers Work?" *Social Service Review* (March 1949): 74–87.

Juster, Norton. *So Sweet to Labor: Rural Women in America, 1865–1895.* New York: Viking Press, 1979.

Kagan, Jerome. *The Growth of the Child: Reflections on Human Development.* New York: W. W. Norton, 1978.

Katzman, David. *Seven Days a Week: Domestic Service in Industrializing America.* New York: Oxford University Press, 1978.

Kauffman, Reginald Wright. *The House of Bondage.* New York: Grosset and Dunlap, 1910.

Kelley, Florence. *Modern Industry in Relation to the Family, Health, Education, Morality.* New York: Longmans, Green and Co., 1914.

Kellor, Francis A. "The Immigrant Woman." *Atlantic Monthly,* September 1907, pp. 401–7.

———. "The Inter-Municipal Research Committee." *Annals of the American Academy of Political and Social Science* 27 (March 1906): 193–200.

———. *Out of Work: A Study of Unemployment.* New York: Knickerbocker Press, 1915.

———. "The Rights of Patrons of Employment Agencies." *Bulletin of the Inter-Municipal Committee on Household Research,* December 1904.

———. "Southern Colored Girls in the North." *Bulletin of the Inter-Municipal Committee on Household Research,* May 1905, pp. 5–9.

Kessler-Harris, Alice. *Out to Work: A History of Wage-Earning Women in the United States.* New York: Oxford University Press, 1982.

———. "Stratifying by Sex: Understanding the History of Working Women." In *Labor Market Segmentation,* edited by Richard C. Edwards, Michael Reich, and David M. Gordon, pp. 217–55. Lexington, Mass.: D. C. Heath, 1975.

———. "Women's Wage Work as Myth and History." *Labor History* 19 (Spring 1978): 287–307.

Klapp, Louise. "Relation of Social Vice to Industry." *Proceedings of the Minnesota State Conference of Charities and Correction, 21st Annual Meeting.* Minneapolis: Minnesota State Board of Control, 1912.

Klink, Jane Seymour. "The Housekeeper's Responsibility." *Atlantic Monthly,* March 1905, pp. 372–81.

———. "Put Yourself in Her Place." *Atlantic Monthly,* February 1905, pp. 169–77.

Kneeland, George. *Commercialized Prostitution in New York City.* New York: Century Co., 1913.

Komarovsky, Mirra. *Blue-Collar Marriage.* 1962. Reprint. New York: Vintage Books, 1967.

———. *Women in the Modern World: Their Education and Their Dilemmas.* Boston: Little, Brown, 1953.

Kowalewska, Monica. "Conditions of Work for Immigrant Girls in Restaurants." *Proceedings of the Minnesota State Conference of Charities and Correction, 25th Annual Meeting.* St. Paul: Minnesota State Board of Control, 1917.

Kraditor, Aileen S., ed. *Up from the Pedestal: Selected Writings in the History of American Feminism.* 5th ed. New York: New York Times Book Co., Quadrangle Books, 1968.

Kreps, Juanita. *Sex in the Marketplace: American Women at Work.* Policy Studies in Employment and Welfare no. 11. Baltimore: Johns Hopkins University Press, 1971.

LaFollette, Cecile Tipton. *A Study of the Problems of 652 Gainfully Employed Married Women Homemakers.* Contributions to Education no. 619. New York: Columbia University Press, 1934.

Laughlin, Clara E. *The Work-a-Day Girl: A Study of Some Present-Day Conditions.* New York: Fleming H. Revell, 1913.

Lerner, Gerda. "The Lady and the Mill Girl: Changes in the Status of Women in the Age of Jackson." *Midcontinent American Studies Journal* 10 (Spring 1969): 5–14.

Levitan, Sar A., and Alderman, Karen Cleary. *Child Care and ABC's Too.* Baltimore: Johns Hopkins University Press, 1975.

Lewis, Ervin Eugene. *Personnel Problems of the Teaching Staff.* New York: Century Co., 1925.

Littell, Jane. "Meditations of a Wage-Earning Wife." *Atlantic Monthly,* December 1924, pp. 728–34.

Long, Clarence D. *The Labor Force under Changing Income and Employment.* Princeton, N.J.: Princeton University Press, 1958.

Lundberg, Emma O. "Aid to Mothers with Dependent Children." *Annals of the American Academy of Political and Social Science* 98 (November 1921): 97–104.

Lundberg, Ferdinand, and Farnham, Marynia. *Modern Woman: The Lost Sex.* New York: Harper and Brothers, 1947.

Lynd, Robert, and Lynd, Helen M. *Middletown in Transition.* New York: Harcourt, Brace and Co., 1937.

McCullogh, Oscar. "Poor Widows with Dependent Children." *Proceedings of the National Conference of Charities and Correction, 15th Annual Meeting.* Boston: Geo. H. Ellis, 1888.

MacLean, Annie Marion. "The Eleanor Clubs of Chicago." *Survey,* 11 April 1914, pp. 60–61.

————. *Women Workers and Society.* Chicago: A. C. McClurg, 1916.

Macy, John. "Equality of Woman with Man: A Myth." *Harper's Monthly Magazine,* November 1926, pp. 705–10.

Marx, Leo. *The Machine in the Garden: Technology and the Pastoral Ideal in America.* New York: Oxford University Press, 1964.

Masnick, George, and Bane, Mary Jo. *The Nation's Families: 1960–1990.* Boston: Auburn House Publishing, 1980.

Masteller, Jean Carwile. "Marriage or Career, 1880–1914: A Dilemma for American Women Writers and Their Culture." Ph.D. dissertation, University of Minnesota, 1978.

Mativity, Nancy Barr. "The Wife, the Home, and the Job." *Harper's Monthly Magazine,* July 1926, pp. 189–99.

May, Henry F. *Protestant Churches and Industrial America.* New York: Harper and Brothers, 1949.

Mechling, Jay. "Advice to Historians on Advice to Mothers." *Journal of Social History* 9 (Fall 1975): 44–63.

Meserve, H. C. *Lowell—An Industrial Dream Come True.* Boston: National Association of Cotton Manufacturers, 1923.

Meyer, Annie Nathan, ed. *Women's Work in America.* New York: Henry Holt, 1891.

Miles, Henry Adolphus. *Lowell, As It Was, and As It Is.* Lowell, Mass.: Nathaniel L. Dayton, Merrill, and Heywood, 1846.

Minnesota Bureau of Labor. *Eighth Biennial Report of the Bureau of Labor of the State of Minnesota, 1901–02.* N.p.: Great Western Printing, 1902.

————. *Ninth Biennial Report of the Bureau of Labor of the State of Minnesota, 1903–04.* 2 vols. N.p.: Great Western Printing, 1904.

————. *Twelfth Biennial Report of the Bureau of Labor, Industries and Commerce of the State of Minnesota, 1909–10.* N.p.: Great Western Printing, 1910.

Minnesota Bureau of Labor Statistics. *First Biennial Report of the Bureau of Labor Statistics of the State of Minnesota, 1887–88.* N.p.: Thos. A. Clark, 1888.

Minnesota Minimum Wage Commission. *First Biennial Report, 1913–1914.* St. Paul, Minn., 1914.

Moore, Elizabeth Payne. "Life and Labor: Margaret Dreier Robins and the Women's Trade Union League." Ph.D. dissertation, University of Illinois at Chicago, 1981.

Morgan, Marabel. *The Total Woman.* Old Tappan, N.J.: Fleming H. Revell, 1973.

Mulry, J. M. "The Care of Destitute and Neglected Children." *Proceedings of the National Conference of Charities and Correction, 26th Annual Meeting.* Boston: Geo. H. Ellis, 1900.

"My Experiences in New York: The True Story of a Girl's Long Struggle." *Ladies' Home Journal*, March 1910–December 1910.

Nash, Gary B. "The Failure of Female Factory Labor in Colonial Boston." *Labor History* 20 (Spring 1979): 165–88.

Nathan, Maude. *The Story of an Epoch-making Movement*. New York: Doubleday, Page and Co., 1926.

———. "Women Who Work and Women Who Spend." *Annals of the American Academy of Political and Social Science* 27 (May 1906): 646–50.

National Bureau of Economic Research. *Aspects of Labor Economics*. Princeton, N.J.: Princeton University Press, 1962.

National League of Girls Clubs. *History of the National League of Women Workers, 1914*. New York: Pearl Press, 1914.

New York Bureau of Social Hygiene. *Housing Conditions of Employed Women in the Borough of Manhattan*. New York: Bureau of Social Hygiene, 1922.

New York Conference of Charities and Correction. *Proceedings, 1912*. Albany, New York: J. B. Lyon, 1912.

Nye, F. Ivan, and Hoffman, Lois Wladis. *The Employed Mother in America*. Chicago: Rand McNally, 1963.

Oettenger, Katherine Brownell. "Maternal Employment and Children." In *Work in the Lives of Married Women*, edited by the National Manpower Council. New York: Columbia University Press, 1958.

Ogburn, William F. "The Family and Its Functions." In *Recent Social Trends in the United States*, 1:661–708. New York: McGraw-Hill, 1933.

Ohio Board of State Charities. *Twenty-third Annual Report*. Columbus, Ohio: Westbote Co., 1899.

Oppenheimer, Valerie Kincade. "Demographic Influence on Female Employment and the Status of Women." In *Changing Women in a Changing Society*, edited by Joan Huber. Chicago: University of Chicago Press, 1973.

———. *The Female Labor Force in the United States: Demographic and Economic Factors Governing Its Growth and Changing Composition*. Population Monograph 5. Berkeley, Calif.: University of California Press, 1970.

Parker, Cornelia Stratton. *Working with the Working Woman*. New York: Harper and Brothers, 1922.

Penny, Virginia. *Think and Act: A Series of Articles Pertaining to Men and Women, Work and Wages*. Philadelphia: Claxton, Remsen, and Haffelfinger, 1869. Reprint. New York: Arno Press, 1971.

Peters, David Wilbur. *The Status of the Married Woman Teacher*. Contributions to Education no. 603. New York: Columbia University Press, 1934.

Pivar, David. *Purity Crusade: Sexual Morality and Social Control, 1868–1900*. Contributions in American History no. 23. Westport, Conn.: Greenwood Press, 1973.

Pleck, Elizabeth. "Two Worlds in One: Work and Family." *Journal of Social History* 10 (Winter 1976): 178–95.

Popenoe, Paul. *The Conservation of the Family*. Baltimore: Williams and Wilkins, 1926.

Post, Emily. *Etiquette: The Blue Book of Social Usage*. New York: Funk and Wagnalls, 1935.

Powell, Aaron M., ed. *The National Purity Congress; Its Papers, Addresses, Portraits*. New York: American Purity Alliance, 1896.

Pruette, Lorine. *Women and Leisure: A Study of Social Waste*. New York: E. P. Dutton, 1924.

———. *Women Workers through the Depression*. New York: Macmillan, 1934.

Rauschenbusch, Walter. *Christianizing the Social Order*. New York: Macmillan, 1917.

Raybeck, Joseph G. *A History of American Labor*. New York: Free Press, 1966.

Rayne, Martha Louise. *What Can a Woman Do? Or, Her Position in the Business and Literary World*. Petersburg, N.Y.: Eagle Publishing, 1893.

"Report of the Committee on Vagrancy of the Conference of Charities of New York City."
Charities Review, May 1896, p. 244.

Report and Testimony Taken before the Special Committee of the Assembly Appointed to Investigate the Condition of Female Labor in the City of New York. 2 vols. Albany, N.Y.: Wynkoop, Hallenbeck Crawford, 1896.

Rhine, Alice Hyneman. "Women in Industry." In *Women's Work in America*, edited by Annie Nathan Meyer. New York: Henry Holt, 1891.

Richardson, Anna Steese. *The Girl Who Earns Her Own Living.* New York: B. W. Dodge, 1909.

Richardson, Dorothy. "The Difficulties and Dangers Confronting the Working Woman." *Annals of the American Academy of Political and Social Science* 27 (May 1906): 624–26.

_____. *The Long Day: The Story of a New York Working Girl as Told by Herself.* 1905. Reprint. New York: Century Co., 1911.

_____. "Trades-Unions in Petticoats." *Leslies Monthly* (March 1904).

Richmond, J. F. *New York and Its Institutions, 1609–1872.* New York: E. B. Treat, 1872.

Richmond, Mary E., and Hall, Fred S. *A Study of Nine Hundred and Eighty-Five Widows Known to Certain Charity Organization Societies in 1910.* New York: Russell Sage Foundation, 1913.

Robinson, Harriet Hanson. *Loom and Spindle: Or Life among the Early Mill Girls.* New York: Thomas Y. Crowell, 1898.

Roosevelt, Eleanor. *It's Up to the Women.* New York: Frederick A. Stokes, 1933.

Roosevelt, Theodore. *The Foes of Our Own Household.* New York: George H. Doran, 1917.

Rosen, Ruth. *The Lost Sisterhood: Prostitution in America, 1900–1918.* Baltimore: Johns Hopkins University Press, 1982.

_____, and Davidson, Sue, eds. *The Maimie Papers.* Old Westbury, N.Y.: Feminist Press, 1977.

Rosenau, Nathaniel S. "Day Nurseries." *Proceedings of the National Conference of Charities and Correction, 21st Annual Meeting.* Boston: Geo. H. Ellis, 1894.

_____. "Schemes for the Self-Help of the Poor." *Proceedings of the National Conference of Charities and Correction, 13th Annual Meeting.* Boston: Geo. H. Ellis, 1886.

Rothman, Sheila M. *Woman's Proper Place: A History of Changing Ideals and Practices, 1870 to the Present.* New York: Basic Books, 1978.

Rupp, Leila J. *Mobilizing Women for War: German and American Propaganda, 1939–1945.* Princeton, N.J.: Princeton University Press, 1978.

Russell, Thomas H. *The Girl's Fight for a Living: How to Protect the Working Woman from Dangers Due to Low Wages.* Chicago: M. A. Donahue, 1913.

Salmon, Lucy Maynard. *Domestic Service.* New York: Macmillan, 1897.

Sanger, William. *The History of Prostitution: Its Extent, Causes and Effects throughout the World.* 1858. Reprint. New York: Eugenics Publishing, 1939.

Schaffer, Rudolph. *Mothering.* Cambridge, Mass.: Harvard University Press, 1977.

Schiffman, Jacob. "Marital and Family Characteristics of Workers, March 1960." *Monthly Labor Review* 84 (April 1961): 355–64.

Schneider, Eric C. "In the Web of Class: Youth, Class and Culture in Boston, 1840–1940." Ph.D. dissertation, Boston University, 1980.

Scoresby, William. *American Factories and Their Female Operatives, with an Appeal on Behalf of the British Factory Population, and Suggestions for the Improvement of Their Condition.* Boston: William D. Ticknor, 1845.

Scott, Joan W., and Tilly, Louise A. "Women's Work and the Family in Nineteenth-Century Europe." *Comparative Studies in Society and History* 17 (January 1975).

Shreve, Anita. "Careers and the Lure of Motherhood." *New York Times Magazine*, November 21, 1982.

Simms, Mary. *The Natural History of a Social Institution: The Young Women's Christian Asso-*

ciation. New York: Women's Press, 1936.

Sklar, Kathryn Kish. *Catharine Beecher: A Study in American Domesticity.* New Haven: Yale University Press, 1973.

Smith-Rosenberg, Carroll, and Rosenberg, Charles. "The Female Animal: Medical and Biological Views of Woman and Her Role in Nineteenth-Century America." *Journal of American History* 60 (September 1973): 332–56.

Smuts, Robert W. *Women and Work in America.* 1959. New York: Schocken, 1971.

Sorokin, Pitirim, and Zimmerman, Carle C. *Principles of Rural-Urban Sociology.* New York: Henry Holt, 1929.

Spencer, Anna Garlin. *The Family and Its Members.* Philadelphia: J. B. Lippincott, 1923.

————. "What Machine-Dominated Industry Means in Relation to Women's Work: The Need of New Training and Apprenticeship for Girls." *Proceedings of the National Conference of Charities and Correction, 37th Annual Meeting.* Fort Wayne, Ind.: Archer Publishing, 1910.

————. *Women's Share in Social Culture.* 1912. Reprint. Philadelphia: J. B. Lippincott, 1925.

Stansell, Mary Christine. "Women of the Laboring Poor in New York City, 1820–1860." Ph.D. dissertation, Yale University, 1979.

Steinfels, Margaret O'Brien. *Who's Minding the Children?: The History and Politics of Day Care in America.* New York: Simon and Schuster, 1973.

Stewart, William Rhinelander. *The Philanthropic Work of Josephine Shaw Lowell.* New York: Macmillan, 1911.

Stigler, George. *Domestic Servants in the United States, 1900–1940.* New York: National Bureau of Economic Research, 1946.

Stokes, Rose H. Phelps. "The Condition of Working Women, from the Working Woman's Viewpoint." *Annals of the American Academy of Political and Social Science* 27 (May 1906): 627–37.

Stoltz, Lois Meek. "Effects of Maternal Employment on Children: Evidence from Research." *Child Development* 31 (1960): 749–82.

Straub, Eleanor. "United States Government Policy toward Civilian Women during World War I." *Prologue* 5 (Winter 1973): 240–54.

Sum, Andrew M. "Women in the Labor Force: Why Projections Have Been Too Low." *Monthly Labor Review* 100 (July 1977): 18–24.

Suransky, Valerie Polakow. *The Erosion of Childhood.* Chicago: University of Chicago Press, 1982.

Sutherland, Daniel E. *Americans and Their Servants: Domestic Service in the United States, 1880–1920.* Baton Rouge, La.: Louisiana State University Press, 1981.

Sweet, James A. *Women in the Labor Force.* New York: Seminar Press, 1973.

Taeuber, Conrad, and Taeuber, Irene. *The Changing Population of the United States.* New York: John Wiley and Sons, 1958.

Talcott, Mrs. H. B. *Madge; Or, Night and Morning.* New York: D. Appleton, 1863.

Tentler, Leslie Woodcock. *Wage-Earning Women: Industrial Work and Family Life in the United States, 1900–1930.* New York: Oxford University Press, 1979.

Terhune, Mary Hawes [Marion Harland, pseud.]. "Counting-Room and Cradle." *North American Review,* September 1893, pp. 334–40.

Thernstrom, Stephen. *Poverty and Progress: Social Mobility in a Nineteenth-Century City.* Cambridge, Mass.: Harvard University Press, 1964.

Thurston, Henry W. *The Dependent Child.* New York: Columbia University Press, 1930.

Tilly, Louise A. "Urban Growth, Industrialization, and Women's Employment in Milan, Italy, 1881–1911." *Journal of Urban History* 3 (August 1977): 467–84.

Tolman, William Howe, and Hemstreet, Charles. *The Better New York.* New York: Baker and Taylor, 1904.

Trattner, Walter L. *Crusade for the Children: A History of the National Child Labor Committee and Child Labor Reform in America.* Chicago: Quadrangle Books, 1970.

Travis, Anthony R. "The Origins of Mothers' Pensions in Illinois." *Journal of the Illinois State Historical Society* 67 (November 1975): 421–28.

Tyson, Helen Glenn. "The Fatherless Family." *Annals of the American Academy of Political and Social Science* 77 (May 1918), pp. 79–90.

———. "The Professional Woman's Baby." *New Republic*, 7 April 1926.

Valesh, Eva McDonald [Eva Gay, pseud.]. *St. Paul Globe*, 26 March 1888–3 August 1891.

Van Duzer, Adelaide Laura. *Everyday Living for Girls*. Philadelphia: J. B. Lippincott, 1936.

Vanek, Joann. "Time Spent in Housework." *Scientific American*, November 1974, pp. 116–21.

Van Vorst, Mrs. John, and Van Vorst, Marie. *The Woman Who Toils: Being the Experiences of Two Ladies as Factory Girls*. New York: Doubleday, Page and Co., 1903.

Wagner, Richard Roland. "Virtue against Vice: A Study of Moral Reformers and Prostitution in the Progressive Era." Ph.D. dissertation, University of Wisconsin, 1971.

Wald, Lillian D. "The Immigrant Young Girl." *Proceedings of the National Conference of Charities and Correction, 36th Annual Meeting*. Fort Wayne, Ind.: Archer Publishing, 1909.

Waldman, Elizabeth, et al. "Working Mothers in the 1970s: A Look at the Statistics." *Monthly Labor Review* 102 (October 1979): 39–49.

Walsh, Mary Roth. *Doctors Wanted: No Women Need Apply: Sexual Barriers in the Medical Profession, 1835–1975*. New Haven: Yale University Press, 1977.

Wandersee, Winifred D. *Women's Work and Family Values, 1920–1940*. Cambridge, Mass.: Harvard University Press, 1981.

Ware, Norman Joseph. *The Industrial Worker, 1840–1860: The Reaction of American Industrial Society to the Advance of the Industrial Revolution*. 1924. Reprint. New York: Quadrangle Books, 1964.

Watson, John B. *Psychological Care of Infant and Child*. New York: W. W. Norton, 1928.

Weiner, Lynn. " 'Our Sister's Keepers': The Minneapolis Woman's Christian Association and Housing for Working Women." *Minnesota History* (Spring 1979): 189–200.

"Widows' Pension Legislation." *Municipal Research* 85 (May 1917).

Wiebe, Robert H. *The Search for Order, 1877–1920*. New York: Hill and Wang, 1967.

Williams, Robin M. "Rural Youth Studies in the United States." *Rural Sociology* 4 (June 1939): 166–78.

Wilson, Elizabeth. *Fifty Years of Association Work among Young Women, 1866–1916: A History of Young Women's Christian Associations in the United States of America*. New York: Young Women's Christian Association, 1916.

Wisconsin Bureau of Labor and Industrial Statistics. *Third Biennial Report of the Bureau of Labor and Industrial Statistics, Wisconsin, 1887–88*. Madison, Wis.: Democratic Printing, 1888.

———. *Tenth Biennial Report of the Wisconsin Bureau of Labor and Industrial Statistics, 1900–1901*. Madison, Wis.: Democratic Printing, 1901.

Wisconsin Bureau of Labor Statistics. *First Biennial Report of the Bureau of Labor Statistics of Wisconsin, 1883 and 1884*. Madison, Wis.: Democratic Printing, 1884.

Wishy, Bernard. *The Child and the Republic: The Dawn of Modern American Child Nurture*. Philadelphia: University of Pennsylvania Press, 1968.

Wolcott, Louise. "Discussion: Poor Widows with Dependent Children." In *Proceedings of the National Conference of Charities and Correction, 15th Annual Meeting*. Boston: Geo. H. Ellis, 1888.

Wolfe, Albert Benedict. *The Lodging House Problem in Boston*. Harvard Economic Studies. Boston: Houghton Mifflin, 1906.

Woods, Robert A., and Kennedy, Albert J. *Young Working Girls: A Summary of Evidence from Two Thousand Social Workers*. Boston: Houghton Mifflin, 1913.

Wright, Carroll D. *The Working Girls of Boston*. 1889. Reprint. New York: Arno and the New York Times, 1969.

Wylie, Philip. *Generation of Vipers*. New York: Farrar and Rinehart, 1942.

Yans-McLaughlin, Virginia. *Family and Community: Italian Immigrants in Buffalo, 1880–1930.* Ithaca, N.Y.: Cornell University Press, 1977.

Yates, Gayle Graham. *What Women Want.* Cambridge, Mass.: Harvard University Press, 1975.

Zimmerman, Carle C. "The Migration to Towns and Cities." *American Journal of Sociology* 32 (November 1926): 450–55.

Index